BUSINESS MATHEMATICS

BUSINESS MATHEMATICS

BUSINESS MATHEMATICS

SECOND EDITION

RICHARD S. THORN
University of Pittsburgh

HARPER & ROW, Publishers

New York   Hagerstown   Philadelphia   San Francisco   London

To my children
Bettina, Clifford, and Eric

Sponsoring Editor: *John W. Greenman*
Project Editor: *Karla Philip/Pamela Landau*
Designer: *Frances Torbert Tilley*
Production Manager: *Jeanie Berke*
Compositor: Syntax International Pte., Ltd.
Printer and Binder: The Murray Printing Company

BUSINESS MATHEMATICS, *Second Edition*

Library of Congress Cataloging in Publication Data

Thorn, Richard S
  Business mathematics.

  Includes index.
  1. Business mathematics. I. Title.
HF5691.T5 1979   513'.93   79-10018
ISBN 0-06-046613-8

CONTENTS

TO THE STUDENT

When you have completed studying the chapters in this book and done the assignments following them, you will have attained the ability to deal with most of the mathematical problems that you will confront in the business world. To be assured that you attain this goal, observe the following procedures:

Read each section of the text carefully and be sure you understand the examples following each explanation.

Do all the problems yourself. When you do not understand something, go back to the appropriate example in the text and see if you can find your error. If this does not clear up the difficulty, ask the assistance of your instructor or a friend.

Work deliberately and methodically. The answers to the lettered problems are given at the end of the book so that you may check your understanding as you go along.

The knowledge that you gain through the successful completion of this course will provide you with skills necessary to compete successfully in the business world.

Good luck on your adventure.

TO THE INSTRUCTOR

This book is designed to enable the student to deal effectively with the great majority of mathematical problems encountered in business. It embodies the most modern techniques for the teaching of business mathematics. The following features of the book are distinctive:

The mathematical principles and their application to business have been carefully selected to embrace the widest possible variety of problems encountered in business.

The book has been organized around a carefully chosen number of mathematical concepts, and their business applications have been presented in order of their increasing difficulty.

Each mathematical concept is first explained verbally, then symbolically, and then numerically. Each concept introduced is presented from the viewpoint of modern mathematical education so the students will have no conceptual difficulty if they choose to pursue mathematical studies further.

The initial applications are simple uses of the particular mathematical principle introduced. The subsequent applications make more sophisticated use of the mathematical principle. In the latter part of the book, the problems also combine the use of two or more mathematical operations.

Following each chapter is a set of problems, arranged in order of increasing difficulty. In each assignment section, answers to selected problems are provided at the end of the book so that the students may immediately check themselves to see that they are applying the correct method in solving the problems.

After each major section of the book, a graded review and evaluation is given to help the students judge how well they have absorbed the material and to pinpoint any misunderstanding so that they may review the relevant sections of the book.

After the first few exercises, review problems are inserted in the exercises to reinforce the students' progress.

Realistic records, business papers, and tables are employed throughout the text as examples and as parts of exercises. The tables enable the students to work with similar tables in business and in other courses.

This book also contains several unique features such as sections on balance sheet analysis, income statement analysis, and financial ratios and their analysis. A special section is devoted to the metric system.

All tables necessary to complete the problems are included in the book and their use is explained. Four-place tables are employed in the exercises requiring mathematical tables for their solution. This may mean that the last digit in the answer is not exact. This sacrifice in accuracy was accepted in order not to burden the students with an excessive amount of computation. The transition to more accurate tables should cause no difficulty.

An appendix contains a sample quantitative section of the Federal Professional and Administrative Careers Examination (PACE) coded to pertinent chapters in the book.

PART ONE

Useful Fundamentals

CHAPTER 1
The number system and basic operations

Very early in the development of civilization, there arose a necessity for some system of measurement. When the ancients became concerned with the concepts of "how much" and "how many," they developed symbols to represent this abstract quality of one-ness, two-ness and so on. They then developed the ability to count by using these symbols and the science of mathematics began.

Because of the variety of civilizations and the time and distance that separated them, several different systems were developed. The system we use is the Arabic Decimal System in which ten basic digits or numbers are used. These are the familiar 0, 1, 2, 3, 4, 5, 6, 7, 8, 9. Although this system is widely used, there are times when we encounter symbols from the Roman System. While the Arabic has ten symbols, the Roman System has only seven. These are given below with their values expressed in the Arabic System.

Roman	English	Arabic
I	one	1
V	five	5
X	ten	10
L	fifty	50
C	one hundred	100
D	five hundred	500
M	one thousand	1000

The use of these seven symbols is quite simple. If a symbol is repeated, then its value is added. For example, II is I plus I, or 2. XXX is X plus X plus X, or 30. If two unlike symbols are together, the position of the symbol with the lesser value is important. When the lesser value is on the left, it is subtracted from the symbol on the right.

$$IV = 5 - 1 = 4$$
$$IX = 10 - 1 = 9$$
$$XL = 50 - 10 = 40$$

When the lesser value is to the right, it is added to the symbol on the left.

$$VI = 5 + 1 = 6$$
$$XI = 10 + 1 = 11$$
$$LX = 50 + 10 = 60$$

When there are more than two symbols, these rules still hold true. For example, what is the value of XIV? Here, the lesser value IV is to the right and must be added to X. Since IV is made up of two symbols with the lesser value to the left, the I must be subtracted from the V. Written in the Roman notation, this would be

$$X + (V - I) = XIV$$

In the Arabic System this would be

$$10 + (5 - 1) = 14$$

One final rule to remember is for Roman numbers that are multiples of 1000. Placing a bar over a number, such as $\overline{XX}$, multiplies the number by 1000. Thus, $\overline{XX}$ is 20,000.

NUMBERS AND THE NUMBER LINE

The counting numbers, such as the Arabic 1, 2, 3, 4, 5 . . . , are called the *natural numbers*. If we include the negatives of the natural numbers (indicated by a minus sign before the number, such as -1 or -2) and zero in our list, we have defined a new set of numbers called the *integers*.

All of these numbers can be plotted on a line such as the one below, where 0 is called the *origin*.

Negative ←——————————Origin ——————————→ Positive

$$-5 \quad -4 \quad -3 \quad -2 \quad -1 \quad 0 \quad 1 \quad 2 \quad 3 \quad 4 \quad 5$$

Any number to the right of the origin is *positive*. Moving from left to right is said to be moving in a positive direction. A number to the left of the origin is *negative*. Moving from right to left is said to be moving in a negative direction.

FUNDAMENTAL RULES

For greater generality, letters may be substituted for numbers. Using this more general notation, we can establish the following rules for mathematical operations.

Rule 1. **Given any two numbers a and b, *only one* of the following relationships can be true.**

　　1. $a = b$ (read "a equals b")
　　2. $a > b$ (read "a is greater than b")
　　3. $a < b$ (read "a is less than b")

Example. If a is equal to 2 and b is equal to 3, then 2 is not equal to 3 and 2 is not greater than 3. Thus, only the third relationship is true: 2 is less than 3.

Rule 2. **For each pair of numbers c and d, there exists *one* and only one sum, $c + d$, and one and only one product, $c \times d$.**

Example. $5 + 2 = 7$　　　Here 7 is the one and only sum of $5 + 2$.
　　　　　　$3 \times 2 = 6$　　　Here 6 is the one and only product of 3×2.

Rule 3. **There exists a number 0, such that the addition of any number *d* and 0 is equal to *d*.**

Example. $d + 0 = d$

$$2 + 0 = 2 \qquad 0 + 2 = 2$$
$$3 + 0 = 3 \qquad 0 + 3 = 3$$

There also exists a number 1, such that the multiplication of *d* times 1 is equal to *d*.

Example. $d \times 1 = d$

$$5 \times 1 = 5 \qquad 1 \times 5 = 5$$
$$8 \times 1 = 8 \qquad 1 \times 8 = 8$$

Rule 4. **The order of operation for addition and multiplication has no effect on the result.**

Example. $a + b = b + a \qquad\qquad a \times b = b \times a$

$$3 + 2 = 2 + 3 = 5 \qquad 4 \times 3 = 3 \times 4 = 12$$
$$6 + 3 = 3 + 6 = 9 \qquad 2 \times 4 = 4 \times 2 = 8$$

Rule 5. **When the problem involves more than two *terms*, such as *a* + *b* + *c*, the number of operations increases. Therefore, to add *a* + *b* + *c*, we have two additive operations: first, we find the sum of *a* and *b*; and second, we add this sum to *c*. This is written algebraically as (*a* + *b*) + *c*. However, the result would be no different had we added *a* and *c* or *b* and *c* first.**

Example. $(a + b) + c = a + (b + c)$

$$(2 + 3) + 6 = 2 + (3 + 6) \qquad (7 + 6) + 5 = 7 + (6 + 5)$$
$$(5) + 6 = 2 + (9) \qquad\quad (13) + 5 = 7 + (11)$$
$$11 = 11 \qquad\qquad\qquad 18 = 18$$

The same rule holds true for multiplication. The example below illustrates this extension of the rule.

Example. $(a \times b) \times c = a \times (b \times c)$

$$(2 \times 3) \times 4 = 2 \times (3 \times 4) \qquad (5 \times 2) \times 3 = 5 \times (2 \times 3)$$
$$(6) \times 4 = 2 \times (12) \qquad\quad (10) \times 3 = 5 \times (6)$$
$$24 = 24 \qquad\qquad\qquad 30 = 30$$

Rule 6. **When the sum of two numbers *b* + *c* is to be multiplied by another number *a*, the result is the same as multiplying each of the numbers separately and adding the products.**

Example. $a(b + c) = (a \times b) + (a \times c)$

$$2 \times (4 + 3) = (2 \times 4) + (2 \times 3)$$
$$2 \times (7) = 8 + 6$$
$$14 = 14$$

$$6 \times (1 + 3) = (6 \times 1) + (6 \times 3)$$
$$6 \times (4) = 6 + 18$$
$$24 = 24$$

Rule 7.   For each number *c*, except 0, there exists a number $-c$, called the *negative* of *c*, such that the sum of *c* and $-c$ equals 0. If a number is written without a sign, its sign is assumed to be positive: $c = +c$.

Example. $c + (-c) = 0$

$$8 + (-8) = 0 \qquad 6 + (-6) = 0$$
$$8 - 8 = 0 \qquad\quad 6 - 6 = 0$$

Rule 8.   For each number *h*, except 0, there exists a number $1/h$, called the *reciprocal* of *h*, such that the multiplication of *h* times $1/h$ equals 1.

Example. $h \times \dfrac{1}{h} = 1$

$$2 \times \frac{1}{2} = 1$$

$$6 \times \frac{1}{6} = 1$$

In addition to these general rules, there are other important rules that relate to specific operations.

SUBTRACTION

A simple definition of subtraction can be derived from the operation of addition given in Rule 2. First, however, another important rule must be established.

Rule 9.   This rule simply states that the negative of a negative number is positive. (See Rule 7 for the definition of a negative number.)

Example. $[-(-a)] = a$

$$-(-8) = 8 \qquad -(-6) = 6$$

Rule 10.   If we keep this in mind, the subtraction of *b* from *a* is the same as adding $-b$ to *a*.

Example. $a - b = a + (-b)$

$$8 - 5 = 8 + (-5) = 3$$
$$6 - 4 = 6 + (-4) = 2$$
$$6 - 1 = 6 + (-1) = 5$$

Perhaps an easier way to visualize subtraction is to think of it as "taking away." For example, $8 - 5$ means to take 5 away from 8. The result is 3.

Rule 11.   Similarly, to subtract a negative number $-f$ from a positive number *g*, means to add the negative of $-f$ to *g*. Rule 9 tells us that the negative of a negative number is positive; thus the negative of $-f$ is *f*. When we subtract we obtain the following results, in which we see that subtracting a negative number is the same as adding the number.

Example. $g - (-f) = g + f$

$$7 - (-2) = 7 + 2 = 9$$
$$4 - (-3) = 4 + 3 = 7$$
$$8 - (-4) = 8 + 4 = 12$$

MULTIPLICATION

There are also important rules for multiplication.

Rule 12. **Any number *a* multiplied by 0 is always 0.**

Example. $a \times 0 = 0$

$$9 \times 0 = 0$$
$$0 \times 4 = 0$$

Multiplication by negative numbers sometimes causes difficulties. The following rules hold for this operation.

Rule 13. **The result of a negative number multiplied by a positive number is negative.**

Example. $(-a) \times b = a \times (-b) = -(a \times b)$

$$-4 \times 2 = -8 \qquad -3 \times 5 = -15$$
$$4 \times -2 = -8 \qquad 3 \times -5 = -15$$

From this simple rule a general rule concerning multiplication by negative numbers can be derived.

Rule 14. **If the number of terms (a number with a positive or negative sign) with a negative sign is odd, then the product of the multiplication will be negative.**

Example. $(-1) \times (-1) \times (-2) \times (2) = -4$

The number of terms with a negative sign is three. The rule states that an odd number of negative signs makes the product negative. Thus the answer is -4.

$$(-2) \times (+3) = -6 \qquad (-6) \times (-1) \times (2) = +12$$

If the number of terms with a negative sign is even, the product will be positive.

Example. $(1) \times (-1) \times (2) \times (-2) = +4$

Since the number of negative terms is even, the answer 4 is positive.

$$(-4) \times (-2) = +8 \qquad (-3) \times (-2) \times (-3) = -18$$

DIVISION

Just as we derived the definition of subtraction from the operation of addition, we can derive a definition for division from the operation of multiplication. To divide *a* by *b* means to multiply *a* by the reciprocal of *b*. (See Rule 8 for the definition of reciprocal.)

Rule 15. **To divide c by d, simply multiply c by the reciprocal of d ($1/d$).**

Example. $c \div d = c \times \dfrac{1}{d}$

$$6 \div 3 = 6 \times \frac{1}{3} = 2 \quad \text{or} \quad 3\overline{)6}$$

$$8 \div 4 = 8 \times \frac{1}{4} = 2 \quad \text{or} \quad 4\overline{)8}$$

Because the definition of division is derived from the operation of multiplication, division by negative numbers is similar to multiplication by negative numbers. (See Rules 13 and 14.)

Rule 16. **If either the number to be divided, c, or the dividing number d is negative, the answer will be negative.**

Example. $c \div -d = -\left(c \times \dfrac{1}{d} \right)$

$-c \div d = -\left(c \times \dfrac{1}{d} \right)$

$8 \div -2 = -\left(8 \times \dfrac{1}{2} \right) = -4 \qquad -2\overline{)\,8}^{\,-4}$

$-6 \div 3 = -\left(6 \times \dfrac{1}{3} \right) = -2 \qquad 3\overline{)-6}^{\,-2}$

If both numbers are negative, the answer will be positive.

$-c \div -d = \dfrac{-c}{-d} = +\left(c \times \dfrac{1}{d} \right)$

$-8 \div -4 = \dfrac{-8}{-4} = +\left(8 \times \dfrac{1}{4} \right) = 2 \qquad -4\overline{)-8}^{\,2}$

$-10 \div -2 = \dfrac{-10}{-2} = +\left(10 \times \dfrac{1}{2} \right) = 5 \qquad -2\overline{)-10}^{\,5}$

SOME USEFUL FORMULAS

Many of the everyday problems that need to be solved in the business world require the calculation of the area or perimeter of a space or volume of an object. To make these calculations, one needs to be familiar with certain formulas. The most frequently needed formulas are given below.

Perimeter

The *perimeter* (*P*) of an area is simply the sum of all its sides.

Perimeter = Side 1 + Side 2 + Side 3 + · · ·

$P = S_1 + S_2 + S_3 + \cdots$

Example. The perimeter of a rectangle measuring 5 by 7 feet is 24 feet.

$24 = 5 + 7 + 5 + 7$

7 ft

5 ft   5 ft

7 ft

The perimeter of a hexagon (six-sided figure) with sides measuring 5, 7, 6, 8, 6, and 7 inches is 39 inches.

$P = 5 + 7 + 6 + 8 + 6 + 7$
$P = 39$

6 in.   8 in.

7 in.   6 in.

5 in.   7 in.

A circle is a figure with special properties. All the points of a circle are equally distant from a point in the middle of the circle called its *center* (*O*). The distance from the center to the perimeter of the circle is called the *radius* (*r*) of the circle. The *diameter* (*d*) of the circle is any line going from one point on a circle to another and passing through the center. It is always equal to twice the radius.

Diameter = 2 × Radius
$d = 2 \times r$

radius (*r*)

0   radius (*r*)

0

Diameter
(*d*)

The *perimeter* of a circle has a special name; it is called the *circumference* of the circle. The relation between the circumference of a circle and its diameter is always the same number regardless of the size of the circle. This number is called pi (π) and is approximately equal to 3.1416:

$$\pi = \frac{c}{d} = 3.1416$$

The circumference of a circle is therefore equal to π times its diameter or, an equivalent expression, π times twice the radius.

$$\text{Circumference} = \pi \times \text{Diameter} = \pi \times 2 \times \text{Radius}$$
$$C = \pi \times d = \pi \times 2 \times r$$

Area of a Rectangle

The area of a rectangle is equal to its length times its width.

$$\text{Area of Rectangle} = \text{Length} \times \text{Width}$$
$$A = l \times w$$

Example. Find the area of a rectangle which is 7 feet long and 5 feet wide.

$$A = 7 \text{ ft} \times 5 \text{ ft}$$
$$A = 35 \text{ square feet (sq ft)}$$

5 ft   35 sq ft

7 ft

Area of a Circle

The area of a circle is equal to π times the radius squared.

$$\text{Area of Circle} = \pi \times \text{Radius}^2$$

Example. Find the area of a circle with a radius of 7 inches.

$$\text{Area} = 3.1416 \times (7 \text{ in.})^2$$
$$= 3.1416 \times 49 \text{ sq in.}$$
$$= 153.9364 \text{ sq in}$$

7 in.

0

Volume of a Rectangular Solid

The volume of a rectangular solid is equal to its length times its width times its height.

$$\text{Volume of Rectangular Solid} = \text{Length} \times \text{Width} \times \text{Height}$$
$$V = l \times w \times h$$

Example. A box is 5 feet wide, 7 feet long, and 3 feet high. What is its volume?

$$V = 5 \text{ ft} \times 7 \text{ ft} \times 3 \text{ ft}$$
$$= 105 \text{ cubic feet (cu ft)}$$

5 ft

3 ft

7 ft

Volume of a Cylinder

The volume of a circular cylinder is equal to π times the square of its radius times its height.

Volume of Cylinder $= \pi \times$ Radius$^2 \times$ Height
$$V = \pi \times r^2 \times h$$

Example. A cylinder has a radius of 2 meters and a height of 10 meters. Find its volume in cubic meters.

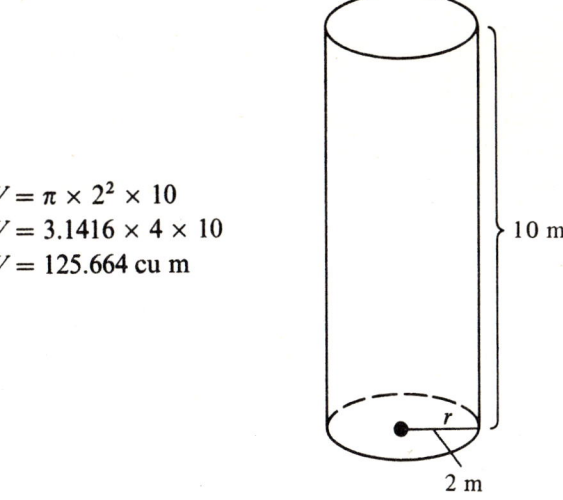

$V = \pi \times 2^2 \times 10$
$V = 3.1416 \times 4 \times 10$
$V = 125.664$ cu m

10 m

2 m

ASSIGNMENT 1 THE REAL NUMBER SYSTEM
AND BASIC OPERATIONS

A. For each of the following Arabic numbers, write the equivalent Roman numeral. (The answers to the problems lettered **a** and **b** are provided at the end of the book.)

a.	28	**b.**	946
1.	46	**2.**	67
3.	127	**4.**	12
5.	1,479	**6.**	18
7.	34	**8.**	93
9.	678	**10.**	248

B. For each of the following Roman numerals, write the equivalent Arabic number.

a.	CII	**b.**	MCCXXVIII
1.	XV	**2.**	XXXIX
3.	LXVI	**4.**	LVIII
5.	LXXXII	**6.**	CXLIV
7.	VII	**8.**	XCIX
9.	XIX	**10.**	DCXIV

C. Find each of the following numbers on the line below and label the points carefully.

a.	10	**b.**	−19
1.	7	**2.**	9
3.	−6	**4.**	4
5.	−2	**6.**	14
7.	−11	**8.**	0
9.	18	**10.**	−15

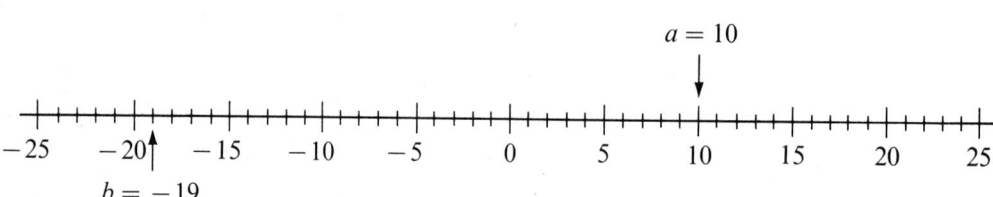

D. Find each of the points on the line provided and then move in the stated direction as many places as given. For example, find 6 and move four places positive.

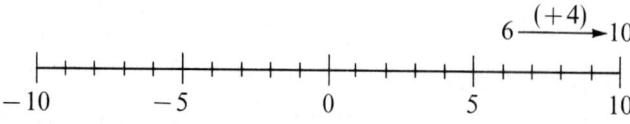

1. Find 2 and move six places positive.

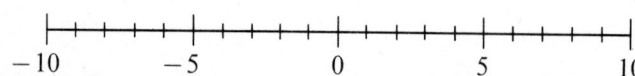

2. Find 0 and move three places negative.

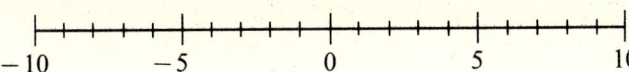

3. Find 9 and move six places negative

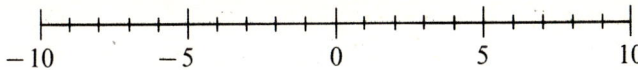

4. Find −3 and move three places negative.

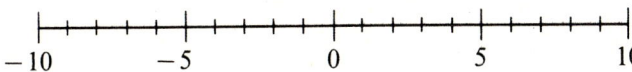

5. Find −5 and move eight places positive.

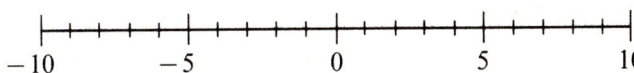

E. For each of the problems below, decide which rules must have been applied to find the answer and indicate the number of the rule.

a. $6 + 2 = 8$ **b.** $-20 \div -5 = 4$

1. $6 + 0 = 6$ **2.** $4 + (-4) = 0$

3. $-(-9) + [-(-8)] = 9 + 8 = 17$ **4.** $5 - 2 = 3$

5. $7(1 + 5) = 7 + 35 = 42$ **6.** $(-6) \times (-1) \times 2 = 12$

7. $-2 \times 8 = -16$ **8.** $21 \times 1 = 21$

9. $15 \div 3 = 5$ **10.** $-6 \times -5 = 30$

F. Perform the indicated operations.

a. $6 + 0 =$ **b.** $1 \times 4 \times 2 \times (-3) \times (-1) =$

1. $5 \times 0 =$ **2.** $9 + (-9) =$

3. $16 - 6 =$ **4.** $12 \times 2 =$

5. $-16 \div 4 =$ **6.** $81 \times 1 =$

7. $18 - (-1) =$ **8.** $26 + 0 - 7 =$

9. $6 \times \dfrac{1}{6} =$ **10.** $33 \div -11 =$

11. $6 \times 2 \times 2 - 4 =$

12. $5(2 + 4) =$

13. $[16 + (-10)] \times 2 =$

14. $(-25 \div -5) + 3 =$

15. $5 \times [-(-5)] =$

16. $(-1) \times (-6) \times 2 \times (-3) =$

17. $[4 \times (-2)] + 6 =$

18. $[6(1 + 5)] - 30 =$

19. $(-6) \times (-5) \div -10 =$

20. $(17 - 7) \times -2 =$

A. Add the following.

	a. 27	1. 96	2. 89	3. 106	4. 119	5. 296
	43	81	12	57	406	137
	82	64	56	82	93	41

	b. 8991	6. 63	7. 101	8. 796	9. 907	10. 3407
	4290	327	643	419	1010	1934
	714	461	790	606	632	2891

B. Solve each of the following.

1. Mr. Stearns bought a tennis racket for $29.95, a can of tennis balls for $3.95, a pair of tennis shoes for $19.95, and a gym bag for $12.50. What was the total cost of these purchases?

2. The St. Clair Sabres football team has played five games so far this season.

GAME	POINTS SCORED (SABRES)	POINTS SCORED (OPPONENT)
1	20	17
2	15	28
3	24	35
4	14	13
5	58	6

   a. What is the total number of points scored by the Sabres so far this year?
   b. How many points have they allowed their opponents to score to date?

3. A freight truck departed from Nelson's Garage carrying 600 pounds of auto body equipment. Its driver then proceeded to make three pickup stops where equipment weighing 50, 436, and 300 pounds respectively was loaded onto the truck. How many pounds of freight was the truck carrying at the end of this trip?

4. During the first week of May, the Printing Department of the McDowell Co. used a total of 171 hours of labor. For the next three weeks respectively, 220, 167, and 336 hours of labor were used. What is the total number of labor hours used by the Printing Department for the month of May?

C. Subtract the following.

a. 78	**1.** 109	**2.** 246	**3.** 367	**4.** 4,610	**5.** 3,700
−19	− 81	−157	− 99	−1,817	− 626

b. 570,470	**6.** 4,218	**7.** 5,661	**8.** 10,004	**9.** 57,002	**10.** 909,012
− 196,693	−3,932	−2,956	− 8,625	−10,098	− 78,944

D. Solve each of the following.

1. Joe and Scott weigh a total of 375 pounds. If Joe weighs 210 pounds, how much does Scott weigh?

2. Mrs. Henry bought 120 candy bars for Halloween treats. After she had finished distributing the candy, 32 bars remained. How many candy bars did Mrs. Henry give away?

3. In January, the supply inventory of a small office included 140 pencils, 35 ball-point pens, 48 legal pads, and 14 typewriter ribbons. In June, inventory of these items was again taken and the office now had 61 pencils, 16 ball point pens, 8 legal pads, and 9 typewriter ribbons. Assuming no purchases were made in the meantime, how many of each item were consumed between January and June?

4. When Nancy arrived in Gateway City, the odometer (mileage meter) reading for her automobile was 25,678. If she had recorded the odometer reading before starting out on her trip as 24,995, how many miles did she drive to reach Gateway City?

E. Multiply the following.

a. 47	**1.** 12	**2.** 59	**3.** 63	**4.** 728	**5.** 589
× 68	× 13	× 81	× 59	× 47	× 88

b. 1926	**6.** 112	**7.** 483	**8.** 633	**9.** 9127	**10.** 6654
× 8407	× 631	× 719	× 517	× 433	× 377

F. Solve each of the following.

1. Mildred Community Church asks each of its 375 members to pledge $5 toward a charity project. If everyone complies with this request, how much money will be raised for the project?

2. A radio station plays 13 songs each hour. How many songs will be played in 12 hours?

3. Dave is paid $4.00 per hour as a lifeguard. If he works 38 hours, how much money will he earn?

4. Jane can assemble 42 components per working day at her factory job. If she works 25 days this month, how many components will she be expected to assemble for the month?

5. If Mr. Jackson earns $150 per week and is paid for 52 weeks each year, what is his annual salary?

6. Each unit of a certain product requires 7 units of raw material A and 3 units of raw material B.
  a. If 350 units of the product are desired, how many units of each raw material are necessary?
  b. If it costs the firm $2 to obtain one unit of raw material A and $1 to obtain one unit of raw material B, what will be the *total* cost of the two raw materials for producing 350 units of the product?

G. Divide the following.

a. $2\overline{)7}$ **1.** $3\overline{)106}$ **2.** $6\overline{)215}$ **3.** $4\overline{)1,070}$ **4.** $7\overline{)4,381}$ **5.** $2\overline{)53,212}$

b. $561\overline{)96,476}$ **6.** $21\overline{)783}$ **7.** $36\overline{)6,041}$ **8.** $83\overline{)5,917}$ **9.** $106\overline{)656}$ **10.** $352\overline{)8,803}$

H. Solve each of the following.

1. Marge's bowling team won a tournament prize of $120, to be distributed equally among the four members. How much did each person on the team receive?

2. Linda spent $16.50 for three neckties, all of which were the same price. How much did one necktie cost?

3. Marcy's compact car averages 30 miles per gallon of gasoline. If she drives 780 miles, how many gallons of gasoline should she expect to use?

4. Terry earns $65 (before deductions) for working 13 hours. What is his hourly salary?

5. An ice cream store orders 18 different flavors of ice cream in equal quantities. If the total number of gallons of ice cream delivered to the store is 270, how many gallons of each flavor are there?

6. If 144 pencils cost $17.28, what is the price of each pencil?

ASSIGNMENT 3 BASIC OPERATIONS APPLIED TO BUSINESS

A. Add the following groups of the values of articles purchased to obtain the total value of each purchase.

	a.		1.		2.		3.		4.		5.
	$19.95		$ 22.31		$78.25		$ 13.92		$52.51		$ 38.97
	12.75		108.64		43.92		84.70		69.18		49.41
	38.50		97.80		10.59		187.59		9.69		212.06
	$		$		$		$		$		$

	a.		6.		7.		8.		9.		10.
	$521.98		$ 769.56		$328.76		$ 62.50		$612.95		$428.82
	20.54		17.18		237.94		300.12		290.19		112.69
	348.86		49.27		76.16		1,707.26		79.70		718.77
	146.00		1,252.05		416.90		875.50		16.25		521.98
	$		$		$		$		$		$

B. Subtract the value of goods returned from the original values of each purchase.

	a.		1.		2.		3.		4.		5.
	$87.16		$19.95		$36.50		$89.95		$76.67		$112.00
	.86		10.14		17.16		54.18		32.90		97.59
	$		$		$		$		$		$

	b.		6.		7.		8.		9.		10.
	$1,900.11		$657.29		$1,284.17		$6,940.89		$72,850.69		$46,512.90
	1,246.73		64.87		1,196.09		1,715.90		947.56		6,943.45
	$		$		$		$		$		$

C. Firms often keep records of sales made by individual salesmen. A sales record is given below for one such firm. Find the amount each person sold and the amount of each product sold. Also find the total sales for the given period (lower right-hand corner).

Weston Brush Co.
Departmental Sales Report
Week Ending May 21, 19X9

ITEM NO.	Smith	Jones	Bryan	Phillips	Thomas	Franklin	ITEM TOTALS
1061	$12.19	$6.70	$4.73	$19.25	$6.53	$3.03	$
1071	7.86	3.28	.89	6.15	1.73	23.27	
1081	34.95	5.75	3.96	.98	18.79	4.19	
1091	18.50	1.59	16.47	1.08	17.49	13.50	
2001	1.59	19.19	22.40	2.98	2.72	14.09	
2011	5.78	41.50	1.61	74.25	3.04	36.20	
SALESMEN TOTALS	$	$	$	$	$	$	$

D. Below is a department store sales slip. Fill in the blanks with the correct answer. The first three are done for you.

			646
Gordon's Bargain Center			
734 VALLEY VIEW			
WILLIAMSBURGH, STATE 46301			

DATE *July 18, 1989*

NAME *Mr. Frank Norsten*

ADDRESS *16 Cresson Road*
Timler, State 46322 .

QUANTITY	ITEM	UNIT COST	TOTAL AMOUNT
6	Ties	$1.50	$
	Cuff Link Sets	2.00	8.00
5	Dress Shirts		25.00
6	Cans Shoe Polish	.27	
2	Belts		7.80
4	Tie Tacks	1.98	
	Slacks	7.35	14.70
	Cardigan Sweaters	12.04	48.16
1	Leather Set		8.16
3	Sport Shirts	4.54	.
		TAX	6.69
		TOTAL	

a. Item 1 (ties) costs $1.50 each. How much do six cost?

$$\begin{array}{r} \$1.50 \\ \times\quad 6 \\ \hline \$9.00 \end{array}$$

b. Item 2 (cuff links) costs $2.00 a set and the total cost of the unknown quantity is $8.00. **How many** sets can we buy for $8.00 at $2.00 apiece?

$$\begin{array}{r} 4 \\ 2.00\overline{)8.00} \\ 8.00 \\ \hline \end{array}$$

c. Item 3 (shorts) costs $25.00 for five. How much does one pair cost?

$$\begin{array}{r} 5.00 \\ 5\overline{)25.00} \\ 25.00 \\ \hline \end{array}$$

E. Solve the following problems.

a. Mrs. Noble bought 5 pounds of ground beef at 79¢ per pound and 2 pounds of chicken at 49¢ per pound. What was the total amount she spent for the meat?

1. Plain cookies sell for $.96 per dozen at Borden's Bakery, while decorated cookies cost $1.32 per dozen.

    a. How much does one plain cookie cost?

    b. How much does one decorated cookie cost?

    c. Mrs. Adams buys $\frac{1}{2}$ dozen of the plain cookies and $1\frac{1}{2}$ dozen of the fancy cookies. How much does she spend altogether?

2. Mr. and Mrs. Stevens took their three children to see a movie and paid the following admissions: $2 per child, $3.50 per adult. What did the Stevens family spend for their movie tickets?

3. Glenfield Ladies' Club is planning its annual ice cream social. They expect to sell 500 ice cream sundaes at $.80 each.

    a. If 25 sundaes can be made using one 2-gallon container of ice cream, how many containers will be needed to serve the expected number of sundaes?

    b. Assuming the Ladies' Club does sell 500 sundaes, what will be the income from the sales?

4. Ray loaded a delivery truck with 36 dozen loaves of white bread, 19 dozen loaves of rye bread, and 22 dozen loaves of whole wheat bread. He has to deliver the following orders before lunchtime.

	LOAVES ORDERED (DOZENS)		
	WHITE	RYE	WHOLE WHEAT
Jasper's Grocery	2	0	2
Serge's Restaurant	4	2	3
City Hospital Cafeteria	10	6	5
Valley Rest Home	7	3	0

Assuming that Ray makes all the correct deliveries, how many dozen loaves of each type of bread will remain on his truck?

F. Solve the following problems, using the formulas learned in this chapter.

    a. What is the area of a parking lot that measures 140 by 70 yards?

1. A circular ice skating rink has a radius of 30 feet.

    a. What is the area of the rink?

    b. What is the circumference of the rink?

2. The measurements of a particular carton are $9 \times 5 \times 3$ inches. What is the volume in cubic inches of this rectangular solid?

3. The semicircles at each end of the ice hockey rink illustrated below represent the goal zones, which are identical in area.

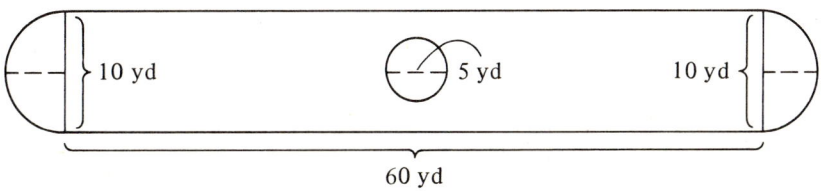

a. What is the area of the *rectangular* portion of the rink (excluding the goal zones)?

b. What is the area of each goal zone? (Hint: the area of a *semi*circle is $\frac{1}{2}$ × total area of the whole circle, or $\frac{1}{2}\pi r^2$.)

c. What is the area of the center (face-off) circle if its diameter is 5 yards?

4. Mr. Deitz's foreman instructs him to split into two equal parts a concrete block with dimensions as follows: $l = 6$ feet, $w = 3$ feet, $h = 1$ foot. What will be the volume of each half when Mr. Dietz has completed this task?

5. A football field (including end zones) is 120 yards long and 15 yards wide.

a. How many square yards of artificial turf are needed to cover this playing area?

b. Suppose the price of the artificial turf (including installation) is $25/sq yd. What will be the total cost to install it?

6. A cylindrical tank holding airplane fuel has a base radius of 1.5 feet and is 3 feet high. What is the volume of this tank in cubic feet?

7. A landscaper wants to plant grass in a plot that is 19 feet wide and 25 feet long. Assume he needs .5 pounds of grass seed to cover each square foot of the plot. How many pounds of grass seed will he need for the entire area?

8. An interior decorator for the Hotel Beaumont wants to cover a circular dancing floor that has a diameter of 36 feet. The price of the covering (including installation) is $4.50 per square foot. How much will it cost the hotel to cover the dancing area?

CHAPTER 2
Fractions and basic operations

Frequently, we encounter numbers that are greater than zero, but at the same time, less than one. Such numbers express parts of a whole. A convenient way to express parts of a whole is by *fractions*. A fraction is written as one number over another.

$$\frac{1}{2} \qquad \frac{2}{3} \qquad \frac{3}{4} \qquad \frac{7}{8}$$

The number below the line is called the *denominator* and is the number of equal parts into which a whole unit is divided. The number above the line is called the *numerator* and is the number of equal parts we wish to express. The denominator and the numerator are called the *terms of the fraction*. If the denominator is larger than the numerator, the fraction is called a *proper fraction*.

$$\frac{7}{9} \qquad \frac{3}{10} \qquad \frac{5}{6} \qquad \frac{1}{2}$$

If the numerator is larger than the denominator, we are expressing a number larger than a whole unit. This type of fraction is called an *improper fraction*.

$$\frac{9}{7} \qquad \frac{5}{3} \qquad \frac{7}{4} \qquad \frac{3}{2}$$

A number that is a combination of whole units and fractions is called a *mixed number*.

$$2\frac{1}{4} \qquad 1\frac{3}{7} \qquad 3\frac{2}{3} \qquad 4\frac{1}{2}$$

Since we have already said that an improper fraction expresses an amount greater than one unit, a relationship must exist between an improper fraction and a mixed number.

Rule 1. (a) **To change an improper fraction to a mixed number, first divide the numerator by the denominator. The integer that results is the whole-number part of the mixed number. The remainder is the numerator of the fraction part. The denominator of the improper fraction is the denominator of the fraction part.**

Example. Convert $\frac{12}{7}$ to a mixed number.

First, divide 7 into 12.

$$7)\overline{12}$$
$$\underline{7}$$
denominator $\qquad$ 5 $\longrightarrow$ numerator

Since the answer is 1 with a remainder of 5, the mixed number is $1\frac{5}{7}$.

Example. Convert $\frac{10}{3}$ to a mixed number.

$$3)\overline{10}$$
$$\underline{9}$$
denominator $\qquad$ 1 $\longrightarrow$ numerator

The mixed number is $3\frac{1}{3}$.

(b) To convert a mixed number to an improper fraction, multiply the whole-number part by the denominator of the fraction. Then add the numerator of the fraction. This result becomes the numerator of the improper fraction. The denominator is the same as the denominator of the mixed number.

Example. Convert $1\frac{5}{7}$ to an improper fraction.

$$1\frac{5}{7} = \frac{(7 \times 1) + 5}{7} = \frac{12}{7}$$

First, multiply 7 times 1 and then add 5. After placing this result over the denominator 7, the conversion is complete.

Example. Convert $3\frac{1}{3}$ to an improper fraction.

$$3\frac{1}{3} = \frac{(3 \times 3) + 1}{3} = \frac{9 + 1}{3} = \frac{10}{3}$$

FRACTIONS IN LOWEST TERMS

Factors are numbers that divide evenly into both terms of a fraction. A number is said to be *prime* when it cannot be divided evenly by any number except itself or 1. In other words, a number is prime if it has no factors except itself or 1.

Example. The number 8 is not prime because it can be divided by 2 and 4. The number 4 in turn can be divided by 2. Factors of 8, then, are 4 and 2, but the *prime factors* are 2, 2, and 2.

The number 7 is prime because there is no number, except 1 or 7, that can be divided into 7 evenly.

The prime numbers from 0 to 25 are

1, 2, 3, 5, 7, 11, 13, 17, 19, 23

A fraction is said to be in *lowest terms* when there are no *common factors* in the denominator and numerator. In other words, as long as both terms can be divided by any number except 0 or 1, the fraction is *not* in lowest terms. The important point to remember here is that *both* terms must be divisible by the same number.

Example. Convert the following to lowest terms: $\frac{3}{9}$; $\frac{8}{12}$; $\frac{5}{6}$.

$$\frac{3}{9} = \frac{1}{3} \qquad\qquad \frac{8}{12} = \frac{2}{3} \qquad\qquad \frac{5}{6}$$

Both terms can be divided by 3.

Both terms can be divided by 4

Although the denominator can be divided by 2, 3, or 6, the numerator cannot. Thus, the fraction is in lowest terms.

Table 2.1 is useful when reducing large fractions.

TABLE 2.1

A NUMBER IS DIVISIBLE BY	
2	if the last number is 0 or even.
3	if the sum of its digits is divisible by 3.
4	if the number represented by its last two digits is divisible by 4 or both are zeros.
5	if the last digit is 5 or 0.
6	if it is an even number whose sum of its digits is divisible by 3.
7	NO KNOWN RULE
8	if the number represented by the last three digits is divisible by 8.
9	if the sum of its digits is divisible by 9.

ADDITION

Fractions with different denominators are called *unlike fractions*.

$$\frac{1}{2} \qquad \frac{2}{3} \qquad \frac{5}{6}$$

To add unlike fractions, the denominators must be made equal. This can be done by finding the *least common denominator* (LCD). The LCD is the smallest number that is exactly divisible by each of the denominators.

Example. The LCD of $\frac{1}{6}$ and $\frac{1}{2}$ is 6 because it is exactly divisible by 6 and 2.

The LCD of $\frac{1}{3}$ and $\frac{1}{4}$ is 12 because 12 is the smallest number that can be divided evenly by 3 and 4.

In the case of small fractions, the LCD can usually be found quite easily. In most cases it is either the largest of the denominators or the product of the denominators.

Example. $\frac{1}{6}$ and $\frac{1}{2}$
LCD = 6

The smallest number that can be divided evenly by *both* denominators is 6. In this case, 6 is the largest of the denominators.

$\frac{1}{3}$ and $\frac{1}{4}$
LCD = 12

The smallest number that can be divided evenly by both denominators is 12. In this case, 12 is the product of the denominators (3×4).

For larger fractions and problems involving more than two fractions, these methods are not always effective. If we wanted to find the LCD of $\frac{1}{12}$, $\frac{2}{21}$, and $\frac{3}{40}$, we could multiply the denominators together. However, the result, 10,080, would not be the least common denominator. There is a much smaller number that is divisible by all the denominators. In this case the LCD is 840. As can be seen, the methods used in finding the LCD for small fractions may not yield the LCD for larger fractions. The following rule can be used for both small and large fractions.

Rule 2. **To find the LCD, first reduce each of the denominators to multiples of prime factors. Arrange these factors by aligning those that are the same number into columns. Then, take one number from each column and multiply them together. The resulting product is the LCD.**

First, to see that the process works for small fractions, find the LCD of $\frac{1}{4}$ and $\frac{1}{3}$.

$$4 = 2 \times 2$$
$$3 = 1 \times 3$$

Taking one number from each column, we have

$$2 \times 2 \times 1 \times 3 = 12 = \text{LCD}.$$

To demonstrate the process for a more complex problem, return to the previous example of $\frac{1}{12}$, $\frac{2}{21}$, and $\frac{3}{40}$.

$$
\begin{array}{l}
12 \text{ can be factored to equal } 2 \times 2 \times 3 \\
21 3 \times 7 \\
40 2 \times 2 \times 5 \times 2 \\
\hline
 2 \times 2 \times 3 \times 7 \times 5 \times 2 = 840
\end{array}
$$

Taking one number from each column, we can compute the LCD.

To change each of the fractions to fractions with a common denominator or *like fractions*, divide the original denominator into the LCD. Then multiply the numerator of the original fraction by this result and place the product over the LCD. This is illustrated as we continue the examples above.

Example. $\frac{1}{4}$ and $\frac{1}{3}$.

The LCD equals 12.

$$\frac{1}{4}, \qquad 12 \div 4 = 3, \qquad \frac{1 \times 3}{12} = \frac{3}{12}$$

$$\frac{1}{3}, \qquad 12 \div 3 = 4, \qquad \frac{1 \times 4}{12} = \frac{4}{12}$$

$\frac{1}{12}$, $\frac{2}{21}$, and $\frac{3}{40}$

The LCD equals 840.

$$\frac{1}{12}, \qquad 840 \div 12 = 70, \qquad \frac{70 \times 1}{840} = \frac{70}{840}$$

$$\frac{2}{21}, \qquad 840 \div 21 = 40, \qquad \frac{40 \times 2}{840} = \frac{80}{840}$$

$$\frac{3}{40}, \qquad 840 \div 40 = 21, \qquad \frac{21 \times 3}{840} = \frac{63}{840}$$

Another way to look at this process is to divide the LCD by the denominator and multiply the original fraction, both the denominator and the numerator, by this result.

$$\frac{1}{12}, \qquad 840 \div 12 = 70, \qquad \frac{1 \times 70}{12 \times 70} = \frac{70}{840}$$

Here, we are multiplying by $\frac{70}{70}$, or 1. Since we have really multiplied by 1, we have not changed the value of the original fraction.

Now, to add these fractions, simply add the numerators and put this sum over the LCD. Completing the examples we have been using, we get the following results.

$$\frac{1}{4} + \frac{1}{3} = \frac{3}{12} + \frac{4}{12} = \frac{3+4}{12} = \frac{7}{12}$$

$$\frac{1}{12} + \frac{2}{21} + \frac{3}{40} = \frac{70}{840} + \frac{80}{840} + \frac{63}{840} = \frac{70+80+63}{840} = \frac{213}{840}$$

To add mixed numbers, add the whole-number part and the fraction part separately. The addition of the fraction part follows the process of addition given above.

Example. $3\frac{7}{8} + 2\frac{1}{2} = \begin{array}{c} 3\frac{7}{8} \\ 2\frac{1}{2} \end{array} = \begin{array}{c} 3\frac{7}{8} \\ 2\frac{4}{8} \end{array} = \begin{array}{cc} 3 & \frac{7}{8} \\ 2 & \frac{4}{8} \\ \hline 5 & \frac{11}{8} \end{array} = 5 + \frac{11}{8} = 5 + 1\frac{3}{8} = 6\frac{3}{8}$

$4\frac{3}{4} + 6\frac{5}{6} = \begin{array}{c} 4\frac{3}{4} \\ 6\frac{5}{6} \end{array} = \begin{array}{c} 4\frac{9}{12} \\ 6\frac{10}{12} \end{array} = \begin{array}{cc} 4 & \frac{9}{12} \\ 6 & \frac{10}{12} \\ \hline 10 & \frac{19}{12} \end{array} = 10 + \frac{19}{12} = 10 + 1\frac{7}{12} = 11\frac{7}{12}$

The process of subtraction is similar to addition. First, change the fractions to like fractions. Second, subtract the numerators and place the difference over the LCD.

Example. Subtract $\frac{3}{4}$ from $\frac{5}{6}$. Changing to like fractions with an LCD of 12, we have $\frac{10}{12} - \frac{9}{12}$. Placing the subtraction of the numerators over the LCD, we obtain $\frac{10-9}{12} = \frac{1}{12}$.

MULTIPLICATION

To multiply two fractions, the following three steps are required.

Step 1. Multiply the numerators.
Step 2. Multiply the denominators.
Step 3. Reduce the result to the lowest terms.

Example. $\frac{2}{3} \times \frac{5}{8} = \frac{2 \times 5}{3 \times 8} = \frac{10}{24} = \frac{5}{12}$

The third step may be eliminated by the process of *cancellation*. Using the previous example, we see that the second step is $\frac{2 \times 5}{3 \times 8}$. From Rule 4 of the previous chapter we can rewrite this step as $\frac{2 \times 5}{8 \times 3}$ without changing the result. This is now equivalent to $\frac{2}{8} \times \frac{5}{3}$. The fraction $\frac{2}{8}$ can be reduced to $\frac{1}{4}$ and the problem completed.

$$\frac{2}{3} \times \frac{5}{8} = \frac{2 \times 5}{3 \times 8} = \frac{\overset{1}{\cancel{2}} \times 5}{\underset{4}{\cancel{8}} \times 3} = \frac{1}{4} \times \frac{5}{3} = \frac{1 \times 5}{4 \times 3} = \frac{5}{12}$$

This entire process can be simplified by using the original problem and determining if both a numerator and a denominator can be divided evenly by the same number. The key point is to divide one numerator and one denominator, regardless of their position, by the same number.

Example. $\quad \dfrac{\overset{1}{\cancel{2}}}{3} \times \dfrac{5}{\underset{4}{\cancel{8}}} = \dfrac{5}{12}$ $\qquad$ Divide by 2.

$\qquad\qquad \dfrac{7}{\underset{3}{\cancel{9}}} \times \dfrac{\overset{1}{\cancel{3}}}{12} = \dfrac{7}{36}$ $\qquad$ Divide the 3 and 9 by 3.

$\qquad\qquad \dfrac{4}{\underset{1}{\cancel{5}}} \times \dfrac{\overset{3}{\cancel{15}}}{16}$ $\qquad$ In this case, two divisions are possible. First, divide by 5.

$\qquad\qquad \dfrac{\overset{1}{\cancel{4}}}{1} \times \dfrac{3}{\underset{4}{\cancel{16}}} = \dfrac{3}{4}$ $\qquad$ Second, divide by 4.

$\qquad\qquad \dfrac{3}{\underset{1}{\cancel{7}}} \times \dfrac{\overset{3}{\cancel{21}}}{25} = \dfrac{9}{25}$

$\qquad\qquad \dfrac{7}{\underset{3}{\cancel{9}}} \times \dfrac{\overset{4}{\cancel{12}}}{17} = \dfrac{28}{51}$

If no divisions are possible, then we cannot use cancellation and must use the three-step method for multiplication, as shown in the first example.

To multiply a whole number times a fraction, make the whole number a fraction by putting it over 1. Then multiply by the process given above.

Example. $\quad 16 \times \dfrac{1}{6}$ $\qquad$ Place the 16 over 1 and multiply.

$\qquad\qquad \dfrac{16}{1} \times \dfrac{1}{6}$

$\qquad\qquad \dfrac{\overset{8}{\cancel{16}}}{1} \times \dfrac{1}{\underset{3}{\cancel{6}}} = \dfrac{8}{3} = 2\dfrac{2}{3}$

$\qquad\qquad 20 \times \dfrac{2}{9} = \dfrac{20}{1} \times \dfrac{2}{9} = \dfrac{40}{9} = 4\dfrac{4}{9}$

$\qquad\qquad 15 \times \dfrac{1}{4} = \dfrac{15}{1} \times \dfrac{1}{4} = \dfrac{15 \times 1}{1 \times 4} = \dfrac{15}{4} = 3\dfrac{3}{4}$

To multiply mixed numbers, change the mixed numbers to improper fractions and multiply.

Example. $6\dfrac{1}{3} \times 4\dfrac{1}{5} = \dfrac{19}{\overset{}{\underset{1}{\cancel{3}}}} \times \dfrac{\overset{7}{\cancel{21}}}{5} = \dfrac{133}{5} = 26\dfrac{3}{5}$

$3\dfrac{2}{3} \times \dfrac{1}{3} = \dfrac{11}{3} \times \dfrac{1}{3} = \dfrac{11 \times 1}{3 \times 3} = \dfrac{11}{9} = 1\dfrac{2}{9}$

$6\dfrac{2}{3} \times 1\dfrac{6}{7} = \dfrac{20}{3} \times \dfrac{13}{7} = \dfrac{260}{21} = 12\dfrac{8}{21}$

DIVISION

To divide by fractions, simply invert the divisor (the dividing number) and multiply according to the rules and the process given for multiplication.

Example. $\dfrac{4}{15} \div \dfrac{2}{5}$ Invert the $\frac{2}{5}$ and multiply.

$\dfrac{4}{15} \times \dfrac{5}{2} = \dfrac{\overset{2}{\cancel{4}}}{\underset{3}{\cancel{15}}} \times \dfrac{\overset{1}{\cancel{5}}}{\underset{1}{\cancel{2}}} = \dfrac{2 \times 1}{3 \times 1} = \dfrac{2}{3}$

$18 \div \dfrac{2}{9}$ First make 18 a fraction. Then invert the $\frac{2}{9}$ and multiply.

$\dfrac{18}{1} \div \dfrac{2}{9} = \dfrac{\overset{9}{\cancel{18}}}{1} \times \dfrac{9}{\underset{1}{\cancel{2}}} = 81$

$\dfrac{15}{16} \div 5$ First make 5 a fraction. Then invert this fraction and multiply.

$\dfrac{15}{16} \div \dfrac{5}{1} = \dfrac{\overset{3}{\cancel{15}}}{16} \times \dfrac{1}{\underset{1}{\cancel{5}}} = \dfrac{3 \times 1}{16 \times 1} = \dfrac{3}{16}$

ASSIGNMENT 4 FUNDAMENTALS OF FRACTIONS

A. Change each of the following improper fractions to whole or mixed numbers.

a. $\dfrac{12}{8}$ 　　　　　　　　　　 b. $\dfrac{310}{93}$

1. $\dfrac{16}{6}$ 　　　　　　　　　　 2. $\dfrac{27}{8}$

3. $\dfrac{147}{21}$ 　　　　　　　　　 4. $\dfrac{126}{7}$

5. $\dfrac{57}{12}$ 　　　　　　　　　 6. $\dfrac{76}{64}$

7. $\dfrac{156}{13}$ 　　　　　　　　　 8. $\dfrac{17}{17}$

9. $\dfrac{510}{260}$ 　　　　　　　　 10. $\dfrac{265}{146}$

B. Change each of the following mixed numbers to improper fractions.

a. $7\dfrac{1}{6}$ 　　　　　　　　　　 b. $71\dfrac{9}{10}$

1. $9\dfrac{5}{8}$ 　　　　　　　　　　 2. $6\dfrac{3}{5}$

3. $3\dfrac{11}{12}$ 　　　　　　　　　 4. $12\dfrac{3}{7}$

5. $22\dfrac{1}{2}$ 　　　　　　　　　 6. $31\dfrac{9}{13}$

7. $6\dfrac{23}{24}$ 　　　　　　　　　 8. $13\dfrac{5}{17}$

9. $7\dfrac{31}{33}$ 　　　　　　　　　 10. $56\dfrac{29}{30}$

C. Reduce each of the following fractions to lowest terms.

a. $\dfrac{9}{21}$ 　　　　　　　　　　 b. $\dfrac{160}{210}$

1. $\dfrac{25}{30}$ 　　　　　　　　　　 2. $\dfrac{32}{56}$

3. $\dfrac{12}{16}$ 　　　　　　　　　　 4. $\dfrac{60}{80}$

5. $\dfrac{63}{66}$

6. $\dfrac{75}{1000}$

7. $\dfrac{318}{424}$

8. $\dfrac{182}{208}$

9. $\dfrac{315}{378}$

10. $\dfrac{375}{2250}$

D. Change each of the following groups to like fractions.

a. $\dfrac{3}{4}, \dfrac{5}{8}$

1. $\dfrac{5}{6}, \dfrac{1}{4}$

2. $\dfrac{3}{4}, \dfrac{1}{4}, \dfrac{1}{16}$

3. $\dfrac{7}{20}, \dfrac{9}{16}, \dfrac{3}{4}$

4. $\dfrac{8}{21}, \dfrac{7}{8}, \dfrac{17}{32}$

5. $\dfrac{15}{24}, \dfrac{11}{18}, \dfrac{19}{27}, \dfrac{9}{11}$

A. Add the following groups of numbers. Reduce the answer to lowest terms.

a. $\dfrac{3}{5} + \dfrac{1}{2} + \dfrac{2}{3} =$

b. $62\dfrac{2}{3} + \dfrac{5}{6} + \dfrac{11}{9} =$

1. $\dfrac{4}{7} + \dfrac{1}{8} + \dfrac{4}{5} =$

2. $\dfrac{7}{15} + \dfrac{2}{15} + \dfrac{7}{15} =$

3. $\dfrac{3}{11} + \dfrac{5}{14} + \dfrac{19}{22} =$

4. $\dfrac{7}{8} + \dfrac{3}{4} + \dfrac{29}{32} =$

5. $\dfrac{5}{6} + \dfrac{1}{4} + \dfrac{11}{12} =$

6. $6\dfrac{9}{13} + 26 + 17\dfrac{5}{6} =$

7. $11\dfrac{1}{4} + 6\dfrac{5}{16} + 5\dfrac{5}{8} =$

8. $\dfrac{11}{7} + \dfrac{23}{9} + \dfrac{31}{16} =$

9. $\dfrac{4}{5} + 5\dfrac{1}{5} + \dfrac{7}{5} =$

10. $46\dfrac{11}{12} + 15\dfrac{3}{4} + 28\dfrac{17}{24} =$

B. Subtract the following groups of numbers. Reduce the answer to lowest terms.

a. $\dfrac{11}{12} - \dfrac{1}{6} =$

b. $7\dfrac{2}{5} - \dfrac{10}{3} =$

1. $\dfrac{15}{16} - \dfrac{5}{16} =$

2. $\dfrac{3}{4} - \dfrac{17}{24} =$

3. $\dfrac{9}{11} - \dfrac{5}{8} =$

4. $28\dfrac{2}{3} - 5\dfrac{3}{8} =$

5. $\dfrac{14}{3} - \dfrac{11}{9} =$

6. $16\dfrac{3}{4} - 6\dfrac{2}{3} =$

7. $5\dfrac{1}{2} - 3\dfrac{4}{5} =$

8. $\dfrac{23}{7} - \dfrac{16}{9} =$

9. $\dfrac{29}{4} - \dfrac{47}{9} =$

10. $\dfrac{9}{11} - \dfrac{7}{33} =$

C. Multiply each of the following. Use cancellation where possible. Reduce the answer to lowest terms.

a. $\dfrac{7}{9} \times \dfrac{4}{11} =$

b. $4\dfrac{1}{5} \times 3\dfrac{4}{7} \times 8\dfrac{1}{2} =$

1. $\dfrac{8}{15} \times \dfrac{3}{5} =$

2. $\dfrac{12}{25} \times \dfrac{5}{7} =$

3. $\dfrac{5}{9} \times \dfrac{4}{5} =$

4. $\dfrac{27}{4} \times \dfrac{6}{21} =$

5. $14 \times \dfrac{2}{9} =$

6. $\dfrac{12}{35} \times \dfrac{31}{32} \times \dfrac{7}{9} =$

7. $\dfrac{21}{25} \times \dfrac{5}{28} \times \dfrac{8}{3} =$

8. $18\dfrac{2}{3} \times 12\dfrac{1}{8} =$

9. $7\dfrac{3}{5} \times 6\dfrac{3}{4} =$

10. $21\dfrac{3}{4} \times 15\dfrac{1}{5} =$

D. Divide each of the following. Use cancellation where possible. Reduce the answer to lowest terms.

a. $\dfrac{1}{2} \div \dfrac{1}{3} =$

b. $43\dfrac{1}{8} \div 19\dfrac{1}{6} =$

1. $\dfrac{5}{6} \div \dfrac{2}{3} =$

2. $\dfrac{11}{4} \div \dfrac{3}{5} =$

3. $\dfrac{7}{13} \div \dfrac{3}{13} =$

4. $\dfrac{21}{75} \div \dfrac{7}{25} =$

5. $2\dfrac{11}{27} \div \dfrac{5}{9} =$

6. $39 \div \dfrac{5}{6} =$

7. $\dfrac{13}{15} \div 3\dfrac{3}{7} =$

8. $151\dfrac{1}{3} \div 16\dfrac{1}{4} =$

9. $44\dfrac{1}{4} \div 29\dfrac{5}{8} =$

10. $95\dfrac{1}{4} \div 21\dfrac{1}{6} =$

E. Solve each of the following problems.

1. Harold Johnson, a part-time employee in a laundry, worked $6\frac{3}{4}$ hours Monday, $7\frac{1}{2}$ hours Wednesday, and $8\frac{1}{4}$ hours Friday. What was the total number of hours he worked those three days?

2. If broadloom carpet is cut from a bolt 12 feet wide to carpet a room $9\frac{2}{3}$ feet wide, how wide is the piece of broadloom remaining on the bolt?

3. If a restaurant manager purchased 54 pounds of steak, how many $\frac{3}{8}$ pound portions could he serve?

4. A carpenter wanted three pieces of wood, each $\frac{5}{8}$ of a foot in length. If he planned to cut them from a single original piece of wood, how long would that piece of wood have to be?

5. George Jones's will instructed that at his death his daughter Susan and his son John were each to receive one-fifth of his estate, his daughter Sharon one-sixth, and his daughter Janet the remainder. What fraction of his estate was Janet to receive?

6. A landscape architect directed that 50 shrubs be distributed around a building as follows: two-fifths in back; and of the remainder, one-half on each side of the front entrance. How many shrubs were to be planted on each side of the front entrance?

7. Paul Reynolds, who owned a $12\frac{2}{5}$ acre tract of land, planned to subdivide the tract into $\frac{1}{4}$ acre lots. If he allotted one-sixth of the land to roads, how many lots would the tract yield?

8. Sarah Smith, a dress manufacturer, purchased 20 bolts of the same cotton print, 19 of which contained 30 yards and 1 of which contained $29\frac{1}{4}$ yards. If, including waste, $3\frac{1}{8}$ yards were needed to make one dress, how many dresses could be cut from the 20 bolts?

9. A room $25\frac{1}{2}$ feet by $17\frac{3}{8}$ feet, with a hall $10\frac{3}{4}$ feet by $8\frac{5}{8}$ feet, was to be air conditioned. If both room and hall had 8-ft ceilings, how many cubic feet did the space contain?

10. Edging was to be tacked around six tables on which merchandise was to be displayed at a sales conference. If two tables were $72\frac{7}{16}$ inches by $29\frac{7}{8}$ inches and four were $59\frac{1}{4}$ inches by $25\frac{1}{8}$ inches, how many inches of edging would be needed?

CHAPTER 3
Decimals and basic operations

Another way to express fractions is by decimal notation. Since *deci-* means ten, a decimal is one or more tenths, hundredths, thousandths, etc., of one unit. In other words, a decimal is a special kind of fraction. In the next chapter, we shall explain the process of converting decimals to fractions and fractions to decimals. However, for the present, it should be remembered that there are two ways to express a fraction: by regular fractional notation and by decimal notation.

$$.5 = \frac{5}{10} = \frac{1}{2} \qquad .6 = \frac{6}{10} = \frac{3}{5} \qquad .25 = \frac{25}{100} = \frac{1}{4} \qquad .75 = \frac{75}{100} = \frac{3}{4}$$

A decimal is denoted by a point placed before the number, such as .5. Here, there is only one number to the right of the decimal point; thus there is only one decimal place. One decimal place is read "tenths," so that our example of .5 is read "five-tenths." A single unit is divided into smaller and smaller parts as we increase the number of decimal places. Two decimal places, such as .05, is read "five-hundredths." In this case, the unit is divided into 100 equal parts, and .05 represents five of these smaller parts. From Table 3.1 you can see how this is carried out further.

TABLE 3.1

NUMBER OF DECIMAL PLACES	NAME	EXAMPLE	READ AS	FRACTIONAL EQUIVALENT
one	tenths	.5	five-tenths	$\frac{5}{10}$
two	hundredths	.05	five-hundredths	$\frac{5}{100}$
three	thousandths	.005	five-thousandths	$\frac{5}{1000}$
four	ten-thousandths	.0005	five ten-thousandths	$\frac{5}{10000}$
five	hundred-thousandths	.00005	five hundred-thousandths	$\frac{5}{100000}$
six	millionths	.000005	five millionths	$\frac{5}{1000000}$

To avoid errors between tenths and tens, hundredths and hundreds, and so forth, we may read decimals such as .058 as "point zero five eight."

Example. Read .6 "six-tenths" or "point six."

Read .27 "twenty seven hundredths" or "point two seven."

Read .313 "three hundred thirteen thousandths" or "point three one three."

ROUNDING OFF

Dollars and cents are generally expressed to two decimal places (hundredths), but from time to time we find them carried out further.

$1.67 $1.675 $7.531 $4.679

In all of these cases, since the smallest value of money we have is $.01, it is impossible to pay or charge someone an amount smaller than $.01 for a single unit. Therefore, if the third decimal number is 5 or greater, we drop it and add $.01 to the number in the second decimal place. If the number in the third decimal place is less than 5, we drop it and everything remains the same.

$1.675 = $1.68 $7.531 = $7.53 $4.679 = $4.68

is 5, so we add   is less than 5,   is greater than 5,

1 cent.   so we just drop the 1.   so we drop it and add 1 cent.

This process, called *rounding off*, can be extended to any decimal by applying the same principle. For example, if we are asked to round off .1763 to three decimal places, we want only that number of places in the answer. We always look at the decimal place immediately to the right of the decimal to which we are rounding off. In this case, we are asked to round off to three places, so we look at the number in the fourth decimal place. Since it is less than 5, we drop it and let everything else remain the same: .1763 rounded off to three decimal places equals .176.

Example. .4329 rounded off to three places equals .433

.76833	to four places	.7683
.57839	to two places	.58
.57839	to four places	.5784

Occasionally, it may be more practical for our purposes to consider only the whole number units to the left of the decimal point, as follows:

Example. How many *full* bags of sugar, each weighing 5 pounds, can be loaded onto a platform with a capacity of 407 pounds?

$$\begin{array}{r} 81.4 \\ 5\overline{)407} \\ 400 \\ \hline 7 \\ 5 \\ \hline 2.0 \\ 2.0 \\ \hline 0 \end{array}$$

Although 81.4 5-pound bags of sugar can actually be loaded onto the platform, we need only consider the portion of this answer to the *left* of the decimal point, which represents the number of *full* bags as specified in the problem.

Example. Michelle has $4.55. How many $.75 bags of popcorn can she buy?

$$\begin{array}{r} 6. \\ .75\overline{)4.55} \\ 4.50 \\ \hline .05 \end{array}$$

She can purchase 6 $.75 bags of popcorn and will have $.05 remaining.

ADDITION

The addition of decimals is exactly the same as the addition of natural numbers. However, there is an important rule to remember if the decimal is found together with a whole number such as 2.063. These combinations of decimals and natural numbers are called *mixed decimals*.

Rule 1. **When adding groups of mixed decimals, remember to keep the decimal points aligned vertically, which is equivalent to filling in the missing places to their right with zeros.**

Example. Add 6.9, 17.42, .006, and 294.

$$\begin{array}{rcl} 6.9 & = & 6.900 \\ 17.42 & = & 17.420 \\ .006 & = & .006 \\ 294. & = & 294.000 \\ \hline 318.326 & = & 318.326 \end{array}$$

SUBTRACTION

As in the addition of decimals, the subtraction of decimals is exactly the same as the subtraction of natural numbers. There is again, however, an important rule to follow.

Rule 2. **When subtracting decimals or mixed decimals, remember to keep the decimal points aligned vertically. The two numbers must also have the same number of decimal places. Therefore, add as many zeros to the right as necessary.**

Example. If .4763 is to be subtracted from 1.062, first vertically align the decimal points. Then add a zero to the 1.062 to make the number of decimal places equal. Finally, subtract.

$$\begin{array}{r} 1.0620 \\ - .4763 \\ \hline .5857 \end{array}$$

Example. 16.481 minus 5.02.

$$\begin{array}{r} 16.481 \\ - 5.020 \\ \hline 11.461 \end{array}$$

MULTIPLICATION

When two decimals are multiplied together, the operation is identical to the multiplication of two natural numbers. What we must know, however, is where the decimal point goes in the answer or product. The following rule explains how the position of the decimal point is determined.

Rule 3. **To find the position of the decimal point in the product of two numbers at least one of which is a decimal or mixed decimal, add the number of decimal places in the decimal number or numbers and count off the same number of places from right to left in the product. If the number of places required is greater than the number of places in the product, add as many zeros to the left of the product as necessary.**

Example.

$$
\begin{array}{r}
.07 \\
\times\ 4 \\
\hline
.28
\end{array}
\qquad
\begin{array}{r}
.6 \\
\times\ .8 \\
\hline
.48
\end{array}
\qquad
\begin{array}{r}
16.22 \\
\times\ \ 1.481 \\
\hline
1622 \\
12976 \\
6488 \\
1622 \\
\hline
24.02182
\end{array}
\qquad
\begin{array}{r}
.45 \\
\times\ .009 \\
\hline
.00405*
\end{array}
\qquad
\begin{array}{r}
.067 \\
\times\ .03 \\
\hline
.00201*
\end{array}
$$

*Here, five places are needed and only three available. Therefore, add two zeros to the left of the product making the answer .00405.

DIVISION

The division of decimals and the position of the decimal point involves two cases. Case 1 occurs when the divisor (the dividing number) is a decimal or a mixed decimal. Case 2 occurs when the divisor is a whole number, but the dividend (the number to be divided) is a decimal or a mixed decimal.

Case 1. If the divisor is a decimal or mixed number, division is performed by moving the decimal point in the divisor as many places to the right as necessary to make the divisor a whole number. The decimal point in the dividend must be moved exactly the same number of places. Zeros may need to be added to the dividend to provide the proper number of places. The decimal point in the answer is then placed directly above the decimal point in the dividend.

Example. $16.389 \div .3 = \dfrac{16.389}{.3} \times \dfrac{10}{10} = \dfrac{163.89}{3}$

$$.3\overline{)16.389} = 3\overline{)163.89}$$

$$
\begin{array}{r}
54.63 \\
3\overline{)163.89} \\
15\ \ \ \ \ \\
\hline
13\ \ \ \ \\
12\ \ \ \ \\
\hline
1\,8\ \ \\
1\,8\ \ \\
\hline
9 \\
9 \\
\hline
0
\end{array}
$$

To make the divisor a whole number, the decimal point must be moved one place to the right; thus, the point in the dividend must be moved one place.

Example. $14 \div .28 = \dfrac{14}{.28} = \dfrac{1400}{28} = 28\overline{)1400}$

$$
\begin{array}{r}
50. \\
.28\overline{)14.00} \\
14\ 0 \\
\hline
00
\end{array}
$$

In this case, zeros must be added to the dividend and the decimal point moved two places to the right in both the divisor and dividend.

$$
\begin{array}{r}
2\ 7.1 \\
2.5\overline{)67.7\ 5} \\
50 \\
\hline
17\ 7 \\
17\ 5 \\
\hline
2\ 5 \\
2\ 5 \\
\hline
\end{array}
\qquad
\begin{array}{r}
6.5 \\
.9521\overline{)6.1886\ 5} \\
5\ 7126 \\
\hline
4760\ 5 \\
4760\ 5 \\
\hline
\end{array}
\qquad
\begin{array}{r}
45\ 3.2 \\
4.2\overline{)1,903.4\ 4} \\
1\ 68 \\
\hline
223 \\
210 \\
\hline
13\ 4 \\
12\ 6 \\
\hline
8\ 4 \\
8\ 4 \\
\hline
\end{array}
$$

Case 2. If the dividend is a decimal or mixed number and the divisor is not, then place the decimal point in the answer directly above the decimal point in the dividend. If necessary, zeros should be added after the decimal point (the addition of zeros after a decimal point does not change the value of a number).

Example.
$$
\begin{array}{r}
.3 \\
7\overline{)2.1} \\
2\ 1 \\
\hline
\end{array}
\qquad
\begin{array}{r}
1.2 \\
4\overline{)4.8} \\
4 \\
\hline
8 \\
8 \\
\hline
\end{array}
\qquad
\begin{array}{r}
18.1 \\
2\overline{)36.2} \\
2 \\
\hline
16 \\
16 \\
\hline
2 \\
2 \\
\hline
\end{array}
$$

Example. $.1 \div 20$

$$
\begin{array}{r}
.005 \\
20\overline{).100} \\
100 \\
\hline
\end{array}
$$

In this case, division is not possible without the addition of zeros.

When it is not stated how far a division problem should be carried out, it is convenient to write the remainder in the form of a fraction. The remainder becomes the numerator, and the divisor becomes the denominator. The fraction is then written as part of the answer.

Example.

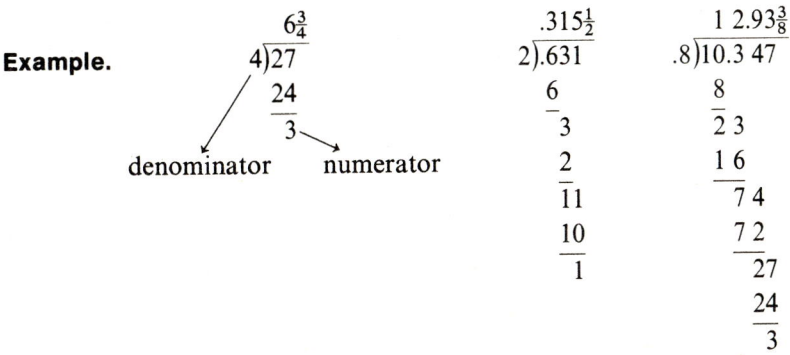

$$
\begin{array}{r}
6\frac{3}{4} \\
4\overline{)27} \\
24 \\
\hline
3
\end{array}
\qquad
\begin{array}{r}
.315\frac{1}{2} \\
2\overline{).631} \\
6 \\
\hline
3 \\
2 \\
\hline
11 \\
10 \\
\hline
1
\end{array}
\qquad
\begin{array}{r}
1\ 2.93\frac{3}{8} \\
.8\overline{)10.3\ 47} \\
8 \\
\hline
2\ 3 \\
1\ 6 \\
\hline
7\ 4 \\
7\ 2 \\
\hline
27 \\
24 \\
\hline
3
\end{array}
$$

denominator   numerator

Sometimes, however, it is desirable to have the answer come out to a decimal with a certain number of places, often two places. Again, zeros can always be added after the decimal point in the dividend without changing its value.

Example. $18.6 \div 20$

$$
\begin{array}{r}
.9 \\
20\overline{)18.6} \\
18.0 \\
\hline
6
\end{array}
$$

$$
\begin{array}{r}
.93 \\
20\overline{)18.60} \\
18\ 0\downarrow \\
\hline
60 \\
60 \\
\hline
\end{array}
$$

Here, if we divide without adding zeros, the division leaves us with an answer with just one decimal place and a remainder of 6. If we add a zero and bring it down, the answer has two decimal places (and, in this instance, the remainder happens to be eliminated).

ASSIGNMENT 6 DECIMALS: ADDITION AND SUBTRACTION

A. Write each of the following as decimal numbers.

   a. seven-tenths

   b. one thousand two, and one hundred two, ten-thousandths

   1. twenty-four hundredths

   2. nine-thousandths

   3. fifty-seven millionths

   4. twelve ten-thousandths

   5. one hundred thirty two thousandths

   6. seventy five and six-tenths

   7. fifteen and fifteen ten-thousandths

   8. sixty-seven thousandths

   9. nine hundred eighty eight millionths

   10. ninety-one hundredths

B. Write each of the following decimals in words.

   a. 74.1

   b. 1,624.1006

   1. 4.23

   2. .112

   3. 3.08

   4. .045

   5. 30.19

   6. .0301

   7. .18

   8. 702.02

   9. .368

   10. .0009

C. Round off the following decimals to hundredths.

   a. .698

   1. .543

   2. .9785

   3. .26582

   4. 1.5729

   5. .89578

D. Round off the following decimals to thousandths.

   a. .0008

   1. .0567

   2. .3692

   3. .37428

   4. .6464

   5. .9459

E. Write the following decimals as fractions.

   a. .85

   1. .6

   2. .25

   3. .94

   4. .005

   5. .365

F. Put each of the following groups of numbers in columns and add.

   a. 7.2, 9.64, .8, 12

   1. 17.8, 5.79, .432, .2

2. 6.47, 3.8, 5.429, .2

3. .99, 10.7, 19.87, 4.892

4. 2.396, 1.8, 229, .004

5. 146.1, .0208, .92, 17.463, .1

G. Perform each of the following subtractions.

a. 2.396 minus .947

1. .578 minus .394

2. 9.502 minus .69

3. 105.3 minus 9.35

4. 4.69534 minus .43596

5. 106.7 minus .7394

ASSIGNMENT 7 DECIMALS: MULTIPLICATION AND DIVISION

A. Multiply each of the following decimals.

a.	.432	1.	9.067	2.	8.0875	3.	.00064	4.	.678	5.	12.96
	× .6		× 75		× .5		× .91		×.076		×.0014

b.	54.39	6.	.0142	7.	72.9	8.	.376	9.	20.7	10.	600.9
	×1.782		× 72.9		×.0142		× .35		×3.0007		× .402

B. Multiply each of the following decimals.

a. 32.746 × .00062   1. .4127 × .0956   2. 361.2 × 16.002

3. 2,368.7 × 26.1   4. .3413 × .0106   5. 2.041 × 72.830

b. 10,009 × .00601   6. 16.096 × 57.063   7. 8.6134 × .0012

8. 710.26 × 10.301   9. 1,926 × .1132   10. 30.19 × .000062

C. Divide each of the following and round off your answer correct to hundredths.

a. .132 ÷ 6   1. 5.4 ÷ 30   2. 67.32 ÷ 5,610

3. 117.6 ÷ 32   4. 1.92 ÷ 276   5. 14.469 ÷ .0013

D. Divide each of the following and round off your answer correct to hundredths.

    a. $168.31 \div 19.43$ **1.** $3.692 \div .0036$ **2.** $2.0856 \div 2.68$

    3. $9.7031 \div .321$ **4.** $96.482 \div 1,346$ **5.** $642.81 \div .406$

E.   Solve each of the following problems.

    a. How many whole shares of American Soap Company can be purchased with $24,775 if the stock is selling at $42 per share? (Disregard the broker's commission.)

    1. The television department of a store sold 117 television sets in June for a total of $31,712.46. What was the average price of the sets sold?

    2. Bill Wilson, who has driven his car 10,012 miles, gets 20.4 miles per gallon. If Bill buys gas at $.615 per gallon, how much has he spent on gas since buying the car?

    3. A subscription to a business magazine, published monthly, costs $9.84 annually. On the news-stand, it costs $1.25 per issue. How much does a reader who buys each issue save by taking out a subscription for one year? How much does he save per issue?

    4. The clerical staff in a small office earned the following monthly salaries: $800.17, $692.56, $582.14, $489.72, and $417.20. What was the average monthly salary paid?

    5. A package containing six 8-ounce cans of fruit juice was selling for $1.49. What was the cost of the juice per ounce? Which was the better buy, the six-pack or an 18.5 ounce can of the same brand priced at $.55?

    6. The owner of Jill's Eatery sold 37 beef dinners, each of which yielded a profit of $.54. On the same night, she also sold 51 chicken dinners, each of which yielded a $.48 profit. On which of the two dinners did she make a greater total profit?

    7. Harold Novak subdivided a tract of land containing 63.007 acres so that lots containing 3.06, 12.2, 1.0575, and 1.27 acres were created. How much of the original tract was left after he had sold the four smaller lots? (Express answer to three decimal places.)

8. Kathy has 145 yards of material in which to make play costumes. If each costume requires 3.75 yards of material, how many whole costumes can be made from her fabric?

9. Mr. Thorpe, a foreman, must assign workers to a project which has been calculated to require 356 man hours.

   a. If he assigns eight workers each to work 37.5 hours, how many man hours of the project will remain to be completed?
   b. Policy states that whatever time is left over after one full week of work (37.5 hours) will be divided equally among the eight workers. How many extra hours of work will each worker contribute to this project?

10. Jack Jones instructed his stockbroker to buy 100 shares of American Machine Tool Company with the $6,707.12 in his account and to buy as many whole shares of United Enterprises stock as possible with the remainder. If American Machine Tool Company stock is selling at $42.25 and United Enterprises stock at $7.50, how many shares of United Enterprises stock can be purchased? How much money will remain in Jack Jones's account after these transactions have been made? (Disregard the broker's commission.)

CHAPTER 4
Fraction-decimal relationships

Since both fractions and decimals express parts of whole units, a fraction can be converted to a decimal and a decimal to a fraction. The methods for these conversions are set forth in the following rules.

Rule 1. *Changing a fraction to a decimal.* **Since the line separating the numerator and denominator represents division, to change a fraction to a decimal, simply divide the numerator by the denominator.**

Example.

$$\frac{3 \text{ dividend}}{4 \text{ divisor}}$$

$$\begin{array}{r} .75 \\ 4\overline{)3.00} \\ 2\,8 \\ \hline 20 \\ 20 \\ \hline \end{array}$$

In this example the numerator 3 is divided by the denominator 4. A decimal is placed after the 3 and two zeros added, just as we did in the division of decimals.

$$\frac{1}{2} = .5 \qquad \begin{array}{r} .5 \\ 2\overline{)1.0} \\ 1\,0 \\ \hline \end{array}$$

$$\frac{4}{5} = .8 \qquad \begin{array}{r} .8 \\ 5\overline{)4.0} \\ 4\,0 \\ \hline \end{array}$$

Rule 2. *Changing a decimal to a fraction.* **First, omit the decimal point and place the number over a denominator that reflects the number of places in the original decimal, that is, 10, 100, 1,000, and so forth. Then reduce the fraction to lowest terms.**

Example. $.7 = \dfrac{7}{10}$

Drop the decimal point and place the 7 over the denominator 10, which expresses the number of places in the original decimal.

$$.8 = \frac{8}{10} = \frac{4}{5} \qquad .55 = \frac{55}{100} = \frac{11}{20} \qquad .325 = \frac{325}{1000} = \frac{65}{200} = \frac{13}{40}$$

Now that we have two ways of expressing parts of a whole and a means to convert them, we can use either form in a given problem.

Example.

	FRACTION		DECIMAL	

$$\frac{3}{5} \times \frac{1}{4} \qquad \frac{3 \times 1}{5 \times 4} = \frac{3}{20} \qquad \frac{3}{5} = .6 \qquad \begin{array}{r} .25 \\ \times \;\; .6 \\ \hline .150 \end{array}$$

$$\frac{1}{4} = .25$$

$$\frac{3}{4} \times \frac{7}{10} \qquad \frac{3 \times 7}{4 \times 10} = \frac{21}{40} \qquad \frac{3}{4} = .75 \qquad \begin{array}{r} .75 \\ \times \;\; .7 \\ \hline .525 \end{array}$$

$$\frac{7}{10} = .7$$

$$\frac{3}{4} + \frac{1}{8} \qquad \frac{6}{8} + \frac{1}{8} = \frac{7}{8} \qquad \frac{3}{4} = .75 \qquad \begin{array}{r} .75 \\ +.125 \\ \hline .875 \end{array}$$

$$\frac{1}{8} = .125$$

$$\frac{1}{2} + \frac{3}{8} \qquad \frac{4}{8} + \frac{3}{8} = \frac{7}{8} \qquad \frac{1}{2} = .5 \qquad \begin{array}{r} .5 \\ +.375 \\ \hline .875 \end{array}$$

$$\frac{3}{8} = .375$$

Table 4.1 gives some of the most commonly encountered fractions with their decimal equivalents.

TABLE 4.1

Common Decimal Equivalents

$\frac{1}{32} = .03125$	$\frac{11}{32} = .34375$	$\frac{11}{16} = .6875$
$\frac{1}{16} = .0625$	$\frac{3}{8} = .375$	$\frac{23}{32} = .71875$
$\frac{3}{32} = .09375$	$\frac{13}{32} = .40625$	$\frac{3}{4} = .75$
$\frac{1}{8} = .125$	$\frac{7}{16} = .4375$	$\frac{25}{32} = .78125$
$\frac{5}{32} = .15625$	$\frac{15}{32} = .46875$	$\frac{13}{16} = .8125$
$\frac{3}{16} = .1875$	$\frac{1}{2} = .5$	$\frac{27}{32} = .84375$
$\frac{7}{32} = .21875$	$\frac{17}{32} = .53125$	$\frac{7}{8} = .875$
$\frac{1}{4} = .25$	$\frac{9}{16} = .5625$	$\frac{29}{32} = .90625$
$\frac{9}{32} = .28125$	$\frac{19}{32} = .59375$	$\frac{15}{16} = .9375$
$\frac{5}{16} = .3125$	$\frac{5}{8} = .625$	$\frac{31}{32} = .96875$
	$\frac{21}{32} = .65625$	

BUSINESS APPLICATIONS

Frequently, the prices of articles are quoted as so many dollars a hundred (sometimes expressed by the Roman symbol C), hundred-weight or hundred pounds (cwt), thousand (expressed by the Roman symbol M) or ton (T).

To find the cost of a quantity priced by the hundred, hundred-weight, thousand, or ton, first divide the quantity by whatever unit the price is expressed in. Then multiply the result by the unit price.

Example. Find the cost of 1200 bricks at $35 per M.
First, divide the quantity 1200 by 1000.

$$\frac{1200}{1000} = 1000\overline{)1200.0} = 1.2$$

$$
\begin{array}{r}
1.2 \\
1000\overline{)1200.0} \\
\underline{1000} \\
200\ 0 \\
\underline{200\ 0}
\end{array}
$$

Then multiply by the price.

$$1.2 \times \$35 =
\begin{array}{r}
\$\ 3\ 5 \\
1.2 \\
\hline
7\ 0 \\
35 \\
\hline
\$42.0 = \text{or } \$42.00
\end{array}
$$

Alternatively, we can combine these operations and simplify.

$$\frac{12\cancel{00}}{10\cancel{00}} \times 35 = \frac{\overset{6}{\cancel{12}}}{\underset{5}{\cancel{10}}} \times 35 = \frac{6}{\cancel{5}} \times \overset{7}{\cancel{35}} = \$42$$

Another way to determine the number of hundreds, or thousands, is simply to move the decimal point. To find hundreds, move the decimal point two places to the left in the quantity figure. To find thousands, move the decimal point three places to the left in the quantity figure.

Example. Find the cost of 512 envelopes at $1.20/C. Since we are to find the cost in terms of hundreds, we move the decimal two places to the left in the quantity figure, making 512 the same as 5.12 C. Now multiply by the price.

$$
\begin{array}{r}
5.12 \\
\times\quad 1.20 \\
\hline
1\ 0240 \\
5\ 12\quad \\
\hline
\$6.1440
\end{array}
$$

Then, rounding off the cents, we obtain $6.14.

Example. Find the cost of 1750 pencils at $8/M.

$$\frac{\overset{35}{\cancel{1750}}}{\underset{\substack{20\\5}}{\cancel{1000}}} \times \overset{2}{\cancel{8}} = \frac{70}{5} = \$14 \quad \text{or} \quad \frac{1750}{1000} = 1.750 \qquad \begin{array}{r} 1.750 \\ \times \quad\quad 8 \\ \hline \$14.000 \end{array}$$

In making out payrolls, salaries or wages sometimes have to be expressed in different time units than the ones in which they were originally expressed. Annual salary divided by 12 is monthly salary. A monthly salary divided by $4\frac{1}{3}$ (52 weeks divided by 12 months) is a weekly salary. A weekly salary divided by days worked per week is daily wages. Weekly salary divided by hours worked per week is the hourly rate.

Example. If a man makes $8400 a year, how much does he make in a month? in a week? If he works eight hours a day, five days a week, how much does he earn in one day, disregarding any unpaid holidays? in one hour?

$$\begin{array}{r} \$700/\text{mon} \\ 12\overline{)8400} \\ 84 \\ \hline \end{array} \qquad 700 \div 4\frac{1}{3} \qquad 700 \times \frac{3}{13} = \frac{2100}{13}$$

$$\begin{array}{r} 161.538 = \$161.54/\text{wk} \\ 13\overline{)2100.000} \\ 13 \\ \hline 80 \\ 78 \\ \hline 20 \\ 13 \\ \hline 7\,0 \\ 6\,5 \\ \hline 50 \\ 39 \\ \hline 110 \end{array}$$

$$\begin{array}{r} 32.308 = \$32.31/\text{da} \\ 5\overline{)161.540} \\ 15 \\ \hline 11 \\ 10 \\ \hline 1\,5 \\ 1\,5 \\ \hline 40 \\ 40 \\ \hline \end{array} \qquad\qquad \begin{array}{r} 4.038 = \$4.04/\text{hr} \\ 40\overline{)161.540} \\ 160 \\ \hline 1\,54 \\ 1\,20 \\ \hline 340 \\ 320 \\ \hline 20 \end{array}$$

ASSIGNMENT 8 FRACTION-DECIMAL RELATIONSHIPS

A. Change each of the fractions to decimals. Round off your answer correct to thousandths. (Note: wherever possible, use Table 4.1, Common Decimal Equivalents, for the problems in Assignment 8.)

a. $\dfrac{5}{7}$

b. $\dfrac{120}{121}$

1. $\dfrac{5}{8}$

2. $\dfrac{11}{12}$

3. $\dfrac{29}{32}$

4. $\dfrac{3}{41}$

5. $\dfrac{17}{51}$

6. $\dfrac{47}{149}$

7. $\dfrac{71}{89}$

8. $\dfrac{101}{121}$

9. $\dfrac{12}{367}$

10. $\dfrac{523}{757}$

B. Change each of the following decimals to fractions.

a. 0.17

b. 0.0080

1. 0.95

2. 0.8

3. 0.075

4. 0.60

5. 0.136

6. 0.0042

7. 0.0275

8. 0.6455

9. 0.3332

10. 0.16524

C. Perform each of the following operations by both the fraction and decimal methods.

	FRACTION	DECIMAL

a. $\left(\dfrac{5}{6} \times \dfrac{1}{3}\right) + \dfrac{5}{8}$

1. $2\dfrac{1}{3} \times 6\dfrac{1}{2}$

2. $5\dfrac{3}{5} \div 2\dfrac{2}{3}$

3. $7\frac{1}{2} + \frac{9}{10} + 1\frac{4}{5}$

4. $\frac{8}{9} - \frac{1}{4}$

5. $16 + 8\frac{1}{2} - \frac{15}{16}$

ASSIGNMENT 9 FRACTION-DECIMAL RELATIONSHIPS

A. Perform the indicated operations by both the fraction and decimal methods.

	FRACTION	DECIMAL

a. $\dfrac{31}{32} - \dfrac{9}{16}$

1. $\dfrac{17}{12} - \dfrac{5}{8}$

2. $6\dfrac{3}{4} - \dfrac{16}{15}$

3. $\dfrac{1}{2} + \dfrac{2}{3} + \dfrac{3}{4} + \dfrac{4}{5}$

4. $\dfrac{5}{8} + \dfrac{5}{6} + \dfrac{13}{16}$

5. $7\dfrac{3}{5} + 2\dfrac{1}{2} + 9\dfrac{1}{4} + \dfrac{11}{16}$

B. Perform the indicated operations by both the fraction and decimal methods. Round off decimals correct to thousandths.

	FRACTION	DECIMAL

a. $\dfrac{7}{16} \times \dfrac{1}{64}$

1. $4\dfrac{1}{5} \times 2\dfrac{1}{3} \times 3\dfrac{4}{7}$

2. $\dfrac{1}{2} \times \dfrac{7}{8} \times \dfrac{3}{4}$

3. $\dfrac{7}{4} \div \dfrac{12}{11}$

4. $\dfrac{7}{8} \div \dfrac{29}{32}$

5. $2\dfrac{19}{32} \div 1\dfrac{3}{4}$

ASSIGNMENT 10 BUSINESS APPLICATIONS OF FRACTIONS AND DECIMALS

A. Find the cost of the following articles.

a. 300 articles at $7/C

b. 13,700 articles at $7.49/C

1. 175 articles at $8/C

2. 350 lb at $6/cwt

3. 750 articles at $12/M

4. 1550 articles at $10/M

5. 60 lb at $4.80/cwt

6. 95 lb at $10.50/cwt

7. 1200 articles at $5/M

8. 9000 lb at $18/T

9. 1800 lb at $20/T

10. 7500 lb at $8/T

11. 6000 lb at $5.50/T

12. 3000 lb at $6.90/T

13. 1775 lb at $3.20/T

14. 100 articles at $20/M

15. 850 articles at $16/M

16. 2500 articles at $17/M

17. 1450 articles at $19/M

18. 864 articles at $4.16/C

19. 4250 articles at $67.70/M

20. 1320 articles at $7.49/C

B. Listed below are the annual salaries of six workers. If all six work eight hours a day and five days a week, find their monthly, weekly, daily, and hourly wage.

Miss Smith: $9600   Mr. Brown: $7800

Mr. Thomas: $5700   Mr. Jackson: $12,500

Mrs. Davis: $10,800   Mr. Carlson: $8500

C. Solve the following problems, using both fraction and decimal methods for each.

1. If 12 workers worked $7\frac{1}{4}$ hours each for five days at $4.10 per hour, what was the total amount they were paid?

2. If $2\frac{1}{4}$ pounds of candy cost $6.50, how much would $7\frac{1}{2}$ pounds cost?

3. Marta Schmidt, a financial advisor, recommended that her client spend one-quarter of his income on shelter and one-fifth on food, that he save one-tenth, and that he use the rest for other goods and services. Assuming an income of $20,000, how many dollars of her client's income are left for other expenditures?

4. If it took seven men 21.4 hours apiece to complete a job, how many hours apiece would it have taken three men?

5. A hardware store had the following items in stock.
    $2\frac{3}{4}$ dozen screwdrivers valued at $25.50 per dozen
    $1\frac{1}{4}$ dozen drills valued at $51.67 per dozen
    $\frac{2}{3}$ dozen pliers valued at $40.40 per dozen
    $3\frac{1}{6}$ dozen wrenches valued at $37.63 per dozen
    $7\frac{5}{6}$ dozen hammers valued at $22.75 per dozen

    What was the total value of these items?

CHAPTER 5
Aliquot parts

In Chapter 2, we defined a number that divides evenly into another number as a *factor* of that number. In business, a common name for a factor is *aliquot part*.

Example. An aliquot part of 9 is 3 because it divides evenly into 9.
An aliquot part of 18 is 6 because it divides evenly into 18.
An aliquot part of 24 is 8 because it divides evenly into 24.

A mixed number may also be an aliquot part of another if it divides evenly into that number.

Example. An aliquot part of 11 is $5\frac{1}{2}$ because it divides evenly into 11.

$$11 \div 5\frac{1}{2} = \frac{11}{1} \div \frac{11}{2} = \frac{\overset{1}{\cancel{11}}}{1} \times \frac{2}{\underset{1}{\cancel{11}}} = 2$$

An aliquot part of 10 is $3\frac{1}{3}$ because it divides evenly into 10.

$$10 \div 3\frac{1}{3} = \frac{10}{1} \div \frac{10}{3} = \frac{\overset{1}{\cancel{10}}}{1} \times \frac{3}{\underset{1}{\cancel{10}}} = 3$$

In business, the time involved in computing costs and prices can be lessened by making use of aliquot parts of $1.00. For example, suppose we were asked to find the cost of 216 ballpoint pens at $.50 apiece. Our first thought would probably be to multiply 216 times $.50.

$$\begin{array}{r} 216 \\ \times \quad 0.50 \\ \hline \$108.00 \end{array}$$

However, it would be much quicker if we thought in terms of aliquot parts. If the price of the pens were $1.00, the cost would have been $216. Since $.50 is $\frac{1}{2}$ of a dollar, we can simply multiply 216 times $\frac{1}{2}$. In this case, the division is simple and can be done mentally.

$$216 \times \frac{1}{2} = \frac{216}{2} = \$108$$

Example. Find the cost of 362 cigars at $.25 apiece. (The symbol @ is used to mean "at." In business, this is sometimes written as "362 cigars @ $.25.")

$$362 \times \frac{1}{4} = \frac{362}{4} = \$90.50$$

240 neckties @ $.75   160 light bulbs @ $.25

$$240 \times \frac{3}{4} = \frac{720}{4} = \$180 \qquad 160 \times \frac{1}{4} = \frac{160}{4} = \$40$$

The most common aliquot parts of $1.00 are found in Table 5.1.

TABLE 5.1

Aliquot Parts of $1.00	
$\frac{1}{20} = \$.05 = 5$ cents	$\frac{1}{6} = \$.16\frac{2}{3} = 16\frac{2}{3}$ cents
$\frac{1}{16} = \$.06\frac{1}{4} = 6\frac{1}{4}$ cents	$\frac{5}{6} = \$.83\frac{1}{3} = 83\frac{1}{3}$ cents
$\frac{1}{15} = \$.06\frac{2}{3} = 6\frac{2}{3}$ cents	$\frac{1}{5} = \$.20 = 20$ cents
$\frac{1}{12} = \$.08\frac{1}{3} = 8\frac{1}{3}$ cents	$\frac{2}{5} = \$.40 = 40$ cents
$\frac{1}{10} = \$.10 = 10$ cents	$\frac{3}{5} = \$.60 = 60$ cents
$\frac{3}{10} = \$.30 = 30$ cents	$\frac{4}{5} = \$.80 = 80$ cents
$\frac{7}{10} = \$.70 = 70$ cents	$\frac{1}{4} = \$.25 = 25$ cents
$\frac{1}{8} = \$.12\frac{1}{2} = 12\frac{1}{2}$ cents	$\frac{3}{4} = \$.75 = 75$ cents
$\frac{3}{8} = \$.37\frac{1}{2} = 37\frac{1}{2}$ cents	$\frac{1}{3} = \$.33\frac{1}{3} = 33\frac{1}{3}$ cents
$\frac{5}{8} = \$.62\frac{1}{2} = 62\frac{1}{2}$ cents	$\frac{2}{3} = \$.66\frac{2}{3} = 66\frac{2}{3}$ cents
$\frac{7}{8} = \$.87\frac{1}{2} = 87\frac{1}{2}$ cents	$\frac{1}{2} = \$.50 = 50$ cents

Many times it is more convenient to solve the problem in terms of aliquot parts of 100 units. For example, we might be asked to find the cost of 60 paperback books at $2.65 apiece. If we had 100 books, the cost would be $265. This is computed mentally; if we multiply by 100, we simply move the decimal point two places to the right. Since 60 is $\frac{3}{5}$ of 100, we can multiply $265 by $\frac{3}{5}$ and find the answer quickly.

$$\overset{53}{\cancel{265}} \times \frac{3}{\cancel{5}} = \frac{53 \times 3}{1} = \$159$$

Example. Find the cost of 25 units @ $1.60.   Find the cost of 50 units @ $36.80.

$$\frac{1}{4} \times \frac{\overset{40}{\cancel{160}}}{1} = \$40 \qquad \frac{\overset{1840}{\cancel{3680}}}{1} = \$1840$$

When the price or cost expressed is greater than $1.00, it can be broken down into a combination of $1.00 and an aliquot part of $1.00. For example, if the price of a book is $1.25, the total cost of 120 books would be $150. This answer was obtained by first finding the cost of 120 units at $1.00 apiece.

120 @ $1.00 = $120

Second, we find the cost of the same 120 units at $.25 apiece.

$$120 \text{ @ } \$.25 = \overset{30}{\cancel{120}} \times \frac{1}{\underset{1}{\cancel{4}}} = \$30$$

Finally, we add the two results to find the total cost.

120
$\underline{30}$
$\overline{\$150} = \text{total cost}$

Example. Find the cost of 412 cartons of cigars at $1.25 a carton.

$$412 \text{ @ } \$1.00 = 412 \times 1.00 = \$412$$
$$412 \text{ @ } \$.25 = 412 \times \frac{1}{4} = \underline{103}$$
$$\overline{\$515} = \text{total cost}$$

Find the cost of 603 pipes at $2.33\frac{1}{3}$ apiece.

$$603 \text{ @ } \$2.00 = 603 \times 2.00 = \$1206$$
$$603 \text{ @ } .33\frac{1}{3} = 603 \times \frac{1}{3} = \underline{201}$$
$$\overline{\$1407} = \text{total cost}$$

Similarly, the quantity can be expressed in terms of a combination of 100 units and an aliquot part of 100 units.

Example. Find the cost of 170 units at $1.65 a unit.

$$100 \text{ units} \times \$1.65 = \$165.00$$
$$70 \text{ units} \times \$1.65 = \frac{7}{10} \times 165 = \underline{115.50}$$
$$\overline{\$280.50}$$

Find the cost of 150 units at $2.90 a unit.

$$100 \times \$2.90 = \$290$$
$$50 \times \$2.90 = \frac{1}{\underset{1}{\cancel{2}}} \times \frac{\overset{145}{\cancel{290}}}{1} = \underline{145}$$
$$\overline{\$435}$$

In many cases, the price or the quantity can be broken down into a combination of aliquot parts.

Example. Find the cost of 45 units at $.85 a unit.
First, we must recognize that we can separate $.85 into $.80 + $.05, whose values as aliquot parts we know.

$$45 \text{ units} \times \$.80 = \overset{9}{\cancel{45}} \times \frac{4}{\underset{1}{\cancel{5}}} = \$36.00 \text{ at } \$.80 \text{ apiece}$$

$$45 \text{ units} \times \$.05 = \overset{9}{\cancel{45}} \times \frac{1}{\underset{4}{\cancel{20}}} = \frac{9}{4} = \$2.25 \text{ at } \$.05 \text{ apiece}$$

Now we add the results to find the cost of 45 units at $.85 apiece.

$36.00
  2.25
‾‾‾‾‾
$38.25 = total cost

We could have done the same problem by separating the 45 units into 20 units + 25 units. Since 20 and 25 are aliquot parts of 100, we could solve the problem in the following manner.

First, we know that 100 units at $.85 a unit would cost $85. We use this to obtain

$$20 \text{ units @ } \$.85 = \frac{1}{5} \times \overset{17}{85} = \$17.00$$

$$25 \text{ units @ } \$.85 = \frac{1}{4} \times 85 = \frac{85}{4} = \$21.25$$

Adding the two results, we get the total cost

$17.00
 21.25
‾‾‾‾‾
$38.25 = total cost

Some other examples follow.

Example. Find the cost of 160 units @ $.65.

$$\$.65 = \$.40 + \$.25$$

$$160 \text{ units} \times .40 = \overset{16}{160} \times \frac{4}{10} = \$64$$

$$160 \text{ units} \times .25 = \overset{40}{160} \times \frac{1}{4} = \$40$$

$ 64
  40
‾‾‾‾
$104 = total cost

Example. Find the cost of 185 units @ $2.50.

$$100 \text{ units} \times \$2.50 = \$250$$

$$80 \text{ units} \times \$2.50 = \frac{4}{5} \times \overset{50}{250} = \$200$$

$$5 \text{ units} \times \$2.50 = \frac{1}{20} \times \overset{25}{250} = \frac{25}{2} = \$12.50$$

$250.00
 200.00
  12.50
‾‾‾‾‾
$462.50 = total cost

It should be remembered that the advantage of using aliquot parts is that some of the multiplication or division can be done mentally. For this reason, the table of aliquot parts of $1.00 should be memorized.

ASSIGNMENT 11 ALIQUOT PARTS

A. Find the cost of the following purchases, using aliquot parts of $1.00.

a. 28 units @ $.25

b. 340 units @ $.50

1. 16 units @ $.50

2. 70 units @ $.50

3. 36 units @ $.25

4. 40 units @ $.25

5. 24 units @ $.75

6. 160 units @ $.25

7. 200 units @ $.75

8. 216 units @ $.50

9. 216 units @ $.25

10. 216 units @ $.75

B. Find the cost of the following purchases, using aliquot parts of $1.00.

a. 27 units @ $.33$\frac{1}{3}$

b. 132 units @ $.83$\frac{1}{3}$

1. 21 units @ $.66$\frac{2}{3}$

2. 36 units @ $.16$\frac{2}{3}$

3. 48 units @ $.83$\frac{1}{3}$

4. 12 units @ $.16$\frac{2}{3}$

5. 60 units @ $.33$\frac{1}{3}$

6. 138 units @ $.16$\frac{2}{3}$

7. 36 units @ $.16$\frac{2}{3}$

8. 36 units @ $.33$\frac{1}{3}$

9. 72 units @ $.83$\frac{1}{3}$

10. 147 units @ $.66$\frac{2}{3}$

C. Find the cost of the following purchases, using aliquot parts of $1.00.

a. 24 units @ $$.12\frac{1}{2}$$

b. 80 units @ $$.87\frac{1}{2}$$

1. 40 units @ $$.87\frac{1}{2}$$

2. 24 units @ $$.8\frac{1}{3}$$

3. 48 units @ $$.37\frac{1}{2}$$

4. 56 units @ $$.62\frac{1}{2}$$

5. 56 units @ $$.12\frac{1}{2}$$

6. 45 units @ $$.6\frac{2}{3}$$

7. 36 units @ $$.8\frac{1}{3}$$

8. 48 units @ $$.6\frac{1}{4}$$

9. 104 units @ $$.87\frac{1}{2}$$

10. 104 units @ $$.37\frac{1}{2}$$

D. Find the cost of the following items, using aliquot parts of $1.00. In some cases, the price is a combination of whole parts and aliquot, while in others it is a combination of aliquot parts.

a. 40 units @ $1.25

b. 20 units @ $1.45

1. 36 units @ $1.75

2. 12 units @ $$2.08\frac{1}{3}$$

3. 56 units @ $2.50

4. 60 units @ $1.33

5. 48 units @ $$2.16\frac{2}{3}$$

6. 80 units @ $.85

7. 60 units @ $.65

8. 54 units @ $$3.83\frac{1}{3}$$

9. 88 units @ $$2.37\frac{1}{2}$$

10. 112 units @ $10.00

E. Find the cost of the following items, using aliquot parts of 100 units.

   a. 75 units @ $.40   **b.** 175 units @ $.48

   1. 50 units @ $.98   **2.** $33\frac{1}{3}$ units @ $.57

   3. $16\frac{2}{3}$ units @ $.36   **4.** $8\frac{1}{3}$ units @ $.48

   5. $62\frac{1}{2}$ units @ $.64   **6.** 250 units @ $.54

   7. $137\frac{1}{2}$ units @ $.24   **8.** 225 units @ $.32

   9. $166\frac{2}{3}$ units @ $.33   **10.** $216\frac{2}{3}$ units @ $.60

F. Below are an invoice from a large builders' supply company and an order from Justin's Florists. Find the cost of each item listed, using aliquot parts where possible. Find the total cost.

EAST SIDE BUILDERS' SUPPLY
116 EAST RIAL STREET
MENDON, STATE 70412

Sold to:
Allsin Contractors
527 Newton Road
Clearview, State 70416

Date: June 13, 1989
Order No. 64312
Terms: n/30
Via: Truck

QUANTITY	DESCRIPTION	UNIT PRICE	AMOUNT
50 lb	1¼ " Galvanized Roof Nails	$ .24	
12 lb	Coated Lath Nails	.08⅓	
18 squares	Grade "A" shingles	8.00	
28 sheets	4 x 8 x 5/8 Plywood	1.75	
125 sheets	4 x 8 Plasterboard	3.20	
14 gal	Flat White Undercoat	6.50	
2	4" Paint Brushes	1.30	
75 sacks	White Portland Cement	4.80	
64'	2" Three-Corner Trim	.12 ½	
60 boxes	½" Flat-head Panning Screws	.83 ⅓	
		SALES TAX	12.63
		TOTAL	

JUSTIN'S FLORISTS
2370 MARSHALL ROAD
CRANTON, STATE 20212

QUANTITY	DESCRIPTION OF ITEM	UNIT COST	TOTAL AMOUNT
150	Small Ivy Plants	$ .64	($ 96.00)
75	Large Ivy Plants	1.04	(78.00)
25	Boston Fern	2.08	(52.00)
12	Large Philodendrons	1.44	(17.28)
100	African Violets	.33 1/3	(33.33)
120	8" Clay Pots	.87 1/2	(105.00)
120	6" Clay Pots	.62 1/2	(75.00)
240	4" Clay Pots	.40	(96.00)
120	8" Clay Saucers	.08 1/3	(10.00)
120	6" Clay Saucers	.06	(7.20)
240	4" Clay Saucers	.04 1/2	(10.80)
12 BOXES	Labels	.83 1/3	(10.00)
8 SACKS	Rose Dust	.66 2/3	(5.33)
		TOTAL	$ 595.94

CHAPTER 6
The metric system and conversions

When people began to measure, they needed some means of expressing units of measurement. The first units used were based on experiences or on parts of the body: a day's journey, the length of a foot, the span or spread of a hand. After relying for centuries on many different and confusing systems, the first uniform system was established in the late eighteenth century in France. This system, called the *metric system*, is used extensively throughout the world with the exception of the United States and England, where the more complicated *English system* is used.

Problems dealing with units of measurement are of two basic types: (1) the conversion of one unit to another and (2) the basic operations of adding, subtracting, multiplying, and dividing units of measure.

CONVERTING UNITS OF MEASURE

The first step in converting one unit to another is to decide on an expression that relates to both units. If we wish to change feet to inches, we must find an expression relating both feet and inches. From Table 6.1, we know that 12 inches is equal to 1 foot.

Often a single expression relating both units does not appear in the table. When this occurs, we must use two or more relationships to convert one unit to another. If we are asked to change rods to inches, we must use two relationships: (1) 1 rod is equal to $16\frac{1}{2}$ feet and (2) 12 inches is equal to 1 foot. Thus, by using two conversion relationships, we can change rods to inches.

One problem in conversions is deciding whether to multiply or to divide. This can be resolved by making the conversion relationship a fraction. Thus, 3 feet = 1 yard can be expressed as

$$\frac{3 \text{ ft}}{1 \text{ yd}} \quad \text{(read as ``feet per yard'')}$$

The numerator of the fraction should always be the unit of measure you wish to convert to; the denominator should be the unit of measure you wish to change. This position is important because it allows us to multiply and use cancellation. Units of measure, such as feet, pounds, seconds, can be cancelled just like numbers.

TABLE 6.1

Common Weights and Measures

MEASURES OF TIME

60 seconds (sec)	= 1 minute (min)	10 years	= 1 decade (dec)
60 minutes	= 1 hour (hr)	100 years	= 1 century (cen)
24 hours	= 1 day (da)	$4\frac{1}{3}$ weeks	= 1 month (mo)
7 days	= 1 week (wk)	30 days	= 1 month (average)
365 days	= 1 year (yr)	29 days, 12 hours, 44 minutes = 1 lunar month	
366 days	= 1 leap year	13 weeks	= 1 quarter (of a yr)
52 weeks	= 1 year	12 months	= 1 year

MEASURES OF LENGTH (DISTANCE)   MEASURES OF AREA (SURFACE)

12 inches (in.)	= 1 foot (ft)	144 square inches (sq in.)	= 1 square ft (sq ft)
3 feet	= 1 yard (yd)	9 square feet	= 1 square yd (sq yd)
$5\frac{1}{2}$ yards	= 1 rod (rd)	$30\frac{1}{4}$ square yards	= 1 square rod (sq rd)
$16\frac{1}{2}$ feet	= 1 rod	160 square rods	= 1 acre (A)
66 feet	= 1 chain	640 acres	= 1 square mile
320 rods	= 1 mile (mi)	36 square miles	= 1 township (twp)
5,280 feet	= 1 mile		

CUBIC MEASURE

1,728 cubic inches (cu in.)	= 1 cubic foot (cu ft)
27 cubic feet	= 1 cubic yd (cu yd)
128 cubic feet	= 1 cord (cd)

DRY MEASURE   LIQUID MEASURE

2 pints (pt)	= 1 quart (qt)	4 gills (gi)	= 1 pint (pt)
8 quarts	= 1 peck (pk)	16 fluid ounces	= 1 pint
4 pecks	= 1 bushel (bu)	2 pints	= 1 quart (qt)
		4 quarts	= 1 gallon (gal)
		231 cubic inches	= 1 gallon
		$31\frac{1}{2}$ gallons	= 1 barrel (bbl)

AVOIRDUPOIS WEIGHT (ORDINARY)   TROY WEIGHT (USED BY JEWELERS IN WEIGHING PRECIOUS METALS AND STONES)

16 drams (dr)	= 1 ounce (oz)	24 grains	= 1 pennyweight (pwt)
16 ounces	= 1 pound (lb)	20 pennyweights	= 1 ounce (oz)
7,000 grams	= 1 pound	12 ounces	= 1 pound
100 pounds	= 1 hundred-weight (cwt)	5,760 grains	= 1 pound
2,000 pounds	= 1 ton (T)	3.168 grams	= 1 carat
2,240 pounds	= 1 long ton		

Example. How many feet in 6 yards?

$$6 \text{ yards} \times \frac{3 \text{ feet}}{1 \text{ yard}} = 18 \text{ feet}$$

Example. How many yards in 9 feet?

$$9 \text{ feet} \times \frac{1 \text{ yard}}{3 \text{ feet}} = 3 \text{ yards}$$

Example. How many ounces in 3 pounds?

$$3 \text{ pounds} \times \frac{16 \text{ ounces}}{1 \text{ pound}} = 48 \text{ ounces}$$

Example. How many gallons in 9 quarts?

$$9 \text{ quarts} \times \frac{1 \text{ gallon}}{4 \text{ quarts}} = \frac{9 \text{ gallons}}{4} = 2\frac{1}{4} \text{ gallons}$$

Example. How many inches in 6 yards?

$$6 \text{ yards} \times \frac{3 \text{ feet}}{1 \text{ yard}} = 18 \text{ feet}$$

$$18 \text{ feet} \times \frac{12 \text{ inches}}{1 \text{ foot}} = 216 \text{ inches}$$

Example. How many gallons equal 462 cubic inches?

$$462 \text{ cubic inches} \times \frac{1 \text{ gallon}}{231 \text{ cubic inches}} = 2 \text{ gallons}$$

Example. How many cubic feet equal 864 cubic inches?

$$864 \text{ cubic inches} \times \frac{1 \text{ cubic foot}}{1728 \text{ cubic inches}} = \frac{1}{2} \text{ or } 0.5 \text{ cubic feet}$$

Example. How many cubic inches in 1 quart?

$$1 \text{ quart} \times \frac{1 \text{ gallon}}{4 \text{ quarts}} \times \frac{231 \text{ cubic inches}}{1 \text{ gallon}} = 57.75 \text{ cubic inches}$$

Note that in the above example, it is necessary to convert 1 quart first to gallons, then to cubic inches, as no direct equivalent of a quart in cubic inches is given in Table 6.1. Similarly,

How many square inches in 4.5 square yards?

$$4.5 \text{ sq yd} \times \frac{9 \text{ sq ft}}{1 \text{ sq yd}} \times \frac{144 \text{ sq in.}}{1 \text{ sq ft}} = 5832 \text{ sq in.}$$

Here again, it is necessary to convert square yards into *square feet* before obtaining the correct equivalent in square inches.

BASIC OPERATIONS

When making calculations with units of measure, it is sometimes necessary to convert them all to one unit and then perform the operation. It is also necessary to perform arithmetic operations with the same units. These ideas are illustrated in the following examples.

Example. Add 10 minutes, 20 seconds to 49 minutes, 12 seconds.

10 min 20 sec
49 min 12 sec
——————
59 min 32 sec

If the number of minutes or seconds had been greater than 60, we would have expressed them in the next higher unit.

Example. 43 min 12 sec

<u>19 min 50 sec</u>

62 min 62 sec

62 seconds is the same as 1 minute, 2 seconds. If we add the 1 minute to the 62 minutes, we get 63 minutes, which is the same as 1 hour, 3 minutes. Thus the answer can be written 1 hour, 3 minutes, 2 seconds.

Subtraction

Example. Subtract 8 gallons, 3 quarts from 10 gallons, 2 quarts.

   10 gal 2 qt   Since 3 cannot be subtracted from 2, we must borrow. We take
  <u>− 8 gal 3 qt</u>   1 gallon from the 10 and convert it to quarts, which we then add
             to the 2 quarts.

   9 gal 6 qt
  <u>−8 gal 3 qt</u>
   1 gal 3 qt

Multiplication

Example. Multiply 2 yards, 2 feet, 8 inches by 2.

   2 yd 2 ft 8 in.
  <u>×   2</u>
   4 yd 4 ft 16 in.

   16 in. = 1 ft 4 in.
   5 ft = 1 yd 2 ft

Answer: 5 yd 2 ft 4 in.

Division

The easiest way to divide is to change all the units expressed to the same unit and then divide.

Example. Divide 4 gallons, 3 quarts, 1 pint by 3.

$$4 \text{ gal} \times \frac{4 \text{ qt}}{\text{gal}} = 16 \text{ qt}, \qquad 16 \text{ qt} + 3 \text{ qt} = 19 \text{ qt}$$

$$19 \text{ qt} \times \frac{2 \text{ pt}}{1 \text{ qt}} = 38 \text{ pt}, \qquad 38 \text{ pt} + 1 \text{ pt} = 39 \text{ pt}$$

$$\begin{array}{r} 13 \text{ pt} \\ \hline 3) 39 \text{ pt} \end{array}$$

$$13 \text{ pt} \times \frac{1 \text{ qt}}{2 \text{ pt}} = 6\frac{1}{2} \text{ qt or } 6 \text{ qt, } 1 \text{ pt}$$

$$6 \text{ qt} \times \frac{1 \text{ gal}}{4 \text{ qt}} = 1\frac{1}{2} \text{ gal or } 1 \text{ gal, } 2 \text{ qt}$$

Answer: 1 gal, 2 qt, 1 pt

Most of the world employs the metric system of measures. Now even the last two important exceptions, the United States and the United Kingdom, have passed laws which will in the future change all their weights and measures to the metric system. Children growing up in a metric world will find the metric system simpler than English measure because it is based on the decimal number system. All the units of the metric system are always related by factors of ten. The four basic units of the metric system, along with their abbreviations in parentheses, are

```
meter  (m)—unit
liter (l)    —unit
gram (g)   —unit
are (a)     —unit
```

Originally, a meter was supposed to be equal to one ten-millionth of the distance from the north pole to the equator. Due to an error in the original calculation, this is not exactly true. The basic metric measures of length, weight, volume and area all have a simple relationship to one another.

A *gram* is the weight of distilled water contained in a cube 1/100 of a meter on each side.
A *liter* is the volume of a cube 1/10 of a meter on each side.
An *are* is the area of a square one meter on each side.

The basic units may be modified by the addition of different prefixes. For example, a *kilo*meter is a thousand meters.

The following are some of the prefixes that, combined with the basic units, complete the system. The equivalent relationships between different metric units can now be easily obtained.

PREFIX	ABBREVIATION	DENOTES
micro	—	.000001
milli	m	.001
centi	c	.01
deci	d	.1
deka	dk	10
hecto	h	100
kilo	k	1,000
mega	—	1,000,000

Example. For grams:

$$10 \text{ milligrams} = 1 \text{ centigram} = .01 \text{ gram}$$
$$10 \text{ centigrams} = .1 \text{ gram} = 1 \text{ decigram}$$
$$1 \text{ gram} = 10 \text{ decigrams}$$

Similarly, for meters:

1 millimeter (mm) =	.1 centimeter (cm) =	.01 decimeter (dm) =	.001 meter (m)
10 millimeters =	1.0 centimeter =	.1 decimeter =	.01 meter
100 millimeters =	10 centimeters =	1.0 decimeter =	.1 meter
1000 millimeters =	100 centimeters =	10 decimeters =	1.0 meters

In the metric system, the conversion from one unit to another is simple, merely requiring the shifting of the decimal point. To show this, let us convert 10 meters to decimeters, first using the method of conversion previously used with the English system. The prefix *deci-* tells us 10 decimeters equal 1 meter.

Example. $10 \text{ meters} \times \dfrac{10 \text{ decimeters}}{1 \text{ meter}} = 100 \text{ decimeters}$

$10.0 \text{ meters} = 100 \text{ decimeters}$

Example. Convert 1500 milliliters to liters. The prefix *mil-* tells us 1000 milliliters equals 1 liter.

$1500 \text{ milliliters} \times \dfrac{1 \text{ liter}}{1000 \text{ milliliters}} = 1.5$

$1500 \text{ milliliters} = 1.5 \text{ liters}$

CONVERSION BETWEEN METRIC SYSTEM AND ENGLISH SYSTEM

The English equivalents of the basic units of the metric system, rounded off to two decimal places, are

$$1 \text{ meter} = 39.37 \text{ inches} = 1.09 \text{ yards}$$
$$1 \text{ liter} - 1.06 \text{ liquid quarts} = .265 \text{ gallon}$$
$$1 \text{ gram} = 15.43 \text{ grains} = .035 \text{ ounce}$$
$$1 \text{ yard} = 3.05 \text{ meters}$$
$$1 \text{ quart} = .94 \text{ liter}$$
$$1 \text{ ounce} = 28.35 \text{ grams}$$

The conversion from the metric system to the English system presents some difficulties since every metric unit has a unique English equivalent which bears no simple relationship to the other units. For example, one meter equals 39.37 inches or 1.09 yards, whereas 1 yard equals 3.05 meters or 30.5 decimeters or 305 centimeters.

To achieve English–metric and metric–English conversions given the equivalents of the basic units, we can apply the same methods of conversion which were applied to go from one unit of English measure to another.

Example. Convert 25 meters to inches.

$25 \text{ meters} \times \dfrac{39.37 \text{ inches}}{1 \text{ meter}} = 984.25 \text{ inches}$

Convert 100 yards to meters.

$100 \text{ yards} \times \dfrac{1 \text{ meter}}{1.09 \text{ yards}} = 91.74 \text{ meters}$

Convert 5 gallons to liters.

$5 \text{ gallons} \times \dfrac{1 \text{ liter}}{.265 \text{ gallon}} = 1.88 \text{ liters}$

It is also possible to convert from one unit of measure to another, even though no direct equivalent is given, provided both units have their equivalents expressed in a common third unit.

Example. No equivalent was given between inches and centimeters, but one was given between inches and meters, and another between centimeters and meters. Therefore, converting 10 inches into meters can be done in two steps.

$$10 \text{ inches} \times \frac{1 \text{ meter}}{39.37 \text{ inches}} = .254 \text{ meter}$$

$$.254 \text{ meter} \times \frac{100 \text{ centimeters}}{1 \text{ meter}} = 25.4 \text{ centimeters}$$

By first converting 10 inches to meters, then centimeters, we find that its metric equivalent is 25.4 centimeters.

Example. Convert 1400 milliliters to liquid quarts.

$$1400 \text{ milliliters} \times \frac{1 \text{ liter}}{1000 \text{ milliliters}} = 1.4 \text{ liters}$$

$$1.4 \text{ liters} \times \frac{1.06 \text{ liquid quarts}}{1 \text{ liter}} = 1.484 \text{ liquid quarts}$$

By first converting 1400 milliliters to liters, then to liquid quarts, we find that its equivalent in the English system is 1.484 liquid quarts.

To simplify the problem of conversion, one may employ a conversion table, such as Table 6.2, which eliminates the necessity of doing any arithmetic operations. Table 6.2 was rounded off to two decimal places, but more accurate tables are readily available when greater precision is required.

TABLE 6.2

English–Metric Conversion Tables

LINEAR MEASURE
1 inch (in = 25.4 mm = 2.54 cm = .25 dm = .03 m
12 in. = 1 foot (ft) = 304.8 mm = 30.48 cm = 3.05 dm = .31 m
3 feet = 1 yard (yd) = 914 mm = 91.40 cm = 9.14 dm = .91 m

SQUARE MEASURE
1 sq in. = 64.5 sq mm = 6.45 sq cm = .65 sq dm = .06 sq m
144 sq in. = 1 sq ft = 93.0 sq mm = 9.30 sq cm = .93 sq dm = .09 sq m
9 sq ft = 1 sq yd = 836.0 sq mm = 83.60 sq cm = 8.36 sq dm = .84 sq m

CUBIC MEASURE
1 cu in. = 163.87 cu mm = 16.39 cu cm = 1.64 cu dm = .16 cu m
1,728 cu in. = 1 cu ft = 28.0 cu mm = 2.80 cu cm = .28 cu dm = .03 cu m
128 cu ft = 1 cu yd = 765 cu mm = 7.65 cu cm = .77 cu dm = .08 cu m

LIQUID MEASURE
1 pint (pt) = 473.0 ml = .47 cl
2 pt = 1 quart (qt) = 946 ml = .946 cl
4 qt = 1 gallon (gal) = 3785.0 ml = 3.79 cl
231 cu in. = 1 gal = 3785.0 ml = 3.79 cl
1 cu ft = 7.50 gal

A. Convert each of the following

a. 36 sq ft to square yards

b. 2 ft 10 in. to inches

1. 9 pt to quarts

2. 36 hr to days

3. 20 oz to pounds

4. 2 rd to feet

5. $2\frac{1}{2}$ lb (avoir.) to ounces

6. 8 qt 1 pt to pints

7. 1 rd 2 yd to feet

8. $7\frac{1}{2}$ gal 1 pt to quarts

9. 6 qt 1 pt to pints

10. 2 da 58 min to minutes

B. Convert each of the following.

a. 200 cm to meters

b. 531 cm to meters

1. 20 dkg to grams

2. 30 ml to liters

3. 20 dkm to hectometers

4. 41 g to decigrams

5. 1 kg to decigrams

6. 6462 dl to liters

7. 812 hg to grams

8. 62.1 g to decigrams

9. 5.16 dkm to meters

10. 172 m to centimeters

C. Perform the indicated operation.

a. Add 1 hr, 16 min, 32 sec to 53 min, 39 sec.

1. Add 2 ft, 11 in. to 1 ft, 6 in.

2. Multiply 2 sq yd, 3 sq ft by 6.

3. Subtract 2 min, 59 sec from 4 min, 3 sec.

4. Divide 6 gal, 3 qt by 3.

5. Add 7 lb, 12 oz to $2\frac{1}{2}$ lb, 4 oz.

6. Subtract 2 pk, 6 qt from 3 pk, 4 qt.

7. Divide 27 yd, 2 ft by 2.

8. Multiply 22 cu ft, 12 cu in. by 8.

D. Convert the following within the metric system.

   1. 305 centimeters = _____ decimeters

   2. 20.47 millimeters = _____ meters

   3. 1.98 meters = _____ centimeters

   4. 1496 millimeters = _____ decimeters

   5. 13.63 decimeters = _____ dekameters

   6. 26 centimeters = _____ meters

   7. .577 decimeters = _____ centimeters

   8. 3284.1 millimeters = _____ centimeters

   9. 126.3 meters = _____ hektometers

 10. 70.33 millimeters = _____ meters

 11. 14 decigrams = _____ grams

 12. 132.99 milligrams = _____ grams

 13. 22.44 grams = _____ centigrams

 14. 8718.29 decigrams = _____ milligrams

 15. 3.81 centigrams = _____ decigrams

 16. 2989 grams = _____ milligrams

 17. 16.02 decigrams = _____ milligrams

 18. 909.09 milligrams = _____ grams

 19. 7.2 grams = _____ decigrams

 20. 318.25 centigrams = _____ milligrams

E. Convert the following from one system to the other.

   1. 6 ounces = _____ grams = _____ centigrams

   2. 13.22 yards = _____ meters = _____ decimeters

   3. 17 quarts = _____ liters

4. 9 inches = _____ meters

5. 3.5 gallons = _____ liters

6. 2.4 liters = _____ liquid quarts

7. 37 grams = _____ ounces

8. 753 grams = _____ ounces

9. 15 meters = _____ yards

10. 4.5 quarts = _____ liters

11. 21 ounces = _____ grams

12. 72.5 ounces = _____ centigrams

13. 8 yards = _____ centimeters

14. 6.2 meters = _____ inches

15. 191 milligrams = _____ ounces

16. 24 centimeters = _____ yards

17. 150 decigrams = _____ ounces

18. 33 liters = _____ quarts

19. 48.5 centigrams = _____ ounces

20. 2 quarts = _____ liters

F. Solve the following problems.

1. A large water jug has a diameter of 8 inches and is 36 inches high. How many gallons of water will it hold?

2. Mrs. Conroy bought a 9 × 12 foot rug for her den. If the carpet sold for $12 per square yard, what was the total cost of her purchase?

3. Pat and Charles want to cover the wall illustrated below (excluding the door) with a type of paneling that comes in 6 foot long strips and is 6 inches wide. The cost of this paneling is $.05 per square inch. The strips can be cut if necessary.

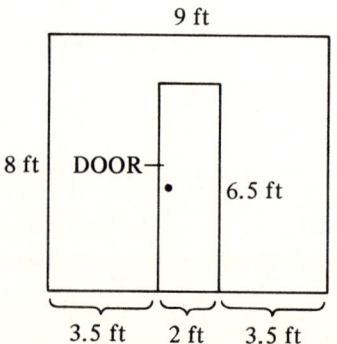

a. How many strips of paneling will they need to buy in order to cover the desired portion of the wall?

b. How much will the paneling cost them?

4. A packer at Jayson's Candy Company must fill a large carton with as many $4 \times 4 \times 4$ inch packages of candy as possible. If the dimensions of the carton are $4 \times 2 \times 2$ feet, how many candy packages can be fitted inside?

5. A large sheet cake is baked in a rectangular pan which measures $48 \times 36 \times 2$ inches. How many 2 inch cube-shaped pieces can be cut from this cake?

6. A kiddie pool has dimensions of $2 \times 8 \times 6$ feet. How many gallons of water are needed to completely fill it?

CHAPTER 7
Banking records

One of the most important services offered by banks is the checking account. Both private individuals and businesses take advantage of this service. The large majority of transactions in the United States are handled by checks. Because of this widespread use, everyone should know how to use a checking account and understand how it operates.

DEPOSITS

When a person makes a deposit into a checking account, he must fill out a deposit slip. This slip states how much he is depositing. The individual is given a deposit receipt, which is his record of the deposit he has made. The deposit slip is the bank's record of the deposit; the information is later transferred to the depositor's account at the bank. The depositor should also record the amount of the deposit in his checkbook. A typical deposit slip is shown below.

Deposited with **UNION NATIONAL BANK** STEELETON, STATE			Dollars	Cents
		CASH	135	55
DATE _July 17, 19X9_		CHECKS	96	20
FOR ACCOUNT OF (print full name and account number)		(LIST SEPARATELY)	212	40
Frank Bensten				
ACCOUNT NUMBER 0 8 9 – 7 1 4 1 3 2		**TOTAL**	444	15

A deposit, such as the one explained here, is known as a checking or *demand deposit*. This means that the bank is liable to the depositor for the amount in his account on demand. The depositor may demand payment for all or part of his account. He can also direct the bank to make payment to a third party by issuing a check. A *check* is simply an order issued by the depositor directing the bank to pay all or part of the funds in his account to another party. A typical check is shown below.

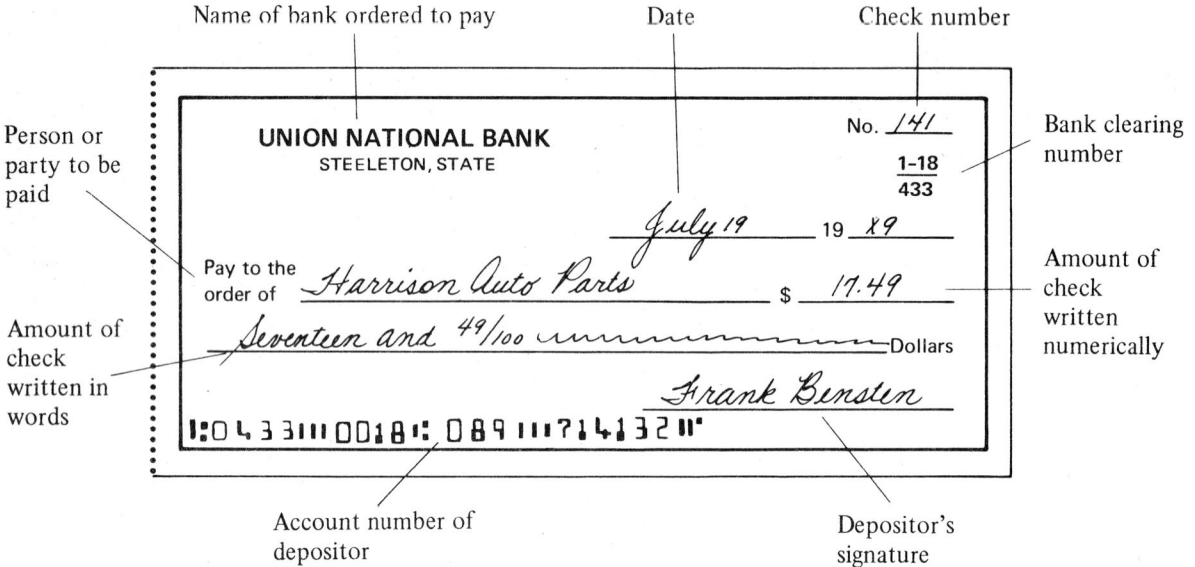

Frequently, the depositor needs cash and may issue the check to himself. He can do this by writing either his name or the word "Cash" on the "Pay to the order of" line.

CHECK STUBS

NO. 141		
DATE July 19 19 x9		
TO Harrison Auto Parts		
FOR Muffler		
BAL. BRO'T FOR'D	713	17
AM'T DEPOSITED	444	15
TOTAL	1,157	32
AM'T THIS CHECK	17	49
BAL. CAR'D FOR'D	1,139	83

It is very important that the individual keep an accurate record of his bank account. This is done by keeping a running account of the balance on the check stubs or record sheets provided with checkbooks. If kept accurately, the stubs should always be up-to-date and should show the deposits and the amounts of the checks drawn, in addition to the current balance. Accuracy in keeping stubs makes easier the reconciliation of the bank statement at the end of the month.

BANK STATEMENTS

At the end of the month, the bank returns the canceled checks paid for that month, plus a statement listing the checks, deposits, service charges deducted from the account and the bank balance. These records should be kept as proof of payment. A typical bank statement is shown below.

Statement of Your Account Union National Bank Steeleton, State			[Mr. Frank Bensten] 1437 Valley View [Harsten, State] Account No. 089-714132		
Checks		Deposits	No. of Checks	Date	Balance
64.50– 19.95–			2	July 1	1069.59
212.00–		250.00+	1	5	1107.59
78.80–			1	6	1028.79
212.62– 103.00–		444.15+	2	10	713.17
17.49– 1.50– SC			1	17	1157.32
				19	1138.33
CM—Credit Memo	RT—Returned Item		SC—Service Charge		

RECONCILIATION OF THE BANK STATEMENT

Often the bank statement does not agree with the balance shown in the checkbook. The reasons for this may be that some checks have been issued but have not yet been cashed, deposits have not yet been credited to the account, and service charges and other costs may not have been recorded in the checkbook. The bank sometimes provides a form to make the checking of any differences easier. This process of checking the bank balance against the checkbook balance is called the *reconciliation of the bank statement*. A sample of this form is shown below.

If such a form is not available, the following steps can be used.

1. Compare the canceled checks with the check stubs and make a list of the checks not yet received by the bank. Subtract these from the balance shown on the bank statement. Add any deposits not yet credited by the bank.

Union National Bank
This form is provided to help you
balance your bank statement

Balance Shown on
Bank Statement $_____

Balance Shown in
Your Checkbook $_____

Add Deposits not
on Statement $_____
                        _____

Add Any Deposits
Not Already
Entered in
Checkbook $_____
                        _____
                        _____
                        _____

            Total $_____

            Total $_____

Subtract Checks Issued
but Not on Statement

No._____ $_____
_____ _____
_____ _____
_____ _____
_____ _____
_____ _____
_____ _____
_____ _____
_____ _____

Subtract Service
Charge and Other
Charges Not in
Checkbook

$_____
_____
_____

            Total $_____

            Balance $_____

            Total $_____

            Balance $_____

These totals should be the same.
Any differences should be reported to the bank.

2. Subtract the service charges and other costs listed on the bank statement from the checkbook balance. All unrecorded credits, such as the collection of a debt by the bank, must be added.
3. If the adjusted checkbook balance is different from the adjusted bank balance, an error has been made either in the checkbook records or by the bank. First, check your records carefully. If no error can be found there, contact the bank immediately.

A. Below are the deposit slips of Ronald Turner, whose account number is 045–816224. With the information given below, fill in the deposit slips completely.

1. On September 5, Mr Turner deposited $131.15 in cash and three checks $212.59, $175.12, and $86.50.

Deposited with **UNION NATIONAL BANK** STEELETON, STATE		Dollars	Cents
	CASH		
DATE _____	CHECKS (LIST SEPARATELY)		
FOR ACCOUNT OF (print full name and account number)			
_____			
_____			
ACCOUNT NUMBER ☐☐☐ – ☐☐☐☐☐☐	TOTAL		

2. On September 12, he deposited $125 in cash, and two checks: $364.78 and $389.19.

Deposited with **UNION NATIONAL BANK** STEELETON, STATE		Dollars	Cents
	CASH		
DATE _____	CHECKS (LIST SEPARATELY)		
FOR ACCOUNT OF (print full name and account number)			
_____			
_____			
ACCOUNT NUMBER ☐☐☐ – ☐☐☐☐☐☐	TOTAL		

3. On September 20, he deposited $186.12 in cash, and four checks: $176.01, $55.00, $96.15, and $316.46.

Deposited with **UNION NATIONAL BANK** STEELETON, STATE				Dollars	Cents
			CASH		
DATE _____			CHECKS (LIST SEPARATELY)		
FOR ACCOUNT OF (print full name and account number)					
_____					
_____					
ACCOUNT NUMBER	☐☐☐ − ☐☐☐☐☐		TOTAL		

4. On September 29, he deposited three checks: $316.40, $167.50, and $171.17. He also had $50 in cash returned to him.

Deposited with **UNION NATIONAL BANK** STEELETON, STATE				Dollars	Cents
			CASH		
DATE _____			CHECKS (LIST SEPARATELY)		
FOR ACCOUNT OF (print full name and account number)					
_____					
_____					
ACCOUNT NUMBER	☐☐☐ − ☐☐☐☐☐		TOTAL		

A. Fill out the following checks for Mr. Turner with the information given below.

1. Check No. 116 to Adams Garden Center on September 3 for $79.16.

UNION NATIONAL BANK
STEELETON, STATE

No. _____

$\frac{1-18}{433}$

_____ 19 _____

Pay to the
order of _____ $ _____

_____ Dollars

⑆0433⑉0018⑆ 045⑈8162241⑈

2. Check No. 120 to Lettan's Upholstery Company on September 10 for $263.27.

UNION NATIONAL BANK
STEELETON, STATE

No. _____

$\frac{1-18}{433}$

_____ 19 _____

Pay to the
order of _____ $ _____

_____ Dollars

⑆0433⑉0018⑆ 045⑈8162241⑈

3. Check No. 124 to Rittan's Service Station on September 16 for $16.80.

```
┌─────────────────────────────────────────────────────────────────┐
│                                                                   │
│   UNION NATIONAL BANK                         No. _____          │
│   STEELETON, STATE                                                │
│                                               1-18                │
│                                               ────                │
│                                               433                 │
│                               _____ 19 _____          │
│   Pay to the                                                      │
│   order of  _____ $ _____        │
│                                                                   │
│   _____ Dollars        │
│                                                                   │
│   ⑈0433⑈⑈00181⑈ 045⑈816224⑈" ─────────────                        │
└─────────────────────────────────────────────────────────────────┘
```

B. Below are Mr. Turner's check stubs for September. The deposit and check amounts are given. Fill in the blanks.

NO. 115		
DATE *September 2* 19 *X9*		
TO *Jason Dept. Store*		
FOR *Shirts*		
BAL. BRO'T FOR'D	1106	12
AM'T DEPOSITED	00	00
TOTAL		
AM'T THIS CHECK	23	18
BAL. CAR'D FOR'D		

NO. 116		
DATE *September 3* 19 *X9*		
TO *Adams Garden Center*		
FOR *Lawn Mower*		
BAL. BRO'T FOR'D		
AM'T DEPOSITED	00	00
TOTAL		
AM'T THIS CHECK	79	16
BAL. CAR'D FOR'D		

NO. 117		
DATE *September 5* 19 *X9*		
TO *Internal Revenue Service*		
FOR *Quarterly Statement*		
BAL. BRO'T FOR'D		
AM'T DEPOSITED	605	36
TOTAL		
AM'T THIS CHECK	264	30
BAL. CAR'D FOR'D		

NO. 118		
DATE *September 5* 19 *X9*		
TO *John Semic*		
FOR *Plumbing*		
BAL. BRO'T FOR'D		
AM'T DEPOSITED	00	00
TOTAL		
AM'T THIS CHECK	22	00
BAL. CAR'D FOR'D		

NO. 119		
DATE September 8 19 X9		
TO Keystone Power		
FOR Electric Bill		
BAL. BRO'T FOR'D		
AM'T DEPOSITED	00	00
TOTAL		
AM'T THIS CHECK	36	15
BAL. CAR'D FOR'D		

NO. 120		
DATE September 10 19 X9		
TO Littan's Upholstering Co.		
FOR Game Room Furniture		
BAL. BRO'T FOR'D		
AM'T DEPOSITED	00	00
TOTAL		
AM'T THIS CHECK	263	27
BAL. CAR'D FOR'D		

NO. 121		
DATE September 12 19 X9		
TO Donaldson Insurance Agency		
FOR Car Insurance		
BAL. BRO'T FOR'D		
AM'T DEPOSITED	878	41
TOTAL		
AM'T THIS CHECK	118	50
BAL. CAR'D FOR'D		

NO. 122		
DATE September 13 19 X9		
TO State Dept. of Revenue		
FOR Registration Plates		
BAL. BRO'T FOR'D		
AM'T DEPOSITED	00	00
TOTAL		
AM'T THIS CHECK	25	00
BAL. CAR'D FOR'D		

NO. 123		
DATE September 16 19 X9		
TO United Finance Co.		
FOR Car Payment		
BAL. BRO'T FOR'D		
AM'T DEPOSITED	00	00
TOTAL		
AM'T THIS CHECK	86	00
BAL. CAR'D FOR'D		

ASSIGNMENT 15 CHECK STUBS AND RECONCILIATION

A. Continue the running account.

NO. 124		
DATE September 16 19 X9		
TO Rittan's Service Station		
FOR Tune Up		
BAL. BRO'T FOR'D		
AM'T DEPOSITED	00	00
TOTAL		
AM'T THIS CHECK	16	80
BAL. CAR'D FOR'D		

NO. 125		
DATE September 18 19 X9		
TO Western Gas Co.		
FOR Gas Bill		
BAL. BRO'T FOR'D		
AM'T DEPOSITED	00	00
TOTAL		
AM'T THIS CHECK	35	18
BAL. CAR'D FOR'D		

NO. 126		
DATE September 20 19 X9		
TO Municipal Water Co.		
FOR Water Bill		
BAL. BRO'T FOR'D		
AM'T DEPOSITED	00	00
TOTAL		
AM'T THIS CHECK	6	00
BAL. CAR'D FOR'D		

NO. 127		
DATE September 20 19 X9		
TO Household Furnishing Ltd.		
FOR Draperies		
BAL. BRO'T FOR'D		
AM'T DEPOSITED	829	74
TOTAL		
AM'T THIS CHECK	59	50
BAL. CAR'D FOR'D		

NO. _128_

DATE _September 22_ 19 _X9_

TO _United Brethren Church_

FOR _Building Fund_

BAL. BRO'T FOR'D		
AM'T DEPOSITED	00	00
TOTAL		
AM'T THIS CHECK	100	00
BAL. CAR'D FOR'D		

NO. _129_

DATE _September 23_ 19 _X9_

TO _Bell Telephone Co._

FOR _Telephone Bill_

BAL. BRO'T FOR'D		
AM'T DEPOSITED	00	00
TOTAL		
AM'T THIS CHECK	11	26
BAL. CAR'D FOR'D		

NO. _130_

DATE _September 26_ 19 _X9_

TO _Dr. Thomas Narch_

FOR _Office Visit_

BAL. BRO'T FOR'D		
AM'T DEPOSITED	00	00
TOTAL		
AM'T THIS CHECK	1	50
BAL. CAR'D FOR'D		

NO. _131_

DATE _September 28_ 19 _X9_

TO _Corner Pharmacy_

FOR _Prescription_

BAL. BRO'T FOR'D		
AM'T DEPOSITED	00	00
TOTAL		
AM'T THIS CHECK	6	13
BAL. CAR'D FOR'D		

NO. _132_

DATE _September 29_ 19 _X9_

TO _Jackson Contractors_

FOR _Roof Repairs_

BAL. BRO'T FOR'D		
AM'T DEPOSITED	605	00
TOTAL		
AM'T THIS CHECK	615	00
BAL. CAR'D FOR'D		

B. Below is the statement Mr. Turner received at the end of September. In the space below, reconcile this statement with the check stubs in the previous assignments.

Statement of Your Account

Union National Bank
Steeleton, State

⌈Mr. Ronald Turner⌉
17 Allan Drive
⌊Glendale, State⌋

Account No. 045-816224

Checks		Deposits	No. of Checks	Date	Balance
23.18–			1	Sept. 2	1082.94
79.17–			1	3	1003.78
264.30–	22.00–	605.36+	2	5	1322.84
36.15–			1	8	1286.69
263.27–			1	10	1023.42
178.50–		878.97+	1	12	1723.89
25.00–			1	13	1698.89
86.00–	16.80–		2	16	1596.09
35.78–			1	18	1560.31
6.00–		829.74+	1	20	2384.05
100.00–			1	22	2284.05
17.26–			1	23	2266.79
		75.00 CM		24	2341.79
7.50–			1	26	2334.29
675.00–	2.50– SC	605.07+	1	29	2261.86

CM—Credit Memo RT—Returned Item SC—Service Charge

CHAPTER 8
Inventories and turnover

An accurate accounting of merchandise inventory is essential for the efficient operation of a business. *Merchandise inventory* is a list of all goods on hand at any given time, valued at either the cost of acquisition or the current selling price. Knowledge of his inventory position helps the businessman make key decisions concerning reordering, pricing, and merchandising, which, in turn, affect profits.

One method of inventory control is the maintenance of a *perpetual inventory*. Each item a firm sells is placed on a separate stock or bin card. This card is always kept up to date. It usually shows the item's stock number, the minimum amount to be kept in stock, the maximum amount that can be kept in stock, and the balance on hand. As the firm acquires more units of the item, the date of purchase, purchase order number, quantity obtained, and cost per unit are specified on the stock card. Similarly, when any number of units of this item are sold, the date, requisition number, and "Quantity Out" are recorded. After each transaction occurs, the remaining inventory

Stock Card
Automotive Department

ITEM _Muffler Clamps_   MAXIMUM ___700___

STOCK NO. _M-162_   MINIMUM ___100___

DATE	P.O. NO.	QUANT. IN	UNIT COST	REQ. NO.	QUANT. OUT	BALANCE
May 9, 19	3121	200	$ .40			200
23	3129	150	.45			350
29				216	75	275
June 3, 19	3135	200	.45			475
6				220	100	375
13				225	75	300
23	3141	175	.50			475

balance is indicated on the stock card, which assists the businessman in deciding which items he needs to reorder.

No matter how complete and accurate the stock cards are kept, the business still must take *physical inventory* at least once during the year. The number of physical inventories is dependent on the size, type, and management of each individual business or company. The physical inventory is the actual counting of each item in stock. These figures are recorded on an inventory sheet like the one shown below.

TALBOTT'S HEALTH NEEDS
INVENTORY SHEET

Counted by *S.A.K*
Priced by *P.G.*
Checked by *B.B.*

July 31, 19X9

QUANTITY	DESCRIPTION	UNIT COST	TOTAL
5 cases	Iodine	$12.60	$63.00
19 cases	Band Aids	4.80	91.20
9 cases	Aspirins	17.50	157.50
11 cases	Shampoo	13.75	151.25
7 cases	Toothpaste	14.00	98.00
4½ doz	Toothbrushes	3.00	13.50

THE VALUE OF INVENTORIES

There are four methods of computing the value of inventories. These are the specific identification method, the average method, the first-in-first-out method (FIFO), and the last-in-first-out (LIFO) method. To illustrate each of these methods, we shall use the stock card shown at the beginning of this chapter.

Specific Identification

This method is the most complex and is usually used by small businesses with small amounts of goods. This involves the stamping or labeling of each shipment, an operation that can be very difficult and time consuming for a large business. In our stock card example, we have a balance of 475. Since no requisition has been filled since the last purchase, we know that 175 of the 475 are from Purchase Order 3141 and are valued at $.50. The remaining 300 clamps could have come from any combination of the preceding purchases but if we have identified each shipment we know exactly how many items remain in each and their actual costs.

In order to illustrate this method, let us assume that in addition to 175 clamps from purchase 3141, 150 clamps were from purchase 3135, 100 from purchase 3129, and 50 from purchase 3121. Remember that the lower the purchase number, the earlier the purchase was made.

Example. 475 balance

Purchase Order No. 3141	$175 \times \$.50 = \$\ 87.50$
3135	$150 \times\ \ .45 = \ \ 67.50$
3129	$100 \times\ \ .45 = \ \ 45.00$
3121	$\underline{\ 50} \times\ \ .40 = \ \ \underline{20.00}$
475	$\$220.00$ = value of inventory

The Average Method

To use the average method the separate purchases are valued at their purchase price. In other words, the cost or value of Purchase Order 3121 is found by multiplying $200 \times \$.40$ and so on. Then the number of units and the value of the units are totalled. The total value of the units divided by the total number of units purchased is the *average cost* of each item in stock. If we multiply this result by the balance in stock, we have the value of the inventory, determined by the *average method.*

Example.

Purchase Order No. 3121	$200 \times \$.40 = \$\ 80.00$
3129	$150 \times\ \ .45 = \ \ 67.50$
3135	$200 \times\ \ .45 = \ \ 90.00$
3141	$175 \times\ \ .50 = \ \ \underline{87.50}$
725	$\$325.00$

$$
\begin{array}{r}
.448 = \text{average cost} \\
725\overline{)325.000} \\
\underline{290\ 0} \\
35\ 00 \\
\underline{29\ 00} \\
6\ 000 \\
\underline{5\ 800} \\
200
\end{array}
\qquad
\begin{array}{r}
475 \\
\times\ \ .448 \\
\hline
3\ 800 \\
19\ 00 \\
\underline{190\ 0} \\
212.800 = \$212.80 = \text{value of inventory}
\end{array}
$$

First-In-First-Out (FIFO)

The assumption in this method is that the first items purchased are the first items sold. If this is assumed to be true, the inventory is made up of the last purchases made and must be valued at their cost price.

Example.

Purchase Order No. 3141	$175 \times \$.50 = \$\ 87.50$
3135	$200 \times\ \ .45 = \ \ 90.00$
3129	$100 \times\ \ .45 = \ \ \underline{45.00}$
475	$\$222.50$ = value of inventory

Last-In-First-Out (LIFO)

The assumption here is that the last items purchased are the first items out; thus, the inventory is made up of the first orders and must be evaluated at their prices.

The LIFO method is advantageous to the company during periods of increasing prices and high tax rates, since it results in lower reported profits and therefore lower taxes than the other methods. The FIFO method is least advantageous in such a period.

Example. Purchase Order No. 3121 $200 \times \$.40 = \$\ 80.00$
                               3129 $150 \times \ \ .45 = \ \ \ 67.50$

                               3135 $\underline{125 \times \ \ .45 = \ \ \ 56.25}$

                                    475        $\$203.75 =$ value of inventory

Example. If we wish to calculate the value of the inventory balance at any particular time, we can use either the LIFO or FIFO methods described above. Referring to the stock card on page 89, we see that on May 29, 19X9, 75 of the 350 units on hand had been sold, leaving a current inventory balance of 275 units. What was the value of the inventory of muffler clamps on May 29?

(1) By using the LIFO method

275 balance = 75 of the units purchased May 23 + 200 units purchased May 9

Value of Inventory on May 29 $= (75 \times \$.45) + (200 \times \$.40)$

                                  $= \$33.75 + \$80.00$

                                  $= \$113.75$

(2) By using the FIFO method

275 balance = 125 of the units purchased May 9 + 150 units purchased May 23

Value of Inventory on May 29 $= (125 \times \$.40) + (150 \times \$.45)$

                                  $= \$50.00 + \$67.50$

                                  $= \$117.50$

Thus, we see that in periods of rising prices, the LIFO metho results in a lesser value for the inventory on hand and a higher cost of goods sold and therefore a lower reported profit and lower income taxes.

TURNOVER

Merchandise turnover is the number of times a business converts its inventories into sales in a given year. The *rate of turnover* may be computed by dividing the total cost of goods sold in the given year by the value of the average inventory. The figure is significant because it indicates how effectively the company is using its assets to generate sales. The average inventory is the total value of all the inventories divided by the number of inventories taken. If the total sales of a business is $606,000 and the average inventory is $202,000, the turnover is 3.

Example.   Beginning Inventory $106,000

               Ending Inventory $\underline{\ \ \ 110,000}$

                                  $\$216,000$

$$\frac{\$ \text{ Total of Inventories}}{\text{Number of Inventories}} = \text{Average of Inventories}$$

$$\frac{\$216,000}{2} = \$108,000$$

$$\frac{\text{Cost of Goods Sold}}{\text{Average Inventory}} = \text{Rate of Turnover}$$

(assume Cost of Goods Sold to be $927,000)

$$\frac{927,000}{108,000} = 8.58$$

Another useful computation is the average number of days for one turnover. This is found by dividing 365 by the rate of turnover.

$$\frac{\text{Days in a Year}}{\text{Turnover}} = \text{Average Number of Days for One Turnover}$$

$$\frac{365}{8.58} = 42.5 \text{ days}$$

A. Fill in each blank in the stock cards below. Then find the value of the balance inventory by the average, FIFO, and LIFO methods.

Stock Card

Household Supplies Department

ITEM *Tumbler Sets* MAXIMUM 500

STOCK NO. *TS-106* MINIMUM 100

DATE	P.O. NO.	QUANT. IN	UNIT COST.	REQ. NO.	QUANT. OUT	BALANCE
9/12/x9	742	150	$2.00			150
9/14/x9				615	60	90
9/21/x9	751	200	2.25			
9/23/x9				621	90	
9/28/x9	759	150	2.50			
10/3/x9				630	100	
10/6/x9	771	100	2.50			

Stock Card

Household Improvement

ITEM *White Paint (gal.)* MAXIMUM 900

STOCK NO. *WP-753* MINIMUM 200

DATE	P.O. NO.	QUANT. IN	UNIT COST	REQ. NO.	QUANT. OUT	BALANCE
1/6/x9	1163	700	$7.95			700
1/9/x9				5563	200	
1/21/x9				5570	250	
1/29/x9	1171	200	8.00			
2/6/x9				5578	200	
2/13/x9	1175	250	8.25			

B. The A. B. Jones Company, a furniture manufacturing company, made purchases of a certain packing material as shown below. The inventory at the end of one year was 2012 units. Fill in the blanks and compute the value of the 2012 units remaining by the average, FIFO, and LIFO methods.

DATE	NO. OF UNITS	UNIT COST	TOTAL COST
1/2/X9	1,200	$5.10	( )
3/1/X9	1,250	( )	$6,240
6/1/X9	( )	$5.30	$6,890
8/25/X9	500	$5.40	( )
9/1/X9	( )	$5.40	$10,800
12/20/X9	2,500	( )	$13,750

Value of 2012 units remaining by: average method _____ ; FIFO method _____ ; LIFO method _____ .

Assuming that reducing taxes rather than increasing reported profits is the company's goal, which method would be most advantageous for A. B. Jones to use? Why?

C. Below is an inventory sheet to be filled in.

COLLEGE PIPE SHOP	Counted by **J.J.K.**		
INVENTORY SHEET	Priced by **R.T.**		
Jan. 27, 19X9	Checked by **M.A.**		

QUANTITY	DESCRIPTION	UNIT COST	TOTAL
26	Snap pipe lighters	$ 2.95	
3 cases	Pipe cleaners		$ 7.20
1 1/2 cases	Polishing cloths	6.20	
	7″ pipe stand	4.95	59.40
10	Walnut pipe rack and humidor	9.50	
52	Pipe tool and knife		67.08
	Tobacco Univ. X-Aromatic, lg. tin	6.00	48.00
7 cases	Tobacco Univ. — regular, lg. tin	5.75	
	Tobacco Univ. — mild, lg. tin	5.75	40.25
9 cases	Tobacco Univ. — blend, lg. tin	6.25	

D. Given the inventories and total cost of goods sold, find the rate of turnover in the problems below.

1. Inventories 4/27/X9 $ 68,000
              10/25/X9   72,000
    Goods sold   612,000

2. Inventories 3/15/X9 $10,500
              7/15/X9   12,500
            11/15/X9   13,000
    Goods sold   92,000

3. Inventories   1/4/X9 $ 73,000
                  4/3/X9   71,000
                  7/5/X9   73,500
                 10/1/X9   70,500
   Goods sold   846,500

4. Inventories   1/30/X9 $ 27,000
                  6/15/X9   30,000
                 12/13/X9   30,000
   Goods sold   367,000

5. Inventories 1/15/X9 $ 36,000
                 9/19/X9   52,000
   Goods sold   112,000

6. Inventories   1/30/X9 $ 61,100
                  6/30/X9   22,000
                  9/28/X9   67,000
                 12/30/X9   5,000
   Goods sold   920,000

E. Below is a stock card for the Hamschlin Company.

THE HAMSCHLIN COMPANY
BOYS' DENIMS
STOCK # 35–209

DATE	PURCHASE ORDER NUMBER	QUANTITY IN	UNIT PRICE	REQ. NO.	QUANTITY OUT	BALANCE
3/1/X4	201	200	$7.50			200
3/7/X4	206	125	$7.75			
3/13/X4				316	80	245
3/16/X4				318	170	75
3/18/X4	208	340	$8.00			415
3/20/X4				322	260	155
3/29/X4	210	100	$8.25			255
3/31/X4				325	200	55

The ending inventory balance for March was 55 pairs of boys' denims.

1. What would the value of the inventory balance be on the following dates if the company had been using the LIFO method of valuation?

    a. March 13? _____

    b. March 18? _____

    c. March 31? _____

2. What would the value of the inventory balance be on the following dates if the company had been using FIFO instead of LIFO?

a. March 13? _____

b. March 18? _____

c. March 31? _____

A. Matching.

_____ **1.** aliquot part

(a) the counting numbers

_____ **2.** check

(b) $\dfrac{1}{C}$

_____ **3.** turnover

(c) the number of equal parts into which the whole unit is divided

_____ **4.** liter

(d) fractions with the denominator larger than the numerator

_____ **5.** prime numbers

(e) numbers made up of whole and fractional parts

_____ **6.** denominator

(f) numbers that cannot be divided evenly by any number except themselves or 1

_____ **7.** reciprocal

(g) fractions with the same denominator

_____ **8.** metric system

(h) numbers made up of whole and decimal parts

_____ **9.** reconciliation of bank statement

(i) the business name given to a mathematical factor

_____ **10.** deposit slip

(j) system of measurements expressed in units of 10

_____ **11.** stock card

(k) unit of volume

_____ **12.** natural numbers

(l) tenth

_____ **13.** deci-

(m) the bank's record of a deposit

_____ **14.** merchandise inventory

(n) liability on the part of the bank to pay on demand

_____ **15.** demand deposit

(o) an order or draft to pay someone a sum of money

_____ **16.** mixed numbers

(p) the process of balancing the checkbook with the bank statement

_____ **17.** kilo-

(q) the list of all goods on hand at any given time

_____ **18.** proper fractions

(r) item used to keep perpetual inventory

_____ **19.** mixed decimals

(s) the number of times a business converts inventories into sales

_____ **20.** like fractions

(t) prefix denoting thousand

B. Perform the indicated operations.

1. $\dfrac{26 + 2(5 - 3) - 12}{2}$

2.
$$163$$
$$57$$
$$+129$$

3.
$$92,101$$
$$-35,872$$

4.
$$362$$
$$\times\ 19$$

5. $21\overline{)5,625}$

6.
$$5\tfrac{1}{3}$$
$$\tfrac{1}{4}$$
$$+16\tfrac{1}{6}$$

7. $\dfrac{16}{3} - \dfrac{9}{11}$

8. $\dfrac{15}{7} \times \dfrac{8}{21} \times \dfrac{3}{4}$

9. $\dfrac{13}{15} \div 3\dfrac{3}{7}$

10. $\dfrac{11}{12} \times \dfrac{5}{6}$

11. $10.06 + 6.3 + .003$

12. $16.06 - 1.125$

13.
$$26.01$$
$$\times 15.12$$

14. $24\overline{)22.6}$ to 3 places

15.
$$13.46$$
$$90.6$$
$$103$$
$$+\ \ \ 0.03$$

C. Perform the indicated operations.

1. Convert $6\tfrac{1}{2}$ gal, 3 qt, 1 pt to quarts.

2. Subtract 2 hr, 59 min from 4 hr.

3. Convert 6,462 dl to liters.

4. Multiply 4 sq yd, 3 sq ft by 4.

5. Add 3 gal, 2 qt, 1 pt to 4 qt, 1 pt.

6. Convert 7 cu ft to gallons.

D. Find the cost of the following mentally, using aliquot parts.

1. 36 units @ $.50

2. 75 units @ $.40

3. 66 units @ $1.33

4. 125 units @ $.48

5. 24 units @ $.08$\tfrac{1}{3}$

E. Below is another sample invoice. Fill in the blanks, using shortcuts where possible. Remember to add the amounts.

```
                    PENNANT SPORTING GOODS
                      363 TOWNSEND PLACE
                    CLANTON, STATE 91202

    Sold to:                                Date    May 22, 19X9
        Clanton Baseball Association        Order   No. 14-363
        Milton Memorial Field               Terms   n/30
        Clanton, State 91202                Via     Picked up
```

QUANTITY	DESCRIPTION	UNIT PRICE	AMOUNT
19	Complete Uniforms	$17.95	$
19	Harvard Baseball Caps		56.05
48	Wilson Baseballs	1.33 1/3	
28	Louisville Slugger Bats	2 for $5.00	
25 lb	Lime	$8.80 /cwt	
6	Wilson Protective Helmets	$21.00 /doz	
1	Rawlings Catcher's Mitt		15.75
1	Rawlings First Base Mitt	17.95	17.95
8 pr.	Spalding Baseball Spikes	11.95	
2	Johnson & Johnson Medicine Kits	5.95	
		Net Total	
		Sales Tax	38.22
		TOTAL	$

F. Solve each of the following problems.

1. Dr. Weston's bank balance at the beginning of July was $8927.15. If he deposited a total of $7412.89 in July and wrote checks for a total of $6989.46, what was his balance at the end of July? (Disregard any service charges, credits, and so forth.)

2. Mrs. Flaherty wishes to wallpaper her living room walls. If the areas of the walls (less windows and doors) are 102, 102, 85, and 68 square feet, what is the total area of the area to be wallpapered in square yards?

3. On a five-day trip, a salesman traveled the following distances: 108 miles, 186 miles, 92 miles, 216 miles, and 154 miles. What was the average distance he traveled each day?

4. If a firm recorded inventories of $12,000, $11,500, and $13,500 during 19X9 and the total cost of all goods sold was $97,500, what was the rate of turnover and how many days did each turnover take?

PART TWO

Percentage in Business

CHAPTER 9
Percentage

The term *percent* is derived from the Latin word "centum," which means "a hundred." Percent is another way to express hundredths. The symbol "%" is frequently used to denote percent. In previous chapters, we learned two other ways to express hundredths—fractions and decimals. Thus, $\frac{13}{100}$, .13, and 13% are all equivalent.

CONVERTING PERCENTS TO FRACTIONS AND DECIMALS

To change a percent to a decimal, move the decimal point two places to the left and drop the percent sign. If the percent consists of only one digit, a zero is added to the left in order to fill two places.

Example. $14\% = 14.\% = .14$ $36\% = 36.\% = .36$ $2\% = 02.\% = .02$

$29\% = .29$ $37\% = .37$ $53\% = .53$

The opposite of the above is applied to change a decimal to a percent. Move the decimal point two places to the right and add the percent sign.

Example. $.42 = .42 = 42\%$ $.49 = .49 = 49\%$ $.08 = .08 = 8\%$

$.91 = 91\%$ $.64 = 64\%$ $.73 = 73\%$

To change a percent to a fraction, drop the percent sign and place the number over 100. To complete the conversion, reduce the fraction to lowest terms.

Example. $17\% = \frac{17}{100}$ $32\% = \frac{32}{100} = \frac{8}{25}$

$2\% = \frac{2}{100} = \frac{1}{50}$ $89\% = \frac{89}{100}$

If the percent contains a decimal, move the decimal point two places to the left, drop the percent sign, and place the number over the appropriate multiple of 10.

Example. $17.5\% = \underset{\frown}{17.5\%} = .175 = \dfrac{175}{1000} = \dfrac{7}{40}$

$23.71\% = \underset{\frown}{23.71\%} = .2371 = \dfrac{2371}{10,000}$

To change a fraction to a percent, we could apply the opposite of the above: expand the fraction to hundredths, drop the denominator, and then add the percent sign to the numerator.

Example. $\dfrac{1}{5} = \dfrac{20}{100} = 20\%$ $\qquad$ $\dfrac{3}{4} = \dfrac{75}{100} = 75\%$

$\dfrac{1}{3} = \dfrac{33\frac{1}{3}}{100} = 33\frac{1}{3}\%$ $\qquad$ $\dfrac{7}{10} = \dfrac{70}{100} = 70\%$

Many fractions cannot, however, be expanded exactly to hundredths. Another method that frequently must be applied is first to convert the fraction to a decimal and then to a percent.

Example.

$$\frac{4}{9} = 9\overline{)4.000} \quad .444 = 44.4\%$$
$$\frac{3\;6}{40}$$
$$\frac{36}{40}$$

$$\frac{7}{8} = 8\overline{)7.000} \quad .875 = 87.5\%$$
$$\frac{6\;4}{60}$$
$$\frac{56}{40}$$

$$\frac{13}{16} = 16\overline{)13.0000} \quad .8125 = 81.3\%$$
$$\frac{12\;8}{20}$$
$$\frac{16}{40}$$
$$\frac{32}{80}$$

$$\frac{21}{23} = 23\overline{)21.0000} \quad .9130 = 91.3\%$$
$$\frac{20\;7}{30}$$
$$\frac{23}{70}$$
$$\frac{69}{10}$$

There are other important points to remember about percents. A percent value that is greater than 100 or a decimal with more than two places can also be converted by the rules given above.

Example. $512\% = \underset{\frown}{512.\%} = 5.12$ $\qquad$ $206\% = \underset{\frown}{206.\%} = 2.06$

$.589 = 58.9\%$ $\qquad\qquad$ $.108 = 10.8\%$

Percents can be a combination of whole and fractional parts.

Example. $12\dfrac{1}{3}\%$ $\qquad$ $89\dfrac{11}{12}\%$ $\qquad$ $45\dfrac{1}{2}\%$ $\qquad$ $28\dfrac{5}{8}\%$

Some percents that are combinations of whole and fractional parts can be changed to exact fractions, but not to exact decimals.

Example. $8\frac{1}{3}\% = \frac{1}{12} = .08333$

$41\frac{2}{3}\% = \frac{5}{12} = .41667$

The above examples were rounded off to five decimal places, but the number of places is dependent on the degree of accuracy needed. Table 9.1 lists the most common percent–fraction–decimal equivalents.

TABLE 9.1

Percent-Fraction-Decimal Equivalents		
$5\% = \frac{1}{20} = .0500$	$33\frac{1}{3}\% = \frac{1}{3} = .3333$	$60\% = \frac{3}{5} = .6000$
$8\frac{1}{3}\% = \frac{1}{12} = .0833$	$37\frac{1}{2}\% = \frac{3}{8} = .3750$	$62\frac{1}{2}\% = \frac{5}{8} = .6250$
$12\frac{1}{2}\% = \frac{1}{8} = .1250$	$40\% = \frac{2}{5} = .4000$	$75\% = \frac{3}{4} = .7500$
$16\frac{2}{3}\% = \frac{1}{6} = .1667$	$41\frac{2}{3}\% = \frac{5}{12} = .4167$	$80\% = \frac{4}{5} = .8000$
$20\% = \frac{1}{5} = .2000$	$50\% = \frac{1}{2} = .5000$	$83\frac{1}{3}\% = \frac{5}{6} = .8333$
$25\% = \frac{1}{4} = .2500$	$58\frac{1}{3}\% = \frac{7}{12} = .5833$	$87\frac{1}{2}\% = \frac{7}{8} = .8750$

We have seen that a fraction can be expressed as a percent. This is often a convenient way of expressing fractional relationships, since individuals will often have a clearer understanding of a percentage relationship than a fractional one.

Example. A survey showed that of 176 people interviewed, 44 had not visited a dentist in the last five years. Expressing this result as a *percentage* of persons interviewed would be more readily understandable. One could say, for example, that of 176 persons surveyed, 25% had not visited a dentist in the last five years.

$\frac{44}{176} = 25\%$

A percentage, therefore, is another way of expressing the ratio or fractional relationship between two numbers.

FUNDAMENTALS OF PERCENTAGE

Percentage problems involve three basic elements: (1) the *base*—the number which is multiplied by the rate, (2) the *rate*—the percent, and (3) the *percentage*—the product of the base and the rate. Given any two of these basic elements, we can easily find the third.

The formula expressing the relationship between these three elements, base, rate, and percentage, is

Percentage = Base × Rate (percent)
$$P = B \times R$$

Example. An employee earns $180 per week and decides to save 10% (rate) of his salary (base) each week. What is the amount (percentage) he saves?

$$P = \$180 \times 10\%$$
$$P = \$180 \times .10$$
$$P = \$18$$

We have just seen how to find the percentage; to find the rate (percent), we employ the formula

$$\frac{P}{B} = R$$

Example. If an employee earns $90 per week and saves $9 of his salary each week, what percent of his salary does he save?

$$\frac{\$18}{\$180} = R = 10\%$$

Note that if the percentage is larger than the base, the rate will be greater than 100.

Example. Mrs. Jones earns $12,000 per year as a librarian. Her husband's teaching job pays $9600 annually. What percentage of Mr. Jones' salary does his wife earn at her position?

$$\frac{P}{B} = \frac{12,000}{9600} = R$$

```
         1.25 = 125%
9,600)12,000.00
       9,600.00
       2,400.00
       1,920.00
         480.00
         480.00
              0
```

Mrs. Jones' annual salary is 125% of her husband's.

To find the base, we employ the formula

$$\frac{P}{R} = B$$

Example. If an employee saves 10% of his salary and saves $9 per week, what is his salary?

$$\frac{\$9}{.10} = B = \$90$$

INCREASE OR DECREASE

Many numbers are made more meaningful by the use of a percent to indicate a change up or down from some base figure. To find the rate (%) of increase or decrease, first find the amount of change. In the case of an increase, subtract the base from the figure representing the base plus the increase. In the case of a decrease, subtract the figure representing the base less the decrease from the base itself. Then divide the amount of change obtained in the first step by the base.

In this second step we are finding the percent the base has increased, or decreased, using the formula

$$R = \frac{P}{B}$$

Example. Mr. Traner's income last year was $11,000. This year he made $13,500. What was the amount and rate of increase?

$$
\begin{array}{r}
\$13,500 \\
-\ 11,000 \\
\hline
\$\ 2,500 = \text{amount of increase}
\end{array}
$$

$$R = \frac{P}{B} \qquad P = \$2,500$$
$$B = 11,000$$

$$R = \frac{\$2,500}{11,000}$$

$$
\begin{array}{r}
.227 = 22.7\% = \text{rate of increase} \\
11,000\overline{)2,500.000} \\
2,200\ 0 \\
\hline
300\ 00 \\
220\ 00 \\
\hline
80\ 000 \\
77\ 000 \\
\hline
\end{array}
$$

Example. Alpine ski boots now sell for $78 a pair. If the company plans to increase the price 9%, what is the amount of increase and the new cost?

$$P = R \times B$$
$$P = .09 \times \$78$$
$$P = \$7.02 = \text{amount of increase}$$

$$
\begin{array}{r}
\$78.00 = \text{old price} \\
+\ 7.02 = \text{increase} \\
\hline
\$85.02 = \text{new price}
\end{array}
$$

Example. Mr. Bliton received a raise of $35 a week. If this was a 5% increase, what was his weekly salary before and after the raise?

$$B = \frac{P}{R} \qquad B = \frac{35}{.05}$$

$$
\begin{array}{r}
700 \\
5\overline{)3,500} \\
3\ 5
\end{array}
\qquad
\begin{array}{l}
\$700/\text{wk} = \text{old salary} \\
\$700 + \$35 = \$735/\text{wk} = \text{new salary}
\end{array}
$$

Example. The Saudi Oil Company was pleased to announce that its profits for 1978 were $4,500,000. This was a 150% increase over the previous year's profits. What were the Saudi Company's profits in 1977?

A very easy error to make in this situation would be to solve for B using the standard formula $B = P/R$ with values inserted as follows: $B = \$4,500,000/1.5$. However, a closer look at the problem indicates that one of these is not the correct figure. Profits for 1978 (\$4,500,000) amounted to a 150% *increase* over the previous year's achievement. This means that the Saudi Oil Company not only *matched* its 1977 profits in 1978 (100%) but earned an *additional* 150% of the 1977 figure as well. Therefore, the 1978 profits for the Saudi Oil Company (\$4,500,000) were equal to

$100\% + 150\% = 250\%$ of the 1977 profits

Thus, $R = 250\%$. We can now solve for B using the standard formula:

$$\frac{P}{R} = \frac{\$4,500,000}{2.5} = \$1,800,000 = \text{Saudi Oil Company's 1977 profits}$$

Had the company announced that 1978 profits were 150% of 1977 profits—not a 150% increase over 1977 profits—the $B = 4,500,000/1.5$ would of course be correct.

ALLOCATION OF OVERHEAD COSTS

All costs that cannot be readily attributed to the production of a specific item of output are called *overhead costs*. The total cost of producing a product is equal to the cost of materials plus the cost of labor plus the amount of *overhead*. Overhead or *indirect costs* of production include rent, depreciation, insurance, taxes, administrative expenses, and, in the case of a manufacturing enterprise, the salaries of all employees not directly engaged in the manufacturing process, such as office staff, maintenance workers, and foremen.

There are several methods of allocating overhead costs among the various departments of a firm. Three methods widely used are to distribute overhead costs according to total floor space occupied, total net sales, and direct labor costs.

Example. A large insurance company selling both life and health insurance occupies a ten-story building. The lower six floors are occupied by the life insurance staff, while the top four floors are occupied by the health insurance staff. When the costs of processing the two kinds of insurance are to be determined, the costs of maintaining the building are apportioned on the basis of the number of floors occupied by each of the two staffs:

$\dfrac{6}{10} = 60\%$ to life insurance

$\dfrac{4}{10} = 40\%$ to health insurance

Example. Doherty Stationery Shop allocates to each of its departments a share of the monthly overhead of \$2450 on the basis of total net sales.

	Total July Sales
Greeting cards	$13,400
Books	8,280
Stationery	7,670
Office supplies	5,490
	$34,840

Overhead will be distributed as follows:

$13,400 ÷ $34,840 = 38.4%	$ 2,450 × 38.4% = $ 940.80	(Greeting cards)
8,280 ÷ 34,840 = 23.8%	2,450 × 23.8% = 583.10	(Books)
7,670 ÷ 34,840 = 22.0%	2,450 × 22.0% = 539.00	(Stationery)
5,490 ÷ 34,840 = 15.8%	2,450 × 15.8% = 387.10	(Office supplies)
$34,840	100.0% $2450.00	(Total overhead)

Example. In manufacturing there are three basic costs: (1) raw materials, (2) direct labor, and (3) factory overhead. Raw materials are the commodities which directly become a part of the finished product. *Direct labor* is the cost of the labor of the people who work on the materials that are converted into finished products. Factory overhead includes all manufacturing costs other than those expended on direct labor and raw materials.

A predetermined overhead rate is sometimes charged against all jobs (or projects) in a factory. The rate is calculated by dividing total overhead costs for a given period, often a year, by total direct labor costs for the same period. The predetermined rate is then multiplied by the direct labor costs of a particular job in order to arrive at the amount of overhead to be charged against that job.

For the Ace Zipper Company, total factory overhead costs for the year were estimated at $48,000 and total direct labor costs at $60,000. Based on this data, the predetermined rate to be applied to all jobs in order to recover all factory overhead is

$$\frac{\$48,000}{\$60,000} = .80 = 80\%$$

The actual overhead allocated to a special order which used $2000 worth of direct labor would therefore be

$$\$2000 \times .80 = \$1600$$

ASSIGNMENT 17 PERCENTAGE AND USES

A. Change each of the following fractions to percents and each of the percents to fractions.

a.	$\frac{1}{10}$	b.	20%
1.	$\frac{2}{5}$	2.	$\frac{7}{8}$
3.	$\frac{13}{16}$	4.	$\frac{1}{3}$
5.	$\frac{3}{4}$	6.	47%
7.	52%	8.	85%
9.	19%	10.	44%

B. Change each of the following decimals to percents and each of the percents to decimals.

a.	.15	b.	33%
1.	.762	2.	.094
3.	.3652	4.	.009
5.	.03	6.	79%
7.	43%	8.	12.7%
9.	93.62%	10.	114%

C. Change each of the following percents to fractions and then to decimals.

a.	30%	b.	125%
1.	26%	2.	25%
3.	$66\frac{2}{3}\%$	4.	$58\frac{1}{3}\%$
5.	75%	6.	$83.33\frac{1}{3}\%$
7.	12.5%	8.	$83\frac{1}{3}\%$
9.	41.67%	10.	$37\frac{1}{2}\%$

D. Given the value of two terms of the percentage formula, find the value of the third. If necessary, round off to two places.

    a. $R = 75\%$, $B = 4800$, $P =$ _____

    b. $R =$ _____, $B = 1500$, $P = 3050$

    1. $R =$ _____, $B = 125$, $P = 95$

    2. $R = 12\%$, $B =$ _____, $P = 50$

    3. $R = 32\%$, $B = 91$, $P =$ _____

    4. $R = 61\%$, $B =$ _____, $P = 18$

    5. $R =$ _____, $B = 910$, $P = 900$

    6. $R = 27\%$, $B = 1003$, $P =$ _____

    7. $R = 93\%$, $B =$ _____, $P = 107$

    8. $R = 175\%$, $B = 65$, $P =$ _____

    9. $R =$ _____, $B = 850$, $P = 900$

    10. $R = 78\frac{1}{2}\%$, $B =$ _____, $P = 1000$

E. Solve each of the following, rounding off the answers to two decimal places.

    a. The price of copper rose by 5%. If the old price of copper was $.70 a pound, what is the new price?

    b. Phil's Garage sales increased by $5,200 this year, representing a 4% increase over last year's sales. What are *this* year's sales?

    1. Roberta Johnson receives a 6% commission on each used car she sells. If she sold a car for $2875, what would be her commission?

    2. Robert Clement's batting average improved .020 points this year. If this is a 10% improvement over last year, what is his batting average this year?

    3. The price of gasoline rose 8%. If the old price was $.65 a gallon, what is the new price?

    4. Harold Vadim wishes to buy a new house. He can obtain a loan for 65% of the price of the house. If the house he wants costs $28,500, how much cash does he need to purchase it?

5. The population of Elm City rose from 110,600 to 450,000 in ten years. What was the percent increase in population?

6. The Campus Shop's sales this year were $85,600, representing a 25% increase from last year. What were last year's sales?

7. John Harris had an income of $8560 this year, and he paid $428 in real estate taxes. What percent of his income went for real estate taxes?

8. Charles Roberts receives a commission of 10% on the brushes he sells. If he received $3280 in commissions last year, what were his sales?

9. Peter Rogers receives 5% interest a year on his savings account. If he keeps $5000 in his savings account this year, how much interest will he receive?

10. The Easy Bounce Mattress Company has a Chicago sales office whose annual cost is allocated between its Cleveland plant and its St. Louis plant, each of which manufactures a different type of bedding. The cost of the sales office is allocated according to the orders filled by each factory. If in 19X9 the Cleveland plant filled orders worth $986,000 and the St. Louis plant orders worth $550,000, what percent of the cost of the Chicago office must be allocated to the St. Louis plant?

11. The Greens, a young couple, have a combined monthly income of $1200 per month. For the month of June, their budgeting resulted in the following table. Supply the omitted amount and percent figures, using the formulas learned in this chapter.

	ITEM	JUNE BUDGET AMOUNT ALLOTED	PERCENT OF MONTHLY INCOME
a.	Rent	_____	25%
b.	Food	$420	_____
c.	Savings	$252	_____
d.	Clothing	_____	6%
e.	Entertainment	$60	_____
f.	Misc.	_____	8%
	Totals	$1200	100%

12. Mrs. Scott, a consumer, recorded supermarket prices of her favorite brands of various items each month. The following is a sample of her records.

ITEM	JANUARY PRICE	FEBRUARY PRICE	MARCH PRICE	APRIL PRICE
Coffee (lb)	$2.49	$2.89	$3.49	$3.19
Milk (qt)	.42	.38	.45	.48
Bread (loaf)	.33	.39	.36	.39

Answer the following questions given the information on page 112.

   a. What percent increase (or decrease) occurred in the price of her coffee from February to March? From March to April?

   b. What percent increase occurred in the price of milk from January to March?

   c. In April, the prices of milk and bread both increased by $.03 over the March price. Which item, milk or bread, had the higher rate of increase? (Compare percent changes.)

13. Ms. Thompson purchased $400 in clothing from the New Leaf store on July 1. She paid for 35% of the merchandise in cash and charged the remainder to her store account.

   a. How much cash did Ms. Thompson pay the New Leaf store that day? _____

   b. Assume that this was her first purchase using the charge account. If 15% of the account total must be paid by July 31, how much will Ms. Thompson owe at that time, provided that she makes no other purchases charged to her account?

14. Mr. Young is a commission salesman for American Dairy Farmers. He receives a certain percentage of the value of different products he sells. Complete the table below.

	PRODUCT	RATE OF COMMISSION (R)	AMOUNT OF SALE ($)	AMOUNT RECEIVED BY MR. YOUNG (R × $)
a.	Butter	6%	375	_____
b.	Milk	8%	295	_____
c.	Eggs	11%	650	_____
d.	Cheese	7%	420	_____

15. The Sporting Goods Department of Simmons' Department Store sold $67,575 worth of merchandise during the month of April. Total sales for Simmons' in April amounted to $420,500 and various overhead expenses totaled $18,680. Based on sales, how much of the overhead should be allocated to the Sporting Goods Department?

16. Suppose the same department store were to allocate the overhead expenses on the basis of floor space. The Sporting Goods Department occupies 1700 of the total 38,500 square feet in the store. The Women's Clothing Department occupies 6600 square feet. Using the information for the month of April given above, determine the allocation of overhead for the Sporting Goods and Women's Clothing Departments on a floor space basis.

17. The Kramer Department Store uses the floor space method to determine the distribution of its overhead expenses. The department space in square feet is as follows: Men's Department, 3450;

Women's Department, 11,400; Children's Department, 4,660; Housewares, 1390. The total overhead expenses for 1977 are $351,300. What is the distribution of overhead for each department?

18. The Keystone Tool Company allocates its factory overhead by the direct labor cost method. In its most recent accounting period, its factory overhead costs were $335,000, and its direct labor costs were $670,000. How much overhead should be allocated for a tool die order that utilized $4000 worth of direct labor costs?

CHAPTER 10
Markup and markdown

One of the most important decisions a businessman must make is at what price he will sell his product. To arrive at a price, a businessman must use the cost of the goods sold, the total expenses incurred in selling the goods, and the amount (or percent) of profit he desires. The selling price must be high enough to cover all three factors. In fact, the selling price can be defined as the amount the cost price is "marked up" in order to cover selling expenses and the businessman's profit on an item.

Also, sometimes the original selling price is reduced, or "marked down" to a new selling price, thus decreasing the profit on the item but increasing the rate of turnover.

MARKUP AND COST PRICE

Markup is sometimes based on the cost price. In this case, the net cost price is equal to 100% and the selling price is equal to 100% plus the percent of markup. The relationships between the price, markup, and selling price, when the markup is based on cost, are given below

c = percent cost price $= 100\%$ C = cost price $= \$\ 86.50$
m = percent markup $= \underline{\ \ 30\%}$ M = markup $= \underline{\ \ 25.95}$
s = percent selling price $= 130\%$ S = selling price $= \$112.45$

There are three general types of problems related to cost and markup.

Case 1. The percent markup and the cost price are given. Find the selling price and the amount of markup. The amount of markup is equal to the percent markup times the cost price.

$$M = m \times C$$

The selling price is equal to the amount of markup plus the cost price.

$$S = M + C$$

Example. The cost price is $86.50 and the percent markup is 30%. Find the amount of markup and the selling price.

$$\begin{array}{ll} \text{percent cost price} = 100\% & \text{cost price} = \$86.50 \\ \text{percent markup} = \underline{\ \ 30\%\ } & \text{markup} = \underline{\hspace{2cm}} \\ \text{percent selling price} = 130\% & \text{selling price} = \underline{\hspace{2cm}} \end{array}$$

$M = m \times C$
$M = .30 \times \$86.50 = \$25.95$
$S = M + C$
$S = \$25.95 + \$86.50 = \$112.45$

Case 2. The percent of markup (30%) and the selling price ($112.45) are given. Find the amount of markup and the cost price. The cost price is equal to the selling price divided by the selling price as a percent of the cost price.

$C = S \div s$
$C = \$112.45 \div 130\% = 112.45 \div 1.30 = \$86.50$

The amount of markup is simply the difference between the selling price and the cost price.

$M = S - C$
$M = \$112.45 - \$86.50 = \$25.95$

Alternatively, one may wish to find the amount of markup directly. It is equal to the selling price multiplied by the percent markup divided by the percent selling price.

$$M = S \times \frac{m}{s}$$

$$M = \$112.45 \times \frac{30\%}{130\%} = 112.45 \times \frac{.30}{1.30} = \$25.95$$

Example. The selling price is $119.75 and the percent of markup is 25%. Find the cost price and the amount of markup.

$$\begin{array}{ll} \text{percent cost price} = 100\% & \text{cost price} = \underline{\hspace{2cm}} \\ \text{percent markup} = \underline{\ \ 25\%\ } & \text{markup} = \underline{\hspace{2cm}} \\ \text{percent selling price} = 125\% & \text{selling price} = \$119.75 \end{array}$$

$C = S \div s$
$C = \$119.75 \div 125\%$
$C = \$95.80$

$M = S - C$
$M = \$119.75 - \$95.80 = \$23.95$

or, alternatively,

$$M = S \times \frac{m}{s}$$

$$M = \$119.75 \times \frac{25\%}{125\%}$$

$$M = \$119.75 \times \frac{1}{5} = \$23.95$$

Case 3. The cost price and the selling price are given. Find the amount and percent of markup. Markup is equal to selling price minus the cost price.

$M' = S - C$

Since the markup is based on the cost price, the percent of markup is equal to the amount of markup divided by the amount of cost price.

$m = M \div C$

Example. The cost price is $99.70 and the selling price is $129.61. Find the percent and the amount of markup and the percent selling price.

percent cost price	= 100%	cost price	= $99.70
percent markup	= _____	markup	= _____
percent selling price	=	selling price	= $129.61

$M = S - C$
$M = \$129.61 - \$99.70$
$M = \$29.91$

$m = M \div C$
$m = \$29.91 \div \$99.70$
$m = 30\%$

MARKUP AND SELLING PRICE

More often, the markup is based on the selling price. In this case the selling price is equal to 100%. The cost price, then, is equal to 100% minus the selling expenses and percent of profit desired. To point out the difference between basing markup on cost price or selling price, we shall use the same cost price and percent markup as in the previous examples.

The relationships between cost, markup, and selling price when the markup is based on the selling price are given below.

c' = percent cost price	= 70%	C = cost price	= $ 86.50
m' = percent markup	= 30%	M' = markup	= 37.07
s' = percent selling price	= 100%	S = selling price	= $123.57

Here again, the problems associated with this method are of three types.

Case 1. The percent of markup and the cost price are given. Find the amount of markup and the selling price. The selling price is equal to the cost price divided by the percent of cost price.

$S = C \div c'$

The markup is equal to the cost price times the fraction of percent of markup to percent of cost price.

$M' = C \times \dfrac{m'}{c'}$

Example. The percent of markup is 30% and the cost price is \$86.50. Find the amount of markup and the selling price.

$$
\begin{array}{ll}
c' = 70\% & C = \$86.50 \\
m' = 30\% & M' = \underline{} \\
\overline{s' = 100\%} & S =
\end{array}
$$

$S = C \div c'$
$S = \$86.50 \div .70$
$S = \$123.57$

$M' = S - C$
$M' = \$123.57 - \$86.50 = \$37.07$

or, alternatively,

$$M' = C \times \frac{m'}{c'}$$

$$M' = \$86.50 \times \frac{30}{70} = \$86.50 \times \frac{3}{7} = \frac{\$259.50}{7}$$

$M' = \$37.07$

Case 2. The percent of markup and the selling price are given. Find the amount of markup and the cost price. The amount of markup is equal to the percent of markup times the selling price.

$M' = m' \times S$

The cost price is equal to the selling price minus the amount of markup or the selling price times the percent of cost price.

$C = S - M'$ or $C = S \times (100\% - m')$
$$C = S \times c'$$

Example. The selling price is \$119.75 and the markup is 25%. Find the amount of markup and the cost price.

$$
\begin{array}{ll}
c' = 75\% & C = \\
m' = 25\% & M' = \underline{} \\
\overline{s' = 100\%} & S = \$119.75
\end{array}
$$

$M' = m' \times S$
$M' = 25\% \times \$119.75$
$M' = \$29.9375$ or \$29.94

$C = S \times (100\% - m')$
$C = \$119.75 \times (100 - 25)$
$C = \$119.75 \times .75$
$C = \$89.8125$ or \$89.81

Case 3. The cost price and the selling price are given. Find the amount and percent of markup. The markup is equal to the selling price minus the cost price.

$M = S - C$

The percent of markup is equal to the amount of markup divided by the selling price

$$m' = M' \div S$$

Example. The cost price is $103.68 and the selling price is $129.60. Find the amount and percent of markup.

$$
\begin{array}{ll}
c' = & C = \$103.68 \\
m' = \underline{} & M' = \underline{} \\
 s' = \overline{100\%} & S = \overline{\$129.60}
\end{array}
$$

$$M' = S - C$$
$$M' = \$129.60 - \$103.68$$
$$M' = \$25.92$$

$$m' = M' \div S$$
$$m' = \$25.92 \div \$129.60$$
$$m' = 20\%$$

MARKDOWN

Markdown is used frequently in retailing as a means of reducing the existing selling price of an item. The *rate of markdown* is the percentage by which the original selling price of an item is multiplied to determine the amount of markdown.

If the amount of markdown (d) and the percent markdown (a) are known, the regular selling price (S) can be computed.

$$\text{Regular Selling Price} = \frac{\text{Markdown}}{\text{Rate of Markdown}}$$

$$S = \frac{d}{a}$$

Example. A suit was marked down during a sale by $25. The rate of markdown used was 25%. What was the original selling price of the suit?

$$S = \frac{d}{a} = \frac{\$25}{.25} = \$100 = \text{original selling price}$$

If the regular selling price (S) and the rate of markdown (a) are known, the amount of markdown (d) and the new selling price (S') can be calculated.

Example. A car regularly selling for $3950 will be marked down by 15% in August. What is the amount of markdown and the new selling price?

$$
\begin{array}{ll}
d = a \times S & S' = S - d \\
 = .15 \times \$3950 & = \$3950.00 \\
 = \$592.50 = \text{markdown} & \underline{-\$\ 592.50} \\
& \ \$3357.50 = \text{new selling price of the car}
\end{array}
$$

If the regular selling price (S) and the new selling price (S') are known, the amount of markdown (d) and the rate of markdown (a) can be computed.

Example. A winter coat which regularly sells for $140 is marked down to $95 during a sale. What is the amount and rate of markdown?

$$d = S' - S$$
$$= \$140 - \$95 = \$45 \text{ markdown}$$

$$a = \frac{d}{S} = \frac{\$45}{\$95} = 47\% \text{ rate of markdown}$$

A. In the problems below, assume that the markup is based on the cost price. In each of the problems enough information to fill in the blanks is given.

a. $c =$ cost price $= \$263$
    $m = 20\%$ markup $=$
    $s =$ selling price $=$

1. $c =$ cost price $=$
    $m = 30\%$ markup $=$
    $s =$ selling price $= \$375$

2. $c =$ cost price $= \$153$
    $m =$ markup $=$
    $s =$ selling price $= \$194$

3. $c =$ cost price $= \$150$
    $m = 25\%$ markup $=$
    $s =$ selling price $=$

4. $c =$ cost price $=$
    $m = 40\%$ markup $=$
    $s =$ selling price $= \$400$

5. $c =$ cost price $= \$245$
    $m =$ markup $=$
    $s =$ selling price $= \$300$

B. In the problems below, assume that the markup is based on the selling price.

a. $c' =$ cost price $= \$460$
    $m' = 25\%$ markup $=$
    $s' =$ selling price $=$

1. $c' =$ cost price $=$
    $m' = 40\%$ markup $=$
    $s' =$ selling price $= \$950$

2. $c' =$ cost price $= \$265$
    $m' =$ markup $=$
    $s' =$ selling price $= \$300$

3. $c' =$ cost price $=$
    $m' = 35\%$ markup $=$
    $s' =$ selling price $= \$560$

4. $c' =$ cost price $= \$900$
    $m' = 42\%$ markup $=$
    $s' =$ selling price $=$

5. $c' =$ cost price $= \$1280$
    $m' = 20\%$ markup $=$
    $s' =$ selling price $=$

C. In the problems below, assume that the markdown is made from the regular selling price.

a. $S = \$380$
    $a = 25\%$
    $S' = ?$

b. $S = ?$
    $a = 45\%$
    $S' = \$220$

c. $S = \$22.50$
    $a = ?$
    $S' = \$19.13$

d. $S = ?$
$a = 5\%$
$S' = \$69.45$

e. $S = \$6867$
$a = 16\%$
$S' = ?$

f. $S = \$2.13$
$a = ?$
$S' = \$1.96$

D. Complete the following table.

	REGULAR SELLING PRICE (S)	MARKDOWN RATE (a)	AMOUNT OF MARKDOWN (d)	REDUCED SELLING PRICE (S')
a.	$27.64	15%	_____	_____
b.	$135.40	_____	$27.08	_____
c.	$16.35	25%	_____	$12.26
d.	$58.99	_____	$20.65	_____
e.	_____	_____	$2.85	$6.65
f.	$17.20	12%	_____	_____
g.	$950.25	_____	_____	$570.15
h.	$342.50	_____	$171.25	_____

E. Solve the following problems.

1. Mr. Drew buys a lamp at $9.88 and sells it at a markup of 30% of the cost price. What is the amount of markup and the selling price of the lamp?

2. Daley's Shoe Store buys tennis shoes at $10.35 per pair and sells them for $16.99. What is the amount and percent markup for the shoes if the markup is based on the selling price?

3. The Lee Company advertised a 25% markdown on all stereo equipment. Jeff bought a turntable for $65, a receiver for $119, and a pair of headphones for $38. What were the regular selling prices for each item?

4. The Donaldson Furniture Company recently marked down a sofa regularly selling for $495 to a new price of $420.75. What was the rate of markdown used?

5. A pair of ladies' gloves retails at Swanson's for $12.50. If the markup on them is 16% of the selling price, what is the cost price?

6. The James' Record Store sells all of its albums at a 20% markdown on the regular selling price. If Joe buys three albums normally selling for $12.97, $8.97, and $6.97, how much did he save altogether by buying the records at James'?

7. Mrs. Ryan bought Christmas cards on December 26 which had been marked down by one-third of their original selling price. She paid $1.88, $2.51, $2.34, and $1.34, respectively, for four boxes of cards. Determine the regular selling price for each box of cards.

8. Marshall's Variety Store sells dish towels for $1.89 each, which is a 20% markup from the cost price. What is the amount of markup and the cost price?

9. The Howard Store purchases oxford cloth shirts for $12 and marks them up by 40% of the selling price. What will their selling price be?

10. The Junior Sportswear Department of a large store had purchased shirts for $7.50 each and listed $11 as their individual selling price. These proved to be slow-moving items and were marked down to $6.99 each. The operating expenses charged to each shirt were 15% of its original selling price.

   a. What were the operating expenses for each shirt?
   b. What was the amount of profit (or loss) for each shirt as a result of the markdown?

11. Mr. Charles pays $325 for a color TV set, and his operating expenses for its sale total $35. If he wants to make a 10% profit on the TV, what will he have to charge as a selling price?

12. The Le Blanc Company marks down by 20% a $500 watch which had cost them $370. Operating expenses totaled 16% of the selling price.

   a. What is the amount of markdown and the new selling price?
   b. After the markdown, does the Le Blanc Company incur a profit or a loss? of what amount?

13. The Melwood Sporting Goods Store must sell a certain basketball at no more than $17 to meet its competitors' prices. If overhead expenses are $1.85 per ball, and a 15% profit is desired, what is the highest price the Melwood Store can afford to pay to acquire each basketball?

14. Roger's Tool Shop sells a particular saw for $29. Its competitor sells the same saw for $24.50. What percent markdown would Roger's use to match the selling price of the other store?

15. Mark's Discount Store features a 15% markdown of a cookware set which normally retails for $37.99. Meanwhile, Richman's Department Store is offering a 20% markdown on the same set which normally retails there for $39.99. Where would you pay less if you were to purchase the cookware?

CHAPTER 11
Discounts

Advertisements sometimes appear with phrases such as "20% off list price." This reduction in the listed price, or regular selling price, which a seller offers a buyer is called a *discount*. A discount differs from a markdown in that a discount is normally a certain amount off the regular selling price, often offered not to all but only to some buyers, while a markdown is a change in the regular selling price itself and is thus available to all customers. In practice the two are often indistinguishable.

The *discount rate* is usually quoted as a percent, while the *discount* is the dollars and cents amount of such a reduction.

TRADE DISCOUNTS

One type of discount is that offered by manufacturers to a merchant in the same "trade"; thus, the name *trade discounts*. The manufacturer lists the prices of all his goods in a catalog. This original price is what he asks all customers to pay. Along with this price is a list of discounts that he offers customers entitled to the trade discount. When the manufacturer wants to change his price to the trade, he can simply do so by changing the discount and issuing a new discount list. The price a customer pays after the discount has been subtracted is the *net price*. The following formulas are used in computing trade discounts and net price.

Discount = List Price × Discount Rate
$$D = L \times R$$

Net Price = List Price − Discount
$$N = L - D$$

Example. The Covena Television Company offers a trade discount of 25% on its portable color television with a list price of $425. What is the amount of the discount and the net price?

Method 1. $D = L \times R$
$D = \$425 \times .25$
$D = \$106.25$
$N = L - D$
$N = \$425 - \$106.25$
$N = \$318.75$

Method 2. There is another method that we could use to solve the above problem. Since the discount is 25%, the purchaser must pay 75% of the list price, which is the net price.

Net Price = List Price × (100% − Discount Rate)
$N = L \times (100\% - R)$
$N = \$425 \times .75$
$N = \$318.75$

Since this is the net price, the amount of discount must be the difference between this price and the list price.

Discount = List Price − Net Price
$D = L - N$
$D = \$425.00 - \$318.75$
$D = \$106.25$

Method 3. There is still another method. Frequently, we can change the discount rate to a fraction. The resulting division is often quicker.

$$25\% = \frac{1}{4}$$

$$D = L \times R$$

$$D = \$425 \times \frac{1}{4}$$

$$D = \frac{425}{4} = \$106.25$$

Note: When computing a discount for a purchase of several items, it is not necessary to calculate the discount for each item. For example, a store employee receives a 15% discount on all purchases he makes in his place of employment. He selects several items valued at $3.50, $2.99, $1.25, and $.69.

Calculating the discounts for the items individually, we find

$3.50 × .15 = .53; $3.50 − $.53 = $2.98
$2.99 × .15 = .45; $2.99 − $.45 = $2.54
$1.25 × .15 = .19; $1.25 − $.19 = $1.06
$ .69 × .15 = .10; $ .69 − $.10 = $ .59
$8.43 = list price total $7.17 = discounted prices total

Calculating the discount for the items collectively, we find

$8.43 = list price total $8.43
×   .15 = discount   − 1.26
1.2645 = $1.26 $7.17 = discounted prices total

These two totals will be exactly the same, as shown.

CHAIN DISCOUNTS

Sometimes a company will grant its customers a second discount. The company would then inform its customers that not only are they entitled to the original discount, but also to this new discount. When a company offers two or more discounts, they are known as *chain* or *series discounts*. The important point to remember is that the two discounts are not added together. If a chain discount of 25% and 10% is offered, it is not equivalent to 35%. The 25% discount must be taken on the original list price and the 10% taken on the amount left after the 25% discount has been subtracted. The quoted chain discounts can, however, be applied in any order without affecting the result.

Example. The Gibson Electric Company offers discounts of 25% and 5% on a refrigerator which lists at $375.

$$\text{Discount} = \text{List Price} \times \text{1st Discount Rate}$$
$$D = \$375 \times .25$$
$$D = \$93.75$$

$$\text{1st Net Price} = L - D$$
$$N = \$375.00 - \$93.75$$
$$N = \$281.25$$

$$\text{2nd Discount} = \text{Net Price} \times \text{2nd Discount Rate}$$
$$D = \$281.25 \times .05$$
$$D = \$14.06$$

$$\text{Final Net Price} = \text{1st Net Price} - \text{2nd Discount}$$
$$N = \$281.25 - \$14.06$$
$$N = \$267.19$$

Just as in the case of one discount, we could solve this problem by using Methods 2 and 3 illustrated in the previous example.

Single Equivalent Rate

We have already stated that chain discounts are not added. However, there is a method available to find a single discount rate equivalent to the given chain-of-discount rates. The first discount rate is subtracted from 100%. This results in the percent amount the customer has to pay or the net price rate before the second discount. The second discount rate is then applied to this result. Next, the amount of this discount rate is subtracted from the first net price rate, which results in the net price rate after the second discount. To find the equivalent discount rate, we then subtract this result from 100%.

Example. Find an equivalent discount rate for the chain discounts 20% and 5%.

$$\text{1st Net Price Rate} = 100\% - 20\%$$
$$= 80\%$$

$$\text{2nd Net Price Rate} = 80\% - (80\% \times .05)$$
$$= 80\% - 4\%$$
$$= 76\%$$

$$\text{Equivalent Rate} = 100\% - \text{Final Net Price Rate}$$
$$= 100\% - 76\%$$
$$= 24\%$$

A short method of finding the single equivalent rate is to take the sum of the two discounts and subtract the product of the two discounts.

Example.
$$20\% + 5\% = 25\%$$
$$-(20\% \times 5\%) = -1\%$$
$$\overline{ 24\%}$$

When there are more than two discounts involved, the third is used with the results of the first two.

Example. Find the single equivalent rate of 20%, 5%, and 2%.

$$20\% + 5\% = 25\%$$
$$-(20\% \times 5\%) = -1\%$$
$$\overline{ 24\%}$$

$$24\% + 2\% = 26.00\%$$
$$-(24\% \times 2\%) = -.48\%$$
$$\overline{ 25.52\%}$$

A still easier method is to use a discount table if one is available. To use the table for two discounts, find the first discount in the column and the second in the row. After finding the discount rates, simultaneously move right from the column and down from the row until you come to the number which is in the same row and column as the two discounts you found initially. That number is the equivalent net price rate stated as a decimal. The same basic procedure is followed for chain discounts of three separate discounts. The order of taking the discounts does not affect the results. A discount table, Table 11.1, and example are given.

TABLE 11.1

RATE PERCENT	5	7½	10	15	20	25	30	33⅓	40	50
2	.931	.9065	.882	.833	.784	.735	.686	.6533	.588	.49
2½	.9263	.9019	.8775	.8288	.78	.7313	.6825	.65	.585	.4875
5	.9025	.8788	.855	.8075	.76	.7125	.665	.6333	.57	.475
5–2½	.8799	.8568	.8336	.7873	.741	.6947	.6484	.6175	.5558	.4631
7½	.8788	.8556	.8325	.7863	.74	.6938	.6475	.6166	.555	.4625
7½–5	.8348	.8128	.7909	.7469	.703	.6591	.6151	.5858	.5273	.4394
10	.855	.8325	.81	.765	.72	.675	.63	.60	.54	.45
10–2½	.8336	.8117	.7898	.7459	.702	.6581	.6143	.585	.5265	.4388
10–5	.8123	.7909	.7695	.7268	.684	.6413	.5985	.57	.513	.4275
10–5–2½	.7919	.7711	.7503	.7086	.6669	.6252	.5835	.5558	.5002	.4168
10–10	.7695	.7493	.729	.6885	.648	.6075	.567	.54	.486	.405
10–10–5	.7310	.7118	.6926	.6541	.6156	.5771	.5387	.513	.4617	.3848
20–5	.722	.703	.684	.646	.608	.57	.532	.5067	.456	.38
20–10	.684	.666	.648	.612	.576	.54	.504	.48	.432	.36
25	.7125	.6938	.675	.6375	.60	.5625	.5250	.50	.45	.375
25–5	.6769	.6591	.6413	.6056	.57	.5344	.4988	.475	.4275	.3563
25–10	.6413	.6244	.6075	.5738	.54	.5063	.4725	.45	.405	.3375
25–10–5	.6092	.5932	.5771	.5451	.513	.4809	.4489	.4275	.3748	.3206

Example. An invoice shows merchandise listing at $172 and subject to discounts of 20%, 10%, and 10%. To find the net price rate, follow the row marked 20-10 across to the column headed by 10. The number at the intersection of the row and column, .648, shows that $.648 is owed for each $1.00 of the list price of the merchandise purchased.

$172 × .648 = $111.456 = $111.46 = net price

The trade discount is $172 − $111.46, or $60.54.

CASH DISCOUNTS

A merchant will frequently offer a discount if a customer pays within a certain length of time. This particular conditional or restricted discount is called a *cash discount*. In the invoices used in the previous assignments, there were numbers given after the words *terms*. These numbers and symbols express the conditions of the cash discount. The numbers "2/10, n/30" mean that a 2% cash discount is given if the bill is paid within 10 days; however, the entire bill must be paid within 30 days.

2/10 — rate of discount — no. of days discount is offered

n/30 — entire balance must be paid — no. of days before balance must be paid

Example. 3/15, n/30 = 3% discount if paid within 15 days—entire balance due within 30 days—
2/30, n/90 = 2% 30 days— 90
3/10, n/120 = 3% 10 days— 120

One important point to remember when working with cash discounts is that the discount is not given on goods returned and on freight charges. Often a customer does not have enough cash to pay off the entire bill but will make a partial payment before the expiration of the discount period. He then receives a discount on the portion paid.

Example. Thomas Benton received an invoice totaling $595 with the terms 3/10, n/30. If he paid $250 within 10 days, what balance did he owe at the end of 30 days?

Since the 3% means that he saves $.03 on each dollar paid back, $.97 paid toward the bill cancels $1.00 of the debt.

$$257.731 = \$257.73 \text{ credited to the bill}$$
amount required to cancel $1.00 = 97.)25000.000 amount paid

$595.00 = original total of invoice
− 257.73
$337.27 = balance due

Example. The Ludwig Company received an invoice on January 15 for $5100 with the terms 2/10, n/30. They chose to pay $1700 on January 20. What balance will remain at the end of 30 days?

The 2% means that the Ludwig Company saves $.02 on each dollar paid back. $.98 paid toward the bill cancels $1.00 of the debt.

$$1724.692 = \$1724.69 \text{ credited to invoice total}$$

```
       1724.692 = $1724.69 credited to invoice total
98.)170000.000
    98
    720
    680
    340
    294
    460.
    392.
    68.0
    58.8
    9.20
    8.92
```

$5100.00
− 1724.69
$3375.31 = balance due at end of 30 days

Example. On October 16, Rosen & Sons chose to pay $4000 towards a $6350 invoice, which was received ten days earlier with terms 3/15, n/60. How much will they save by taking advantage of this discount?

A 3% discount means $.97 paid toward the bill cancels $1.00 of the debt.

```
       4123.611 = $4123.61 credited toward amount of invoice.
97)400000.000
   388
   120
    97
   230
   194
   360.
   291.
   69.0
   58.2
   10.8
   9.7
   1.10
   ..97
   .130
```

$6350.00
− 4000.00
$2350.00 = balance of invoice remaining
           before discount is given

$6350.00
− 4123.61
$2226.39 = balance of invoice remaining
           when discount is given

$2350.00
− 2226.39
$ 123.61 = amount saved by making payment of $4000
           while discount is offered

ASSIGNMENT 19 DISCOUNTS

A. From the information given below, find the discount and the net price by using Method 1.

	LIST PRICE	DISCOUNT RATE	DISCOUNT	NET PRICE
a.	$750	25%		
1.	$450	15%		
2.	$395	25%		
3.	$825	20%		
4.	$970	13%		
5.	$78	10%		
b.	$1,560	15%		
6.	$78.50	18%		
7.	$13,613	32%		
8.	$264.30	28%		
9.	$160	18%		
10.	$412.50	21%		

B. From the information given below, find the discount and the net price by using Method 2.

	LIST PRICE	DISCOUNT RATE	DISCOUNT	NET PRICE
a.	$435	15%		
1.	$715	40%		
2.	$930	23%		
3.	$112.50	20%		
4.	$356.75	10%		
5.	$269	$14\frac{1}{2}$%		
b.	$1,526	15%		
6.	$716	29%		
7.	$1,000	$21\frac{1}{2}$%		
8.	$14,000	60%		
9.	$989.12	36%		
10.	$10,016.41	18%		

C. The Keystone Electric Distributing Company offers a trade discount of 25% on all items. Recently, they circulated a list of *additional* discounts on certain items. Given the list price and the additional discount, find the net price.

		LIST PRICE	ADDITIONAL DISCOUNT	NET PRICE
a.	Television	$295	10%	
1.	Color TV	$545	8%	
2.	Washer	$215	10%	
3.	Dryer	$215	12%	
4.	Dishwasher	$345	18%	
5.	AM-FM radio	$110	6%	
b.	4-Track tape recorder	$326.50	25%	
6.	Desk lamp	$11.95	10%	
7.	Clock radio	$32.75	8%	
8.	Stereo console	$619.50	5%	
9.	Portable stereo	$126.95	12%	
10.	14 cu ft refrigerator	$385.25	20%	

D. Given the following list prices and chain discounts, find the net price.

	LIST PRICE	DISCOUNTS	NET PRICE
a.	$365	5%, 15%	
1.	$470	25%, 10%	
2.	$812	15%, 8%	
3.	$200	20%, 15%, 5%	
4.	$586	30%, 12%	
5.	$641	20%, 15%	
b.	$1936	30%, 20%, 5%	
6.	$78.50	15%, 10%	
7.	$423.95	10%, 8%, 5%	
8.	$2563	25%, 5%, 15%	
9.	$2563	15%, 25%, 5%	
10.	$929.50	30%, 15%, 10%	

E. Solve the following problems.

1. Recently the Kiddie Korner held a sale of children's clothing, and various items were subject to the following discounts.

Boys' pants	20%
Girls' pants	15%
All shoes	10%
All shirts	25%

Mrs. Clark purchased the items below. Complete the selling prices (after discount) for each.

	ITEM	LIST PRICE	SELLING PRICE
a.	1 Pair Boys' pants	8.00	_____
b.	1 Pair shoes	14.99	_____
c.	2 Pairs Girls' pants	7.98	_____
		11.00	_____
d.	1 Shirt	6.50	_____
e.	1 Shirt	5.50	_____

2. Mr. Johnson receives through his company a 15% discount on the price of local baseball tickets. If he buys four tickets which have a list price of $4.75 each, what will he actually pay for them?

3. The Nu-Value Store normally gives a 12% discount on all stereo equipment. If one particular manufacturer, during a promotional event, then offers an additional 8% discount on its $480 model, what would be its selling price in the Nu-Value store?

4. The Walker Company is holding a three-day special discount on its $495 color televisions. A salesperson is instructed to offer an additional 10% discount to the original 15% of list price for a particular damaged model. What will be the selling price for that television?

5. Ms. Scott is an employee of Mason's Department Store and automatically receives a 20% discount on any purchase she makes there. During a store sale, a 15% discount on all sewing machines is in effect. What will Ms. Scott pay for a $275 (list price) machine?

6. Using Table 11.1, find the net price and trade discount for merchandise valued at $532 and subject to discounts of 20%, 10%, and 5%.

7. Mrs. Matthews ordered some supplies for the Greene Lumber Company. When the invoice arrived, it totaled $228 with the terms 2/15, n/30. She sent out payment three days afterward for the entire amount of purchase, having calculated the discount offered. What was the amount of the check Mrs. Matthews wrote to pay for the supplies?

8. The Greene Lumber Company also received a $500 invoice from the Young Tool Company with the terms 2/10, n/30. Mrs. Matthews sent out a check for $325 the following day. What remaining balance did the Greene Company owe at the end of thirty days?

9. On Senior Citizens Day the Greenwood Amusement Part offers a 20% discount on all concessions and rides to those eligible. Mrs. Reese spent $7.35 while attending with the Golden Age Club. How much would she have paid had she gone to the Park on some other day?

10. Cindy took advantage of the special offer at her favorite hairstyling salon. She received a 10% discount on a haircut (normally $12), a 15% discount on coloring (normally $20), and a 25% discount on a permanent wave (normally $30). What was the total amount she saved? What if there had been a 20% discount on the *total* regular prices instead? Would she have saved more or less? Why?

ASSIGNMENT 20 DISCOUNTS

A. Using the discount table, find the single equivalent discount rate for the following chain discounts. (*Hint:* Subtract the equivalent net price decimal from 1.0000.)

a. 30%, 25%, 5%

b. 10%, $7\frac{1}{2}$%, 5%

1. 15%, 10%, 5%

2. 20%, 15%, 5%

3. 40%, 10%, $2\frac{1}{2}$%

4. 25%, 10%

5. 33%, 25%, 5%

6. 15%, 10%, $2\frac{1}{2}$%

7. 50%, 10%, 5%

8. 40%, 5%, $2\frac{1}{2}$%

9. 10%, 10%, 10%

10. 30%, 20%, 10%

B. Explain in words what each of the following notations means.

a. 2/15, n/60

b. 5/10, n/60

1. 3/10, n/30

2. 3/20, n/30

3. 5/10, 2/20, n/30

4. 2/60, n/120

5. n/10

6. 10/5, 5/10, 2/30, n/60

7. $2\frac{1}{2}$/30, n/60

8. $7\frac{1}{2}$/10, n/90

9. 2/90, n/1 yr

10. $2\frac{1}{2}$/10, n/90

C. Find the cash discount and the net amount paid, given the information below.

	NET PRICE OF INVOICE	TERMS	DATE OF INVOICE	DATE PAID	CASH DISCOUNT	NET AMOUNT PAID
a.	$650	2/10, n/30	Jan. 12	Jan. 20		
1.	$1,264.50	4/10, n/30	July 23	Aug. 10		
2.	$963.95	3/10, n/60	March 3	March 13		
3.	$316.00	5/30, n/90	Sept. 12	Oct. 3		
4.	$346,615.00	3/10, n/60	Feb. 16	Feb. 25		
5.	$886.15	2/10, n/30	Nov. 27	Dec. 8		
6.	$419.79	2/10, 1/30, n/60	Dec. 15	Dec. 28		
7.	$178.56	2/10, 1/30, n/90	June 6	June 12		
8.	$12,385.48	5/10, 2/30, n/60	April 7	May 12		
9.	$6,783	6/10, 3/30, n/60	Aug. 16	Aug. 25		
10.	$2,632.09	3/10, 1/30, n/60	May 12	May 28		

CHAPTER 12
Commission and consignment

Manufacturers and producers frequently do not market their own goods. Instead they hire intermediaries known as *commission merchants* or *factors* to handle the distribution. The factors receive a commission for their services. A *commission* is the allowance or payment made to a factor for rendering a service such as selling or buying for another party.

Gross proceeds is the total amount for which the goods were sold. However, the manufacturer or producer, who is called the *principal*, does not receive this amount. The commission merchant must first deduct his commission, freight and storage costs, insurance allowance, and any other costs incurred in the sale. The resulting amount after the deductions, the *net proceeds*, is then forwarded to the principal along with a

	CLARIDGE COMMISSION AGENTS		14-1761
ACCOUNT SALES	CLARIDGE, STATE 74326		
	FOR [Dayton Produce Co. 7326 Rayden Blvd. Dayton, State 74382]		DATE: June 18, 1919
June 3	200 Crates Pears @ $2.75	$ 550.00	
7	150 Crates Plums @ 3.15	472.50	
7	100 Crates Peaches @ 2.50	250.00	
10	500 doz Corn @ .40	200.00	
15	250 crates apples @ 3.50	875.00	
	Gross Proceeds		$ 2,347.50
	Charges:		
	Freight	$112.75	
	Storage	36.50	
	Commisson, 4% of $2,347.50	93.90	243.15
	Net Proceeds		$ 2,104.35

135

statement called the *account of sales*, which shows all the details of the transaction. Such a statement is shown above.

CONSIGNMENT

Merchandising in the manner we have just described is generally known as *selling on consignment*. The principal is the *consignor* and the commission merchant is the *consignee*. The consignor retains ownership of the goods throughout the process until the consignee sells the goods to someone else and receives payment. This is why we referred to the commission merchant earlier as an intermediary. We not only find the consignment method used by commission merchants, but also by some retailers and wholesalers who deal directly with manufacturers.

The commission merchant is not confined simply to selling; he may also buy products for someone else on a commission basis. In this case the price he pays for the goods purchased is called the *prime cost*. To this amount he adds his commission, freight and storage and other costs. The total amount, the *gross cost*, is what he receives from the principal for whom he is buying. When he delivers the goods, he encloses a statement called an *account purchase*, which again shows all the details of the transaction. Such an account purchase is shown below.

PALMER AND SONS
COMMISSION MERCHANTS
TILTON, STATE 41906   64-169

ACCOUNT
PURCHASE
FOR Franklin's Super-Mart
     16 Royal Mall
     Greenville, State 41708   DATE: Sept. 15, 19X9

Sept. 1	700 lbs bacon @ $.79	$ 533.00	
3	350 lbs boiled ham @ .95	332.50	
3	1,100 lbs sausage @ .86	946.00	
6	1,550 lbs salami @ .63	976.50	
8	575 lbs calves liver @ 1.19	684.25	
	Prime Costs		$3,472.25
	Charges:		
	Insured Freight	260.15	
	Handling	46.80	
	Storage	42.70	
	Commission: 3½% of $3,472.25	121.53	471.18
	Gross Cost		$3,943.43

The commission is generally stated as a percent or rate. To compute the commission, simply multiply the prime cost, or gross proceeds, by the rate of commission.

Example. Mr. Roberts, a commission merchant, sells $1050 worth of produce for a farmer. His rate of commission is 4%. Therefore, he will receive 4% × $1050 or $42.00 for that particular sale.

In order to avoid making errors in transactions involving consignment and commission, it is important to remember that gross proceeds (GP) minus commissions (C) and other costs (OC) incurred equals net proceeds (NP):

$$GP - (C + OC) = NP$$

Example. We also know that in Example A, freight costs of $164 were incurred. With this information, it is easy to compute the *net proceeds* for the farmer.

$$GP = \$1050$$
$$C = \$42$$
$$OC = \$164$$
$$NP = \$1050 - (\$42 + 164) = \$744$$

The farmer received $744 net proceeds from this transaction.

Prime cost (PC) plus commission and other costs incurred equals gross cost (GC):

$$PC + (C + OC) = GC$$

Example. Mr. Roberts then purchased 2500 pounds of potatoes at $.30 per pound for Safeway Markets. His commission was 4%, freight costs $52, and storage costs 2%. What was the gross cost of the potatoes to Safeway Markets?

$$PC = 2500 \times \$.30 = \$750.00$$
$$C = 4\% \times \$750 = \$30$$
$$OC = 2\% \times \$750 = \$15 + \$52 \text{ freight}$$
$$GC = \$750 + (\$30 + \$15 + \$52)$$
$$= \$847$$

Safeway Markets incurred a gross cost of $847 for the purchase of potatoes from Mr. Roberts.

A. The following salesmen all receive 6% commission on their sales. In addition, they receive a salary of $550 a month. Given their sales for one month, find their wages for the month.

a. Mr. Thompson

$1654.00
983.00
2460.00
2934.00
563.50

1. Mr. Pendleton

$4326.00
2615.00
1973.75

2. Mrs. Townsend

$ 590.50
3419.00
3887.00
2043.00

3. Mr. Carson

$ 432.03
562.40
3000.06

4. Mr. Crawdin

$9512.75
218.00

5. Mrs. Henderson

$4132.00
1908.50
652.00
819.75
1004.00

6. Miss Justin

$ 4560.75
10,216.00

B. Solve each of the following problems. Read them carefully.

1. Mr. Fredericks makes $700 a month salary as a salesman. In addition, he receives a 5% commission on his sales over $15,000, 4% from his sales $10,000 to 15,000, and 3% on his sales from $5000 to $10,000. If his sales for June amounted to $19,550, what were his earnings for the month?

2. A salesman received a commission check for $720. If this reflects his sales for one month and he receives a 5% commission, what were his sales for the month?

3. Tate Commission Merchants had account sales of $57,413.00 and account purchases of $73,000.75 for the month of January. If they receive a 5% commission on sales and $4\frac{1}{2}\%$ on purchases, what amount of commission did they earn for January?

4. The gross proceeds of an account sale are $10,472.50. If the rate of commission is $4\frac{1}{2}\%$ and the freight, storage, and handling charges total $372.15, what are the net proceeds?

5. Miss Hill must sell $1200 in ladies' wear for the month of August. Her monthly salary is $500, and she receives 2% on all sales up to her quota. For sales above her target of $1200, she receives 4% commission. At the end of the month, her sales total $1675. What will Miss Hill earn as total income (salary plus commission) for August?

6. Mr. Lewis is an advertising executive and receives 5% commission on the value of each business account which he secures for his company. Last month he landed $68,500 worth of advertising accounts. What was the amount of his commission?

7. Mr. Egan receives a commission of 4% on all daily sales over $250. If his total sales each day from Monday through Friday were $365, $285, $410, $320, and $330, what would his commission total be for the week's work?

8. The total sales of the Home Appliance Department in the La Grange Store were $186,400 for February. Complete the following commission totals for the three department employees.

NAME	TOTAL SALES, %	COMMISSION, %	COMMISSION AWARDED
Mr. Benson	36	5	
Mr. Hunt	22	4	
Ms. Wilson	42	6	

A. Given below are the entries for an account sales statement for T. R. Roberts Distributors, 117 N. Bradford, Carrick, State, 91202, which was sent April 30, 19X9. Record the entries on the statement and compute those items not given, that is, gross proceeds, net proceeds, and so on.

700 crates apples @ $3.15 (April 6)
Storage costs, $56.50
575 crates pears @ $2.95 (April 17)
650 crates peaches @ $2.95 (April 13)
Insured freight, $284.15
200 crates oranges @ $6.50 (April 22)
350 crates bananas @ $4.75 (April 29)
Handling, $84.50
Commission, $4\frac{1}{2}\%$

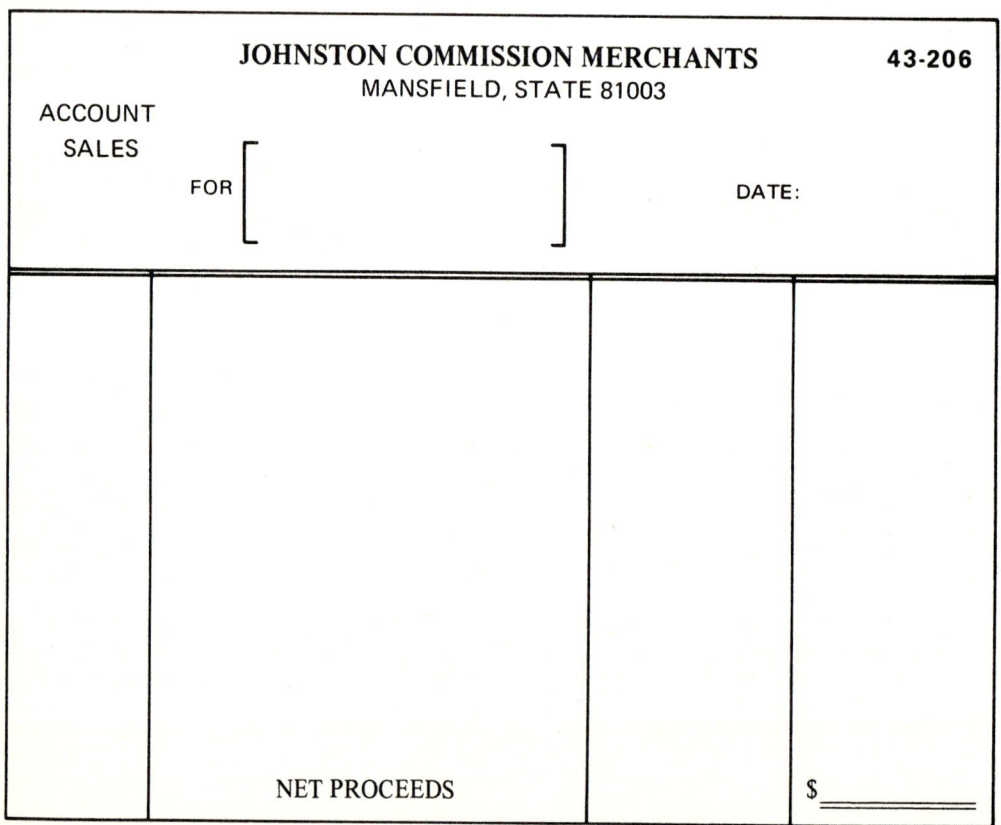

JOHNSTON COMMISSION MERCHANTS 43-206
MANSFIELD, STATE 81003

ACCOUNT SALES FOR [   ]   DATE:

NET PROCEEDS $_____

B. Given below are the entries for an account purchase statement for the One-Stop Food Mart, 7432 Baum Blvd., Nielson, State, 81006, which was sent July 12, 19X9. Record the entries on the statement and compute those items not given.

900 lb bacon @ $0.55 (July 11)
1500 lb assorted lunch meats @ $0.90 (July 2)
Refrigerated storage, $96.00
Refrigerated freight, $595.80
750 lb choice steak @ $1.50 (July 10)
500 lb sausage @ $0.80 (July 8)
Handling, $27.60
Insurance, $\frac{1}{2}\%$
Commission, $3\frac{1}{4}\%$

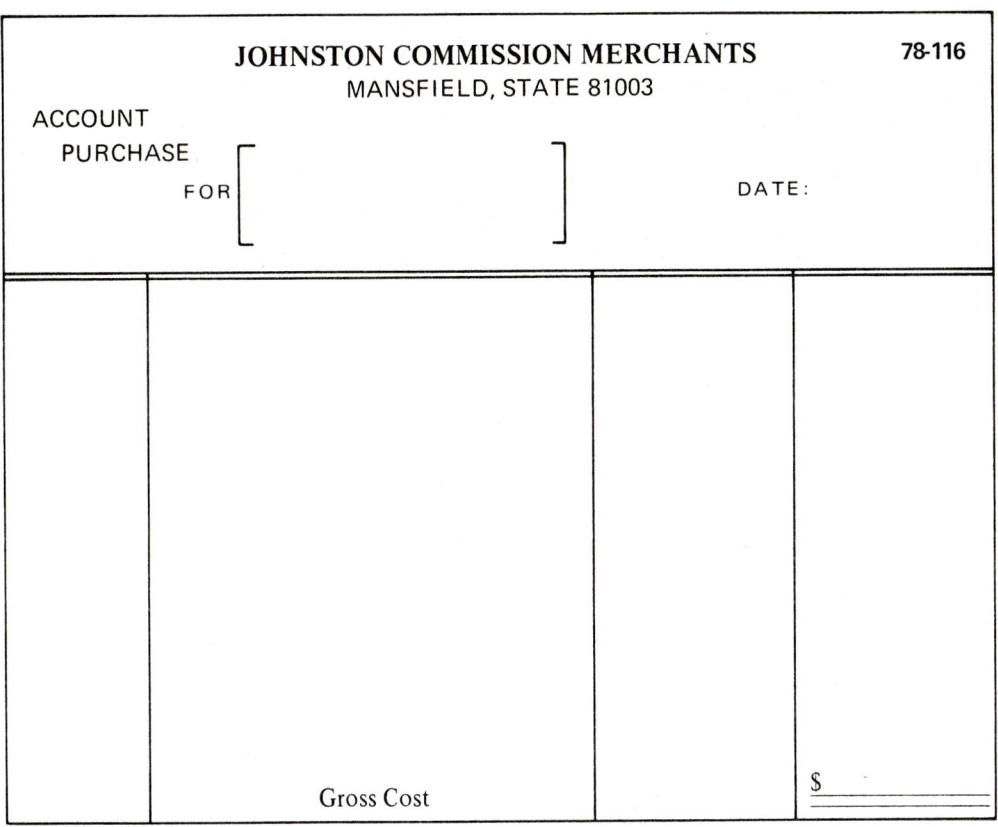

JOHNSTON COMMISSION MERCHANTS   78-116

MANSFIELD, STATE 81003

ACCOUNT
   PURCHASE
      FOR [   ]   DATE:

Gross Cost $

C. Solve the following problems.

1. Sunshine Fruit Market incurred a gross cost of $631 for produce purchased from Mr. Davis, a consignment merchant. Storage costs for the merchandise were $28, freight costs were $43, and Mr. Davis received $20 as his commission.

   a. What was the prime cost of the produce?
   b. What was Mr. Davis's rate of commission?

2. The Miller Dress Factory asked a sales agent to purchase 5000 bolts of fabric at $1.50 per yard (each bolt contained 20 yards of fabric). What was the prime cost of the fabric? The sales agent receives 3% commission. What amount is owed to him for this purchase? Transportation costs for the fabric amounted to $210. What was the gross cost to the Miller Dress Factory for this transaction?

CHAPTER 13
Depreciation

Many assets a firm purchases, such as plant and equipment, have useful lives of many years. If the cost of these assets were deducted from the revenues of the enterprise in a single year, it would destroy the comparability of successive years' profit statements. Profits would be understated in the year the asset was purchased and profits would be subsequently overstated in the following years when no charge would be made for the use of the asset. To resolve this problem the cost of a newly purchased long-lived asset is allocated over the useful life of the asset as an expense item. This allocation is called *depreciation*. To compute the amount of depreciation for each year, a company must know the following:

1. Cost—includes all costs incurred in making the asset ready for use.
2. Salvage Value—the value, if any, the company can get by the sale or disposal of the asset after its estimated life is ended.
3. Estimated Life—the period of time the company expects the asset to be useful.

Once these three factors are known, there are two major ways of computing depreciation: the straight-line method or one of the accelerated methods. The straight-line method allocates the cost equally over the life of the asset, while the accelerated methods allocate more of the cost of the asset to its early years of life than to its later years.

STRAIGHT-LINE DEPRECIATION

The depreciation for the year is equal to the cost price minus the salvage value, all divided by the estimated life.

$$\text{Annual Depreciation} = \frac{\text{Cost Price} - \text{Salvage Value}}{\text{Estimated Life}}$$

Example. Cost price, $10,000
Salvage value, $500
Estimated life, 8 years

$$\text{Annual Depreciation} = \frac{\$10,000 - 500}{8}$$

$$= \frac{\$9500}{8} = \$1187.50$$

This means that the depreciation expense each year for eight years on this particular asset with a life of eight years is $1187.50.

ACCELERATED DEPRECIATION

Sum of the Years Digits (SOYD) Method

In this method, the cost minus the salvage is multiplied by a changing fraction (K).

Annual Depreciation = (Cost Price − Salvage Value) × K

The denominator of the fraction is the sum of all the digits up to the digit representing the estimated life. Thus, if the life is five years, the denominator would be

$$1 + 2 + 3 + 4 + 5 = 15$$

If the asset's life were estimated to be 10 years, the denominator would be

$$1 + 2 + 3 + 4 + 5 + 6 + 7 + 8 + 9 + 10 = 55$$

A shorter method of finding the denominator is to use the formula

$$d = \frac{n \times (n + 1)}{2}$$

where n is the estimated life of the asset. If we had used this formula in the previous examples, we would have derived the same denominators.

Example. Life = 5 years   Life = 10 years

$$d = \frac{5 \times (5 + 1)}{2} \qquad d = \frac{10 \times (10 + 1)}{2}$$

$$= \frac{5 \times 6}{2} \qquad = \frac{10 \times 11}{2}$$

$$= \frac{30}{2} \qquad = \frac{110}{2}$$

$$= 15 \qquad = 55$$

The denominator remains constant; however, the numerator is the remaining years of life and changes each year. Thus,

$$K = \frac{\text{Years of Life Remaining}}{\text{Sum of the Estimated Life's Digits}}$$

Given this equation, we find that the fraction for the first year's depreciation, if the asset's life were 10 years, would be $\frac{10}{55}$. The second year would be $\frac{9}{55}$, and so forth. At the end of 10 years the total sum of the annual depreciations will just equal the cost of the asset less its salvage value.

Example. Cost, $15,000

Salvage value, $3000

Estimated life, 5 years

$$\text{Annual Depreciation for 1st Year} = (15{,}000 - 3000) \times \frac{5}{15}$$

$$= 12{,}000 \times \frac{1}{3} = \$4000$$

$$\text{Annual Depreciation for 2nd Year} = (15{,}000 - 3000) \times \frac{4}{15}$$

$$= 12{,}000 \times \frac{4}{15} = \$3200$$

Double-Declining Balance Method

In this method the salvage value is *not* subtracted. The depreciation expense is equal to the undepreciated balance times some fixed rate.

Depreciation = Undepreciated Balance × R

For tax purposes, a limit is imposed on this fixed rate; the maximum fixed rate is double the straight-line rate. To determine the fixed rate, we use

$$R = 2\left(\frac{100\%}{\text{Estimated Life}}\right)$$

The fixed rate is equal to twice 100% divided by the estimated life. Thus, to find the first year's depreciation, we take the original cost times the fixed rate. To obtain the second year's depreciation, we must first subtract the previous year's depreciation expense from the balance in order to find the balance of undepreciated value. The fixed rate is then applied to this figure.

Example. Cost, $17,000

Salvage value, $2000

Estimated life, 10 years

$$\text{Depreciation for 1st Year} = \$17{,}000 \times 2\frac{(100\%)}{(10)}$$

$$= \$17{,}000 \times 2(10\%)$$
$$= \$3400$$

At end of 1st year, the balance = $17,000 − $3400 = $13,600

$$\text{Depreciation for 2nd Year} = \$13{,}600 \times 20\%$$
$$= \$2720$$

A company must decide for itself which depreciation method to use. The major advantage in the straight-line method is its simplicity. A company may, however, wish

TABLE 13.1

Comparative Depreciation Table for 25-Year Life

Year	STRAIGHT-LINE Annual %	Cum. %	DOUBLE DECLINING BALANCE Annual %	Cum. %	SUM OF DIGITS Annual %	Cum. %
1	4.00	4.00	8.00	8.00	7.69	7.69
2	4.00	8.00	7.36	15.36	7.38	15.08
3	4.00	12.00	6.77	22.13	7.08	22.15
4	4.00	16.00	6.23	28.36	6.77	28.92
5	4.00	20.00	5.73	34.09	6.46	35.38
6	4.00	24.00	5.27	39.36	6.15	41.54
7	4.00	28.00	4.86	44.22	5.85	47.38
8	4.00	32.00	4.46	48.68	5.54	52.92
9	4.00	36.00	4.10	52.78	5.23	58.15
10	4.00	40.00	3.78	56.56	4.92	63.08
11	4.00	44.00	3.48	60.04	4.62	67.69
12	4.00	48.00	3.19	63.23	4.31	72.00
13	4.00	52.00	2.94	66.17	4.00	76.00
14	4.00	56.00 →	2.71	68.88	3.69	79.69
15	4.00	60.00	2.49	71.37	3.38	83.08
16	4.00	64.00	2.29	73.66	3.08	86.15
17	4.00	68.00	2.11	75.77	2.77	88.92
18	4.00	72.00	1.94	77.71	2.46	91.38
19	4.00	76.00	1.78	79.49	2.15	93.54
20	4.00	80.00	1.64	81.13	1.85	95.38
21	4.00	84.00	1.51	82.64	1.54	96.92
22	4.00	88.00	1.39	84.03	1.23	98.15
23	4.00	92.00	1.28	85.31	.92	99.08
24	4.00	96.00	1.17	86.48	.62	99.69
25	4.00	100.00	1.08	87.56	.31	100.00

to decrease reported profits, thereby decreasing taxes, more in the earlier years of the estimated useful life of an asset than in the later years. An accelerated method of depreciation would then be chosen.

For tax purposes, it is permissible, and may be advantageous, to change from one method of depreciation to another before the useful life of the asset expires. Whenever the remaining undepreciated balance divided by the remaining years of useful life (straight line) is greater than the accelerated depreciation, a higher immediate amount of depreciation can be obtained by switching methods. The chart below shows graphically the three main depreciation methods. It relates how much of the cost is recovered each year over a 25-year period for an asset with a 25-year life. The point marked by the arrow shows where a switch from the double-declining balance method to the straight-line method would result in a greater amount of depreciation. Table 13.1 also compares the three main methods.

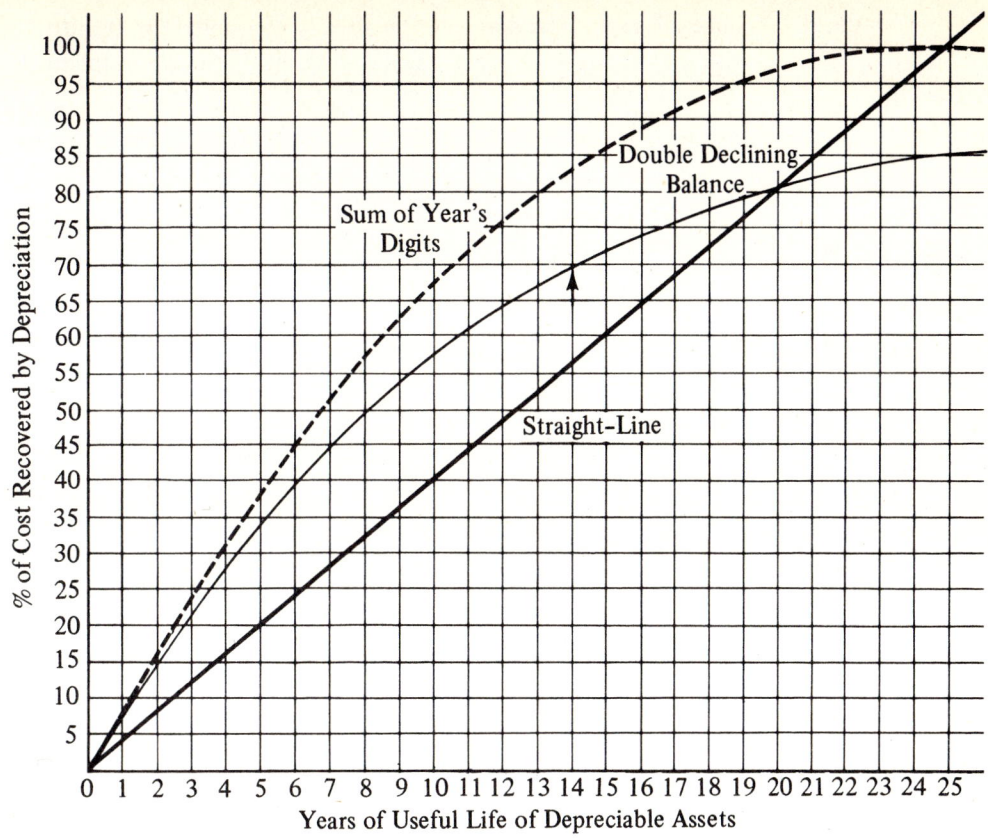

Years of Useful Life of Depreciable Assets

ONE-SHOT INITIAL DEPRECIATION

Before leaving the subject of depreciation, there is one more important consideration. Sometimes the Internal Revenue Service allows a large initial depreciation allowance. The amount and eligibility of this allowance are subject to the following conditions.

1. A set percent is allowed on a limited amount of asset value.
2. The asset must meet a minimum life requirement.

Example. Suppose an initial allowance of 20% were allowed on $10,000 of new or used assets acquired if their remaining years of life were 6 years or more. Compute the depreciation of the following asset using the straight-line method.

Cost, $43,000
Salvage value, $1000
Estimated life, 20 years

The initial allowance is computed first.

$10,000 = limit
  .20 = percent
―――――――――
$2,000.00 = initial depreciation

Since this represents depreciation already accounted for, it must be subtracted along with the salvage value before computing the depreciation for the first year.

$$\text{Depreciation for 1st Year} = \frac{\text{Cost} - (\text{Salvage Value} + \text{Initial Depreciation})}{\text{Estimated Life}}$$

$$= \frac{\$43,000 - (1000 + \$2000)}{20}$$

$$= \frac{\$40,000}{20}$$

$$= \$2000$$

It should be noted that the total depreciation for the first year will be $4000. This includes the $2000 one-shot initial depreciation plus the $2000 regular annual depreciation. It is important to remember that the initial depreciation must be subtracted in *all* cases (including the double-declining balance method) before annual depreciation is computed.

ASSIGNMENT 23 DEPRECIATION

A. Given the information below for XYZ Company, compute the depreciation expense for the first year. No initial allowance is applicable.

	ITEM	COST PRICE	ESTIMATED LIFE	SALVAGE VALUE	METHOD	AMOUNT OF DEPRECIATION
a.	Heavy duty trucks	$32,000	6	$4,000	SOYD	
1.	Automobiles	$12,000	5	$2,000	Straight	
2.	Office furniture	$10,000	10	$400	Declining	
3.	General purpose trucks	$18,000	5	$3,000	SOYD	
4.	Factory building	$70,000	20	$8,000	Declining	
5.	Warehouse	$32,000	30	$2,000	Straight	
6.	Office building	$190,000	20	$10,000	Straight	
7.	Electrical equipment	$8,500	9	$400	SOYD	
8.	Turret lathes	$2,000	5	$250	Declining	
9.	Drill presses	$7,000	5	$400	SOYD	
10.	Sprinkler system	$13,000	10	$100	Declining	
					Total	

B. The Widg-it Company purchased a new machine at a cost of $15,000. If its salvage value is $3,000 and its estimated useful life is five years, find the depreciation for each year by each of the three methods. No initial allowance is applicable.

YEAR	STRAIGHT-LINE	SOYD	DECLINING
1			
2			
3			
4			
5			
Total			

C. Assume that a 20% initial depreciation expense up to a maximum of $10,000 in assets is allowed on all assets having a 5-year life or more. Compute the depreciation for the first two years by the straight-line method and then by the sum of the years digits method.

Straight-Line

	ITEM	COST	LIFE	SALVAGE	20% APPLICABLE YES OR NO	DEPRECIATION YEAR 1	YEAR 2
a.	Factory building	$120,000	10	$20,000			
1.	Machinery	$73,000	10	$3,000			
2.	Automobiles	$17,000	3	$2,000			
3.	Office furniture	$15,000	5	0			
4.	Office machinery	$20,000	5	$2,000			
5.	General purpose trucks	$22,000	3	$4,000			

Sum of Years Digits

	ITEM	COST	LIFE	SALVAGE	20% APPLICABLE YES OR NO	DEPRECIATION YEAR 1	YEAR 2
b.	Factory building	$120,000	10	$20,000			
6.	Machinery	$73,000	10	$3,000			
7.	Automobiles	$17,000	3	$2,000			
8.	Office furniture	$15,000	5	0			
9.	Office machinery	$20,000	5	$2,000			
10.	General purpose trucks	$22,000	3	$4,000			

D. Solve the following problems.

1. A new typewriter purchased by a company's Research Department cost $850. Its estimated life is 6 years. Using the double-declining balance method, compute (a) the fixed annual rate of depreciation, (b) the amount of depreciation for the first year, and (c) the amount of depreciation for the second year.

2. Suppose the IRS allowed a 10% initial allowance on up to $10,000 of new assets acquired, providing they had at least 5 years of life. The ABC Company decides to buy some office furniture. What would be the first year depreciation for the following assets?

   a. New Desk
   Cost, $610
   Est. life, 8 yr
   Salvage, $50

   b. File Cabinet
   Cost, $226
   Est. life, 3 yr
   Salvage, $40

   c. New Mimeograph Machine
   Cost, $2100
   Est. Life, 7 yr
   Salvage, $76

3. A machine was purchased new in 1975 for $1200. At that time it was estimated to have a useful life of 15 years and a salvage value of $40. What would be the book value (cost less accumulated depreciation) after three years of straight-line depreciation have been taken?

4. Using the sum of the years digits method, find the first-year depreciation of an asset which cost $48,600 new, has a salvage value of $3500, and an estimated life of eight years. Also, what would be the second-year depreciation?

5. The Mitchell Company uses a fixed-rate, double-declining balance method of depreciation. Recently it purchased a $4000 automobile to use in making deliveries. It was estimated that the car would have a useful life of five years, after which it could be traded in for $800. What would be the first-year depreciation for the new car?

6. A small office has only a few assets which require computation of depreciation. They are a sofa, originally valued at $539 with a useful life of 10 years; a chair, originally valued at $175 with a useful life of 8 years, and a desk, originally valued at $425 with a useful life of 12 years. The salvage values of the items are, respectively, $65, $30, and $25. What is the total amount of straight-line depreciation for this year for all three assets?

CHAPTER 14
Federal and state taxes

Little has to be said about the purpose of taxes and their effect on our profits or incomes. It is, however, important to understand how each major type of tax is computed. We shall concern ourselves with Federal income taxes, sales and excise taxes, property taxes, and customs duties.

FEDERAL INCOME TAX

The tax with the greatest effect on businesses and on the individual citizen is the Federal income tax. Every person with taxable income over a certain sum in any given year ($2950 for a single individual under 65 in 1977) must file a report to the government by April 15th of the following year. This report, called a *tax return*, shows all the vital information needed to compute the tax. Along with the return, each employed taxpayer must file a *W-2 form*, which shows how much has been withheld from his paychecks during the year and forwarded to the Federal Government. The employee receives this from his employer. Such a form follows.

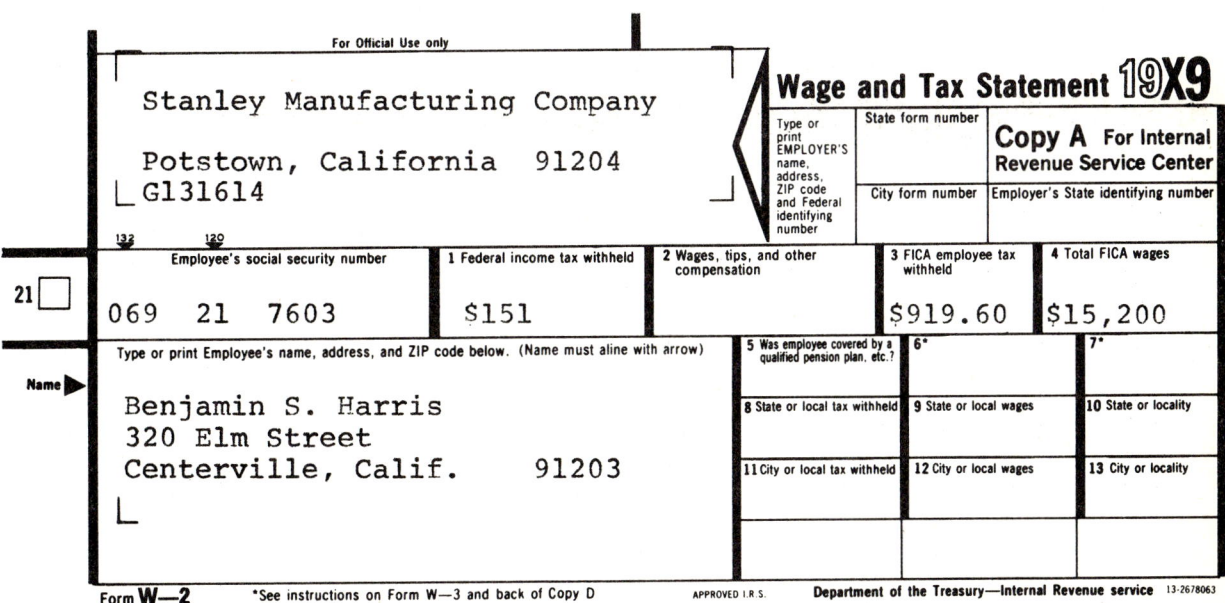

Form **1040** **U.S. Individual Income Tax Return** **19X9**

Department of the Treasury—Internal Revenue Service

For the year January 1–December 31, 1977, or other taxable year beginning _____ , 1977 ending _____ , 19 ___ .

Use IRS label. Otherwise, print or type.

First name and initial (if joint return, give first names and initials of both)	Last name
Benjamin S. and Ruth A.	Harris

Your social security number
069 : 21 : 7603

Present home address (Number and street, including apartment number, or rural route)
920 Oak Street

For Privacy Act Notice, see page 3 of Instructions.

Spouse's social security no.
071 : 32 : 8605

City, town or post office, State and ZIP code
Centerville, California 91204

Occupation — Yours ▶ salesman
Spouse's ▶ homemaker

Presidential Election Campaign Fund ▶

Do you want $1 to go to this fund? . . . . **X** Yes ▨ No

If joint return, does your spouse want $1 to go to this fund? . **X** Yes ▨ No

Note: Checking "Yes" will not increase your tax or reduce your refund.

Filing Status

Check Only One Box

1. ☐ Single
2. **X** Married filing joint return (even if only one had income)
3. ☐ Married filing separately. If spouse is also filing, give spouse's social security number in the space above and enter full name here ▶ ....
4. ☐ Unmarried Head of Household. Enter qualifying name ▶ .... See page 7 of Instructions.
5. ☐ Qualifying widow(er) with dependent child (Year spouse died ▶ 19 ___). See page 7 of Instructions.

Exemptions

Always check the "Yourself" box. Check other boxes if they apply.

6a **X** Yourself ☐ 65 or over ☐ Blind

Enter number of boxes checked on 6a and b ▶ **2**

b **X** Spouse ☐ 65 or over ☐ Blind

c First names of your dependent children who lived with you ▶ John and Betty

Enter number of children listed ▶ **2**

d Other dependents: (1) Name	(2) Relationship	(3) Number of months lived in your home.	(4) Did dependent have income of $750 or more?	(5) Did you provide more than one-half of dependent's support?
Roger Harris	father	12	no	yes

Enter number of other dependents ▶ **1**

7 Total number of exemptions claimed . . . .

Add numbers entered in boxes above ▶ **5**

Income

8 Wages, salaries, tips, and other employee compensation. (Attach Forms W–2. If unavailable, see page 5 of Instructions.)	8	15200
9 Interest income. (If over $400, attach Schedule B.)	9	75
10a Dividends (If over $400, attach Schedule B) .... 50 , 10b less exclusion 50 , Balance ▶	10c	0

*(If you have no other income, **skip** lines 11 through 20 and go to line 21.)*

11 State and local income tax refunds (does not apply if refund is for year you took standard deduction) . . .	11	
12 Alimony received	12	
13 Business income or (loss) (attach Schedule C)	13	
14 Capital gain or (loss) (attach Schedule D)	14	
15 50% of capital gain distributions not reported on Schedule D	15	
16 Net gain or (loss) from Supplemental Schedule of Gains and Losses (attach Form 4797) . .	16	
17 Fully taxable pensions and annuities not reported on Schedule E	17	
18 Pensions, annuities, rents, royalties, partnerships, estates or trusts, etc. (attach Schedule E) .	18	
19 Farm income or (loss) (attach Schedule F)	19	
20 Other (state nature and source—see page 9 of Instructions) ▶	20	
21 **Total income.** Add lines 8, 9, and 10c through 20 . . . . ▶	21	15275

Adjustments to Income   *(If none, **skip** lines 22 through 27 and enter zero on line 28.)*

22 Moving expense (attach Form 3903)	22		
23 Employee business expenses (attach Form 2106)	23		
24 Payments to an individual retirement arrangement (from attached Form 5329, Part III)	24		
25 Payments to a Keogh (H.R. 10) retirement plan	25		
26 Forfeited interest penalty for premature withdrawal	26		
27 Alimony paid (see page 11 of Instructions)	27		
28 **Total adjustments.** Add lines 22 through 27 . . . . ▶		28	0
29 Subtract line 28 from line 21		29	15275
30 Disability income exclusion (sick pay) (attach Form 2440)		30	
31 **Adjusted gross income.** Subtract line 30 from line 29. Enter here and on line 32. If you want IRS to figure your tax for you, see page 4 of the Instructions . . . . ▶		31	15275

(left margin) Please Attach Copy B of Forms W–2 Here

(left margin) Please Attach Check or Money Order Here

If a taxpayer worked for more than one employer, he must file a W-2 form for each job in which Federal taxes were withheld.

A taxpayer may usually file a complete return on the one page Form 1040A (the short form) if

1. all income was from salary or wages, tips, interest (not more than $400), and dividends (not more than $400);
2. there are no adjustments for a disability pension, moving expenses, employee business expenses, payments to an individual retirement plan, or alimony payments;
3. income after these adjustments (*adjusted gross income*) did not exceed a certain maximum (in 1977 the maximum was $20,000, or $40,000 if the taxpayer was married and filing a joint return with his spouse); and,
4. deductions are not itemized.

A taxpayer must use the Form 1040 (the long form) if any of these conditions is not met. The first page of a sample Form 1040 is shown on page 152. Along with it, the taxpayer should file the appropriate additional forms.

Whether the 1040 or the 1040A is filed, the Government allows certain *personal exemptions*. Exemptions are portions of income exempt from tax. For each relative the taxpayer supports and for himself, he may claim one exemption. Exemptions are also granted for dependents other than relatives, for age (over 65), and for blindness.

Businesses, whether they are owned by one person or are partnerships or corporations, must also file tax returns. Corporations are taxed at the following rates: 20% on taxable income through $25,000; 22% on taxable income over $25,000 (normal rate) plus a 26% surtax on all income over $50,000.

Deductions

Each taxpayer has the choice of itemizing his deductions or claiming a *standard deduction*, or zero bracket amount. Items which can be deducted include, among other things, medical expenses above a certain percentage of adjusted gross income, taxes other than the Federal income tax (such as state and local income taxes and property taxes), interest paid, charitable contributions, and casualty losses. A sample Schedule A, the form on which itemized deductions are listed, has been reproduced on page 154.

The flat-rate *standard deductions* for all taxpayers provided by the Tax Reduction and Simplification Act of 1976 are

Taxpayer status	Standard deduction
Married, filing joint return or a qualifying widow(er)	$3200
Single or an unmarried head of household	$2200
Married, filing separate return	$1600

A taxpayer should compare his actual itemized deductions to the standard deduction to which he is entitled, and claim whichever is larger. It is to his advantage *not* to itemize deductions unless their total *exceeds* the flat rate standard deduction for taxpayers in his IRS classification. (*Note:* Because the qualifications for other tax statuses are sometimes complex, the examples and problems which follow include only single taxpayers and married taxpayers filing joint returns.)

Schedules A&B—Itemized Deductions AND Interest and Dividend Income

(Form 1040)
Department of the Treasury
Internal Revenue Service

► Attach to Form 1040. ► See Instructions for Schedules A and B (Form 1040).

19X9

Name(s) as shown on Form 1040
Robert and Mary Waldeman

Your social security number
069 : 44 : 9102

Schedule A Itemized Deductions (Schedule B is on back)

Medical and Dental Expenses (not compensated by insurance or otherwise) (See page 14 of Instructions.)

1 One-half (but not more than $150) of insurance premiums for medical care. (Be sure to include in line 10 below) . . .	150
2 Medicine and drugs	100
3 Enter 1% of line 31, Form 1040 . . .	122
4 Subtract line 3 from line 2. Enter difference (if less than zero, enter zero) . .	0
5 Enter balance of insurance premiums for medical care not entered on line 1 . .	210
6 Enter other medical and dental expenses:	
a Doctors, dentists, nurses, etc. . . .	250
b Hospitals	
c Other (itemize—include hearing aids, dentures, eyeglasses, transportation, etc.) ▶ eyeglasses	75
7 Total (add lines 4 through 6c) . . .	435
8 Enter 3% of line 31, Form 1040 . . .	367
9 Subtract line 8 from line 7 (if less than zero, enter zero)	68
10 Total (add lines 1 and 9). Enter here and on line 33 . . . . ▶	218

Taxes (See page 14 of Instructions.)

11 State and local income	367
12 Real estate	750
13 State and local gasoline (see gas tax tables)	71
14 General sales (see sales tax tables) . .	114
15 Personal property	
16 Other (itemize) ▶ Occupation tax	10
17 Total (add lines 11 through 16). Enter here and on line 34 . . . . . . ▶	1312

Interest Expense (See page 16 of Instructions.)

18 Home mortgage	1200
19 Other (itemize) ▶	
First National Bank loan	50
Master charge	45
ABC Finance Company	30
20 Total (add lines 18 and 19). Enter here and on line 35 . . . . ▶	1325

Contributions (See page 16 of Instructions for examples.)

21 a Cash contributions for which you have receipts, cancelled checks or other written evidence	198
b Other cash contributions. List donees and amounts. Church contributions	104
22 Other than cash (see page 16 of instructions for required statement)	
23 Carryover from prior years	
24 Total contributions (add lines 21a through 23). Enter here and on line 36 . . ▶	302

Casualty or Theft Loss(es) (See page 16 of Instructions.)

25 Loss before insurance reimbursement .	319
26 Insurance reimbursement	219
27 Subtract line 26 from line 25. Enter difference (if less than zero, enter zero) .	100
28 Enter $100 or amount on line 27, whichever is smaller	100
29 Casualty or theft loss (subtract line 28 from line 27). Enter here and on line 37 . ▶	0

Miscellaneous Deductions (See page 16 of Instructions.)

30 Union dues	120
31 Other (itemize) ▶	
professional books & magazines	128
investment service fees	100
32 Total (add lines 30 and 31). Enter here and on line 38 . . . . ▶	343

Summary of Itemized Deductions **A**
(See page 17 of Instructions.)

33 Total medical and dental—line 10 . .	218
34 Total taxes—line 17	1312
35 Total interest—line 20	1325
36 Total contributions—line 24	302
37 Casualty or theft loss(es)—line 29 . .	0
38 Total miscellaneous—line 32	343
39 Total deductions (add lines 33 through 38). ▶	3500
40 If you checked Form 1040, box: 2 or 5, enter $3,200 1 or 4, enter $2,200 3, enter $1,600	3200
41 Excess itemized deductions (subtract line 40 from line 39). Enter here and on Form 1040, line 33. (If line 40 is more than line 39 see "Who MUST Itemize Deductions" on page 11 of the Instructions.) . . ▶	300

19X9 Tax Table A—SINGLE (Box 1)

If line 34, Form 1040 is— Over	But not over	And the total number of exemptions claimed on line 7 is— 1	2	3	If line 34, Form 1040 is— Over	But not over	And the total number of exemptions claimed on line 7 is— 1	2	3	If line 34, Form 1040 is— Over	But not over	And the total number of exemptions claimed on line 7 is— 1	2	3
		Your tax is—					Your tax is—					Your tax is—		
11,000	11,050	1,447	1,282	1,117	14,000	14,050	2,200	1,998	1,804	17,000	17,050	3,053	2,834	2,617
11,050	11,100	1,459	1,293	1,128	14,050	14,100	2,214	2,011	1,816	17,050	17,100	3,069	2,849	2,631
11,100	11,150	1,470	1,304	1,139	14,100	14,150	2,227	2,025	1,829	17,100	17,150	3,084	2,863	2,646
11,150	11,200	1,482	1,315	1,150	14,150	14,200	2,241	2,038	1,841	17,150	17,200	3,100	2,878	2,660
11,200	11,250	1,493	1,326	1,161	14,200	14,250	2,254	2,052	1,854	17,200	17,250	3,115	2,892	2,675
11,250	11,300	1,505	1,337	1,172	14,250	14,300	2,268	2,065	1,866	17,250	17,300	3,131	2,907	2,689
11,300	11,350	1,516	1,348	1,183	14,300	14,350	2,281	2,079	1,879	17,300	17,350	3,146	2,921	2,704
11,350	11,400	1,528	1,359	1,194	14,350	14,400	2,295	2,092	1,891	17,350	17,400	3,162	2,936	2,718
11,400	11,450	1,539	1,370	1,205	14,400	14,450	2,308	2,106	1,904	17,400	17,450	3,177	2,950	2,733
11,450	11,500	1,551	1,381	1,216	14,450	14,500	2,322	2,119	1,917	17,450	17,500	3,193	2,965	2,747
11,500	11,550	1,562	1,392	1,227	14,500	14,550	2,335	2,133	1,930	17,500	17,550	3,208	2,979	2,762
11,550	11,600	1,574	1,403	1,238	14,550	14,600	2,349	2,146	1,944	17,550	17,600	3,224	2,994	2,776
11,600	11,650	1,585	1,414	1,249	14,600	14,650	2,362	2,160	1,957	17,600	17,650	3,239	3,008	2,791
11,650	11,700	1,597	1,425	1,260	14,650	14,700	2,376	2,173	1,971	17,650	17,700	3,255	3,023	2,805
11,700	11,750	1,608	1,436	1,271	14,700	14,750	2,389	2,187	1,984	17,700	17,750	3,270	3,038	2,820
11,750	11,800	1,620	1,447	1,282	14,750	14,800	2,403	2,200	1,998	17,750	17,800	3,286	3,053	2,834
11,800	11,850	1,631	1,459	1,293	14,800	14,850	2,416	2,214	2,011	17,800	17,850	3,301	3,069	2,849
11,850	11,900	1,643	1,470	1,304	14,850	14,900	2,430	2,227	2,025	17,850	17,900	3,317	3,084	2,863
11,900	11,950	1,654	1,482	1,315	14,900	14,950	2,443	2,241	2,038	17,900	17,950	3,332	3,100	2,878
11,950	12,000	1,666	1,493	1,326	14,950	15,000	2,457	2,254	2,052	17,950	18,000	3,348	3,115	2,892
12,000	12,050	1,679	1,505	1,337	15,000	15,050	2,472	2,268	2,065	18,000	18,050	3,363	3,131	2,907
12,050	12,100	1,691	1,516	1,348	15,050	15,100	2,486	2,281	2,079	18,050	18,100	3,379	3,146	2,921
12,100	12,150	1,704	1,528	1,359	15,100	15,150	2,501	2,295	2,092	18,100	18,150	3,394	3,162	2,936
12,150	12,200	1,716	1,539	1,370	15,150	15,200	2,515	2,308	2,106	18,150	18,200	3,410	3,177	2,950
12,200	12,250	1,729	1,551	1,381	15,200	15,250	2,530	2,322	2,119	18,200	18,250	3,425	3,193	2,965
12,250	12,300	1,741	1,562	1,392	15,250	15,300	2,544	2,335	2,133	18,250	18,300	3,441	3,208	2,979
12,300	12,350	1,754	1,574	1,403	15,300	15,350	2,559	2,349	2,146	18,300	18,350	3,456	3,224	2,994
12,350	12,400	1,766	1,585	1,414	15,350	15,400	2,573	2,362	2,160	18,350	18,400	3,472	3,239	3,008
12,400	12,450	1,779	1,597	1,425	15,400	15,450	2,588	2,376	2,173	18,400	18,450	3,487	3,255	3,023
12,450	12,500	1,791	1,608	1,436	15,450	15,500	2,602	2,389	2,187	18,450	18,500	3,503	3,270	3,038
12,500	12,550	1,804	1,620	1,447	15,500	15,550	2,617	2,403	2,200	18,500	18,550	3,518	3,286	3,053
12,550	12,600	1,816	1,631	1,459	15,550	15,600	2,631	2,416	2,214	18,550	18,600	3,534	3,301	3,069
12,600	12,650	1,829	1,643	1,470	15,600	15,650	2,646	2,430	2,227	18,600	18,650	3,549	3,317	3,084
12,650	12,700	1,841	1,654	1,482	15,650	15,700	2,660	2,443	2,241	18,650	18,700	3,565	3,332	3,100
12,700	12,750	1,854	1,666	1,493	15,700	15,750	2,675	2,457	2,254	18,700	18,750	3,580	3,348	3,115
12,750	12,800	1,866	1,679	1,505	15,750	15,800	2,689	2,472	2,268	18,750	18,800	3,596	3,363	3,131
12,800	12,850	1,879	1,691	1,516	15,800	15,850	2,704	2,486	2,281	18,800	18,850	3,611	3,379	3,146
12,850	12,900	1,891	1,704	1,528	15,850	15,900	2,718	2,501	2,295	18,850	18,900	3,627	3,394	3,162
12,900	12,950	1,904	1,716	1,539	15,900	15,950	2,733	2,515	2,308	18,900	18,950	3,642	3,410	3,177
12,950	13,000	1,917	1,729	1,551	15,950	16,000	2,747	2,530	2,322	18,950	19,000	3,659	3,425	3,193
13,000	13,050	1,930	1,741	1,562	16,000	16,050	2,762	2,544	2,335	19,000	19,050	3,676	3,441	3,208
13,050	13,100	1,944	1,754	1,574	16,050	16,100	2,776	2,559	2,349	19,050	19,100	3,693	3,456	3,224
13,100	13,150	1,957	1,766	1,585	16,100	16,150	2,791	2,573	2,362	19,100	19,150	3,710	3,472	3,239
13,150	13,200	1,971	1,779	1,597	16,150	16,200	2,805	2,588	2,376	19,150	19,200	3,727	3,487	3,255
13,200	13,250	1,984	1,791	1,608	16,200	16,250	2,820	2,602	2,389	19,200	19,250	3,744	3,503	3,270
13,250	13,300	1,998	1,804	1,620	16,250	16,300	2,834	2,617	2,403	19,250	19,300	3,761	3,518	3,286
13,300	13,350	2,011	1,816	1,631	16,300	16,350	2,849	2,631	2,416	19,300	19,350	3,778	3,534	3,301
13,350	13,400	2,025	1,829	1,643	16,350	16,400	2,863	2,646	2,430	19,350	19,400	3,795	3,549	3,317
13,400	13,450	2,038	1,841	1,654	16,400	16,450	2,878	2,660	2,443	19,400	19,450	3,812	3,565	3,332
13,450	13,500	2,052	1,854	1,666	16,450	16,500	2,892	2,675	2,457	19,450	19,500	3,829	3,580	3,348
13,500	13,550	2,065	1,866	1,679	16,500	16,550	2,907	2,689	2,472	19,500	19,550	3,846	3,596	3,363
13,550	13,600	2,079	1,879	1,691	16,550	16,600	2,921	2,704	2,486	19,550	19,600	3,863	3,611	3,379
13,600	13,650	2,092	1,891	1,704	16,600	16,650	2,936	2,718	2,501	19,600	19,650	3,880	3,627	3,394
13,650	13,700	2,106	1,904	1,716	16,650	16,700	2,950	2,733	2,515	19,650	19,700	3,897	3,642	3,410
13,700	13,750	2,119	1,917	1,729	16,700	16,750	2,965	2,747	2,530	19,700	19,750	3,914	3,659	3,425
13,750	13,800	2,133	1,930	1,741	16,750	16,800	2,979	2,762	2,544	19,750	19,800	3,931	3,676	3,441
13,800	13,850	2,146	1,944	1,754	16,800	16,850	2,994	2,776	2,559	19,800	19,850	3,948	3,693	3,456
13,850	13,900	2,160	1,957	1,766	16,850	16,900	3,008	2,791	2,573	19,850	19,900	3,965	3,710	3,472
13,900	13,950	2,173	1,971	1,779	16,900	16,950	3,023	2,805	2,588	19,900	19,950	3,982	3,727	3,487
13,950	14,000	2,187	1,984	1,791	16,950	17,000	3,038	2,820	2,602	19,950	20,000	3,999	3,744	3,503

Continued next column   Continued next column

Example. Sally Morris is single and has calculated her itemized deductions on Schedule A to be $1400. Since her flat-rate standard deduction from the table above is $2200, it would certainly be to her advantage *not* to itemize deductions but rather to take the standard deduction.

Example. Jim and June Grayson are married and file a joint return. Their itemized deductions total $5300. Considering the standard deduction above for their taxpayer classification, it would be to their advantage *not* to use that figure ($3200) when filing their return, but instead to *itemize* deductions, which exceed it by $2100.

Computing the Tax

To determine the tax he owes, a taxpayer using the standard deduction first finds the table applicable to persons in his IRS classification (single, married filing jointly, or other). He then finds the column applicable to taxpayers claiming the number of exemptions to which he is entitled; locates the bracket into which his adjusted gross income falls; and finally locates the figure representing his tax (the standard deduction is incorporated in the table).

If a taxpayer itemizes deductions he must subtract from his total itemized deductions the standard deduction to which he would be entitled if he did not itemize. He must then subtract that remainder, "excess itemized deductions," from his adjusted gross income in order to find the reduced amount of income to look up in the tax table. It is important to note that the step-by-step procedure to be followed here is given at the bottom of Schedule A—Itemized Deductions (page 154) and also on the back of Form 1040.

Example. In 1977 Bill Sciulli earned $12,225 as a draftsman, had no income from any other source, and was entitled to no adjustments. Since he had only $500 in itemized deductions, he chose to use the standard deduction. If he is single and has no dependents (hint: one exemption), what is his tax? Using Tax Table A partially reproduced on page 155, his tax is $1729.

Example. Bob Waldman also earned $12,225, had no income from any other source, and was entitled to no adjustments. He had itemized deductions of $3,500, however, and was married and the father of four children (hint: married filing jointly with six exemptions). Using Tax Table B (p. 157), what is his tax?

$3500 = itemized deductions
− 3200 = standard deduction
$ 300 = excess itemized deductions

$12,225 = adjusted gross income
− 300 = excess itemized deductions
$11,925 = taxable income
tax: $453

Once his tax has been determined, the taxpayer offsets it with any credits to which he is entitled and adds to it any additional taxes he may owe. He then compares the amount owed with the amount already paid via withholding, and calculates either the amount to be refunded to him or the additional amount he must pay.

19X9 Tax Table B—MARRIED FILING JOINTLY (Box 2) and QUALIFYING WIDOW(ER)S (Box 5)

(If your income or exemptions are not covered, use Schedule TC (Form 1040), Part I to figure your tax)

If line 34, Form 1040 is— Over	But not over	2	3	4	5	6	7	8	9
					Your tax is—				
11,600	11,650	1,037	910	751	573	397	235	78	0
11,650	11,700	1,046	918	760	583	406	243	86	0
11,700	11,750	1,054	927	770	592	415	252	94	0
11,750	11,800	1,063	935	779	602	424	260	102	0
11,800	11,850	1,071	944	789	611	434	269	110	0
11,850	11,900	1,080	952	798	621	443	277	118	0
11,900	11,950	1,088	961	808	630	453	286	126	0
11,950	12,000	1,097	969	817	640	462	294	134	0
12,000	12,050	1,105	978	827	649	472	303	142	0
12,050	12,100	1,114	986	836	659	481	311	150	0
12,100	12,150	1,122	995	846	668	491	320	158	3
12,150	12,200	1,131	1,003	855	678	500	328	166	11
12,200	12,250	1,139	1,012	865	687	510	337	174	19
12,250	12,300	1,148	1,020	874	697	519	345	183	27
12,300	12,350	1,156	1,029	884	706	529	354	191	35
12,350	12,400	1,165	1,037	893	716	538	362	200	43
12,400	12,450	1,173	1,046	903	725	548	371	208	51
12,450	12,500	1,182	1,054	912	735	557	380	217	59
12,500	12,550	1,190	1,063	922	744	567	389	225	67
12,550	12,600	1,199	1,071	931	754	576	399	234	75
12,600	12,650	1,207	1,080	941	763	586	408	242	83
12,650	12,700	1,216	1,088	950	773	595	418	251	91
12,700	12,750	1,225	1,097	960	782	605	427	259	99
12,750	12,800	1,235	1,105	969	792	614	437	268	107
12,800	12,850	1,245	1,114	979	801	624	446	276	115
12,850	12,900	1,255	1,122	988	811	633	456	285	123
12,900	12,950	1,265	1,131	998	820	643	465	293	131
12,950	13,000	1,275	1,139	1,007	830	652	475	302	139
13,000	13,050	1,285	1,148	1,017	839	662	484	310	148
13,050	13,100	1,295	1,156	1,026	849	671	494	319	156
13,100	13,150	1,305	1,165	1,036	858	681	503	327	165
13,150	13,200	1,315	1,173	1,045	868	690	513	336	173
13,200	13,250	1,325	1,182	1,054	877	700	522	345	182
13,250	13,300	1,335	1,190	1,063	887	709	532	354	190
13,300	13,350	1,345	1,199	1,071	896	719	541	364	199
13,350	13,400	1,355	1,207	1,080	906	728	551	373	207
13,400	13,450	1,365	1,216	1,088	915	738	560	383	216
13,450	13,500	1,375	1,225	1,097	925	747	570	392	224
13,500	13,550	1,385	1,235	1,105	934	757	579	402	233
13,550	13,600	1,395	1,245	1,114	944	766	589	411	241
13,600	13,650	1,405	1,255	1,122	953	776	598	421	250
13,650	13,700	1,415	1,265	1,131	963	785	608	430	258
13,700	13,750	1,426	1,275	1,139	972	795	617	440	267
13,750	13,800	1,437	1,285	1,148	982	804	627	449	275
13,800	13,850	1,448	1,295	1,156	991	814	636	459	284
13,850	13,900	1,459	1,305	1,165	1,001	823	646	468	292
13,900	13,950	1,470	1,315	1,173	1,010	833	655	478	301
13,950	14,000	1,481	1,325	1,182	1,020	842	665	487	310
14,000	14,050	1,492	1,335	1,190	1,029	852	674	497	319
14,050	14,100	1,503	1,345	1,199	1,039	861	684	506	329
14,100	14,150	1,514	1,355	1,207	1,048	871	693	516	338
14,150	14,200	1,525	1,365	1,216	1,058	880	703	525	348
14,200	14,250	1,536	1,375	1,225	1,067	890	712	535	357
14,250	14,300	1,547	1,385	1,235	1,077	899	722	544	367
14,300	14,350	1,558	1,395	1,245	1,086	909	731	554	376
14,350	14,400	1,569	1,405	1,255	1,096	918	741	563	386
14,400	14,450	1,580	1,415	1,265	1,105	928	750	573	395
14,450	14,500	1,591	1,426	1,275	1,115	937	760	582	405
14,500	14,550	1,602	1,437	1,285	1,124	947	769	592	414
14,550	14,600	1,613	1,448	1,295	1,134	956	779	601	424
14,600	14,650	1,624	1,459	1,305	1,143	966	788	611	433
14,650	14,700	1,635	1,470	1,315	1,153	975	798	620	443
14,700	14,750	1,646	1,481	1,325	1,162	985	807	630	452
14,750	14,800	1,657	1,492	1,335	1,172	994	817	639	462
14,800	14,850	1,668	1,503	1,345	1,181	1,004	826	649	471
14,850	14,900	1,679	1,514	1,355	1,191	1,013	836	658	481
14,900	14,950	1,690	1,525	1,365	1,200	1,023	845	668	490
14,950	15,000	1,701	1,536	1,375	1,211	1,032	855	677	500
15,000	15,050	1,712	1,547	1,385	1,222	1,042	864	687	509
15,050	15,100	1,723	1,558	1,395	1,233	1,051	874	696	519
15,100	15,150	1,734	1,569	1,405	1,244	1,061	883	706	528
15,150	15,200	1,745	1,580	1,415	1,255	1,070	893	715	538

Continued next column

If line 34, Form 1040 is— Over	But not over	2	3	4	5	6	7	8	9
					Your tax is—				
15,200	15,250	1,756	1,591	1,426	1,266	1,080	902	725	547
15,250	15,300	1,767	1,602	1,437	1,277	1,089	912	734	557
15,300	15,350	1,778	1,613	1,448	1,288	1,099	921	744	566
15,350	15,400	1,789	1,624	1,459	1,299	1,108	931	753	576
15,400	15,450	1,800	1,635	1,470	1,310	1,118	940	763	585
15,450	15,500	1,811	1,646	1,481	1,321	1,127	950	772	595
15,500	15,550	1,822	1,657	1,492	1,332	1,137	959	782	604
15,550	15,600	1,833	1,668	1,503	1,343	1,146	969	791	614
15,600	15,650	1,844	1,679	1,514	1,354	1,156	978	801	623
15,650	15,700	1,855	1,690	1,525	1,365	1,165	988	810	633
15,700	15,750	1,866	1,701	1,536	1,375	1,176	997	820	642
15,750	15,800	1,877	1,712	1,547	1,385	1,187	1,007	829	652
15,800	15,850	1,888	1,723	1,558	1,395	1,198	1,016	839	661
15,850	15,900	1,899	1,734	1,569	1,405	1,209	1,026	848	671
15,900	15,950	1,910	1,745	1,580	1,415	1,220	1,035	858	680
15,950	16,000	1,921	1,756	1,591	1,426	1,231	1,045	867	690
16,000	16,050	1,932	1,767	1,602	1,437	1,242	1,054	877	699
16,050	16,100	1,943	1,778	1,613	1,448	1,253	1,064	886	709
16,100	16,150	1,954	1,789	1,624	1,459	1,264	1,073	896	718
16,150	16,200	1,965	1,800	1,635	1,470	1,275	1,083	905	728
16,200	16,250	1,976	1,811	1,646	1,481	1,286	1,092	915	737
16,250	16,300	1,987	1,822	1,657	1,492	1,297	1,102	924	747
16,300	16,350	1,998	1,833	1,668	1,503	1,308	1,111	934	756
16,350	16,400	2,009	1,844	1,679	1,514	1,319	1,121	943	766
16,400	16,450	2,020	1,855	1,690	1,525	1,330	1,130	953	775
16,450	16,500	2,031	1,866	1,701	1,536	1,341	1,141	962	785
16,500	16,550	2,042	1,877	1,712	1,547	1,352	1,152	972	794
16,550	16,600	2,053	1,888	1,723	1,558	1,363	1,163	981	804
16,600	16,650	2,064	1,899	1,734	1,569	1,374	1,174	991	813
16,650	16,700	2,075	1,910	1,745	1,580	1,385	1,185	1,000	823
16,700	16,750	2,086	1,921	1,756	1,591	1,396	1,196	1,010	832
16,750	16,800	2,099	1,932	1,767	1,602	1,407	1,207	1,019	842
16,800	16,850	2,111	1,943	1,778	1,613	1,418	1,218	1,029	851
16,850	16,900	2,124	1,954	1,789	1,624	1,429	1,229	1,038	861
16,900	16,950	2,136	1,965	1,800	1,635	1,440	1,240	1,048	870
16,950	17,000	2,149	1,976	1,811	1,646	1,451	1,251	1,057	880
17,000	17,050	2,161	1,987	1,822	1,657	1,462	1,262	1,067	889
17,050	17,100	2,174	1,998	1,833	1,668	1,473	1,273	1,076	899
17,100	17,150	2,186	2,009	1,844	1,679	1,484	1,284	1,086	908
17,150	17,200	2,199	2,020	1,855	1,690	1,495	1,295	1,095	918
17,200	17,250	2,211	2,031	1,866	1,701	1,506	1,306	1,106	927
17,250	17,300	2,224	2,042	1,877	1,712	1,517	1,317	1,117	937
17,300	17,350	2,236	2,053	1,888	1,723	1,528	1,328	1,128	946
17,350	17,400	2,249	2,064	1,899	1,734	1,539	1,339	1,139	956
17,400	17,450	2,261	2,075	1,910	1,745	1,550	1,350	1,150	965
17,450	17,500	2,274	2,086	1,921	1,756	1,561	1,361	1,161	975
17,500	17,550	2,286	2,099	1,932	1,767	1,572	1,372	1,172	984
17,550	17,600	2,299	2,111	1,943	1,778	1,583	1,383	1,183	994
17,600	17,650	2,311	2,124	1,954	1,789	1,594	1,394	1,194	1,003
17,650	17,700	2,324	2,136	1,965	1,800	1,605	1,405	1,205	1,013
17,700	17,750	2,336	2,149	1,976	1,811	1,616	1,416	1,216	1,022
17,750	17,800	2,349	2,161	1,987	1,822	1,627	1,427	1,227	1,032
17,800	17,850	2,361	2,174	1,998	1,833	1,638	1,438	1,238	1,041
17,850	17,900	2,374	2,186	2,009	1,844	1,649	1,449	1,249	1,051
17,900	17,950	2,386	2,199	2,020	1,855	1,660	1,460	1,260	1,060
17,950	18,000	2,399	2,211	2,031	1,866	1,671	1,471	1,271	1,071
18,000	18,050	2,411	2,224	2,042	1,877	1,682	1,482	1,282	1,082
18,050	18,100	2,424	2,236	2,053	1,888	1,693	1,493	1,293	1,093
18,100	18,150	2,436	2,249	2,064	1,899	1,704	1,504	1,304	1,104
18,150	18,200	2,449	2,261	2,075	1,910	1,715	1,515	1,315	1,115
18,200	18,250	2,461	2,274	2,086	1,921	1,726	1,526	1,326	1,126
18,250	18,300	2,474	2,286	2,099	1,932	1,737	1,537	1,337	1,137
18,300	18,350	2,486	2,299	2,111	1,943	1,748	1,548	1,348	1,148
18,350	18,400	2,499	2,311	2,124	1,954	1,759	1,559	1,359	1,159
18,400	18,450	2,511	2,324	2,136	1,965	1,770	1,570	1,370	1,170
18,450	18,500	2,524	2,336	2,149	1,976	1,781	1,581	1,381	1,181
18,500	18,550	2,536	2,349	2,161	1,987	1,792	1,592	1,392	1,192
18,550	18,600	2,549	2,361	2,174	1,998	1,803	1,603	1,403	1,203
18,600	18,650	2,561	2,374	2,186	2,009	1,814	1,614	1,414	1,214
18,650	18,700	2,574	2,386	2,199	2,020	1,825	1,625	1,425	1,225
18,700	18,750	2,586	2,399	2,211	2,031	1,836	1,636	1,436	1,236
18,750	18,800	2,599	2,411	2,224	2,042	1,847	1,647	1,447	1,247

Continued on next page

Example. Using the examples above of the two men earning $12,225, what would be Bill Sciulli's refund (or payment due) if $1630 had been withheld from his earnings?

$$\begin{array}{rl} \$1729 & = \text{tax} \\ -\ 1630 & = \text{amount withheld} \\ \hline \$\ \ \ 99 & = \text{payment due} \end{array}$$

What would be Bob Waldman's refund (or payment due) if $505 had been withheld?

$$\begin{array}{rl} \$505 & = \text{amount withheld} \\ -\ 453 & = \text{tax} \\ \hline \$\ 52 & = \text{refund} \end{array}$$

SALES AND EXCISE TAXES

Sales and excise taxes are levied on specified goods that are sold. They are usually computed as a percent of the value of the sale. Such taxes are imposed at both the Federal and the state level. The major excise taxes, such as the gasoline tax, are computed on the number of units rather than on the value. These taxes are usually included in the selling price rather than added on later. Sales taxes are added on at the time of the sale. To avoid rounding off at the time of purchase, the tax amounts on less than whole dollars are set arbitrarily but on a basis that makes them comparable to the given percent. Tax tables are established to take this into account. Examples of such are given below.

2% tax on sales of:
$.01 to .14 = none
.15 to .64 = .01
.65 to 1.00 = .02

3% tax on sales of:
$.01 to .40 = none
.41 to .70 = .02
.71 to 1.00 = .03

4% tax on sales of:
$.01 to .25 = .01
.26 to .50 = .02
.51 to .75 = .03
.76 to 1.00 = .04

5% tax on sales of:
$.01 to .20 = .01
.21 to .40 = .02
.41 to .60 = .03
.61 to .80 = .04
.81 to 1.00 = .05

Example. Using the tax tables given, what amount of sales tax would be paid on $5.24 if the percent were 3%? 4%? 5%?

At 3%
$$\begin{array}{rl} \$5.00 \times .03 & = \$.15 \\ .24 \quad \text{from table} & = \quad 0 \\ \hline \$5.24 = \text{sale} & \quad \$.15 = \text{sales tax} \end{array}$$

At 4%
$$\begin{array}{rl} \$5.00 \times .04 & = \$.20 \\ .24 \quad \text{from table} & = \quad .01 \\ \hline \$5.24 = \text{sale} & \quad \$.21 = \text{sales tax} \end{array}$$

At 5%
$$\begin{array}{rl} \$5.00 \times .05 & = \$.25 \\ .24 \quad \text{from table} & = \quad .02 \\ \hline \$5.24 = \text{sale} & \quad \$.27 = \text{sales tax} \end{array}$$

PROPERTY TAX

Before property taxes can be levied, a government official known as a *tax assessor* must place a value on the property in the area to be taxed. This property value, usually a fraction of the property's actual market value, becomes the basis of the tax and is termed the *assessed valuation*. Thus, a higher value of property results in a higher tax. The tax rate may be computed by dividing the total amount of revenue needed by the total assessed value of the community.

$$\text{Tax Rate} = \frac{\text{Revenue Needed}}{\text{Assessed Value}}$$

The tax rate, then, can be given as a percent, as cents per dollar, or as dollars per hundred dollars of assessed value. Many times the tax rate is given in "mills." Since 10 mills is equal to $.01, the conversion is quite simple.

Each year the government must estimate its needs, calculate any change in the assessed value, and decide if the needed revenue can be raised by the same tax rate. The officials may have to raise the tax rate or they may be able to lower the rate.

Example. The city of Claridge has a total assessed value of $10,800,000 and a budget of $982,000. What is the tax rate required?

$$\text{Tax Rate} = \frac{\text{Revenue Needed}}{\text{Assessed Value}}$$

$$= \frac{\$982,000}{\$10,800,000}$$

$$= .0909$$

Tax Rate = 9.09% or 9.09 cents/dollar or $9.09/hundred dollars or 90.9 mills/dollar.

If a property owner's holdings are assessed at $8000, the tax is found by multiplying the assessed value times the rate.

Amount of Tax = Assessed Value × Rate
  = $8000 × .0909
  = $727.20

CUSTOMS DUTIES

To protect some of our own industries and to raise revenue, certain commodities imported from foreign countries are subject to taxes upon entry. These import taxes, known as customs duties, consist of two basic types. *Ad valorem duties* are those expressed as a percent of the value of the commodity. *Specific duties* are those stated as a fixed amount per unit. Thus, one is based on value, while the other is based on quantity. It is possible for a commodity to have both types of duty levied upon it. The value of the commodity upon which the duty is assessed usually includes all expenses incurred in its delivery.

Example. Imported pipes carry an ad valorem duty of 15%. What is the customs duty imposed on 4512 cartons of cigarettes?

Duty = $250 × .15
      = $37.50

Imported cigarettes carry a specific duty of $.20 per carton. What is the duty imposed on 4512 cartons of cigarettes?

Duty = 4512 × $.20
      = $902.40

Certain watches carry an ad valorem duty of 20% and a specific duty of $1.25 apiece. If 412 such watches are imported at a value of $3,900, what is the total duty?

Duty = $3900 × .20
      = $780 ad valorem

Duty = 412 × $1.25
      = $515 specific

$ 780.00
   515.00
$ 1295.00 = total duty

A. Using the information below and the standard deductions (Zero Bracket Amounts) on page 153, determine which standard deduction is applicable to each taxpayer and indicate whether deductions should be itemized. If it is to the advantage of the taxpayer to itemize deductions, compute the amount of itemized deductions in excess of the standard deduction. Then determine the tax liability (assume there are no credits or additional taxes) and the amount of tax payment or refund that is due. Make the tax computation using the tables in this chapter.

	TAXPAYER CLASSIFICATION	NO. OF EXEMPTIONS	ADJUSTED GROSS INCOME	ITEMIZED DEDUCTIONS	TAX WITHHELD
a.	Single	2	12,000	3 100	1,740
1.	Single	1	11,075	900	1,356
2.	Single	1	11,400	2,350	1,692
3.	Married, Filing Joint Return	4	12,600	3,450	1,464
4.	Married, Filing Joint Return	2	11,625	1,500	1,092
5.	Married, Filing Joint Return	3	13,525	3,700	1,040

A. Given each of the total sales figures below, compute the amount of sales tax for rates of 3%, 4%, and 5%. Use the tables in this chapter.

a.	$27.60	b.	$6412.52
1.	$48.00	2.	$96.16
3.	$54.57	4.	$16.80
5.	$73.03	6.	$153.92
7.	$463.85	8.	$980.15
9.	$1800.51	10.	$4903.49

B. Given the import information below, compute the amount of the customs duty.

a.	$700 of merchandise: 15% ad valorem	b.	472 cartons: $.10/carton specific
1.	$950 of merchandise: 20% ad valorem	2.	$3,512.00 of merchandise: 10% ad valorem
3.	$5,600.80 of merchandise: 25% ad valorem	4.	$2,412.50 of merchandise: 15% ad valorem
5.	$16,260.42 of merchandise: 2% ad valorem	6.	500 boxes: $.80/box specific
7.	1725 cases: $.52/case specific	8.	5850 barrels: $1.10/barrel specific
9.	7750 cans: $.75/can specific	10.	10,525 bottles: $.90/bottle specific

C. Given the needed revenue and the total assessed value, find the property tax rate in mills for the following.

	NEEDED REVENUE	ASSESSED VALUE	TAX RATE
a.	$530,250	$10,500,000	
1.	$204,000	$5,100,000	
2.	$876,800	$13,700,000	
3.	$256,000	$8,000,000	
4.	$1,973,820	$982,000,000	
5.	$900,000	$15,000,000	
b.	$176,400	$4,200,000	
6.	$528,500	$7,550,000	
7.	$219,480	$3,720,000	
8.	$667,850	$18,050,000	
9.	$2,669,610	$36,570,000	
10.	$1,478,520	$26,640,000	

D. Use each of the tax rates above to compute the tax amount payable on a piece of property assessed at $12,500.

a.		b.	
1.		2.	
3.		4.	
5.		6.	
7.		8.	
9.		10.	

E. Solve the following problems, using the tables in this chapter.

1. Janet Brown is married and files a joint return with her husband. Their itemized deductions are calculated to be $1300.

   a. What is their standard deduction?
   b. Is it advantageous to them to itemize deductions?
   c. If the Browns' adjusted gross income is $13,025 and they claim two exemptions, what is their tax?

2. Lindsay Crane is single and calculates his itemized deductions to be $3160.

   a. What is his standard deduction?
   b. Should he itemize his deductions or take the standard deduction?
   c. If his adjusted gross income is $12,060 and he claims only the exemption for himself, what is his tax?

3. The Gunthers' commercial property in Whiteview has an assessed value of $58,500. If the local property tax rate is 6.8%, how much revenue will Whiteview receive from the Gunthers?

4. Springton currently has an assessed total property value of $48,256,000 and a budget of $2,171,520.

   a. What is the tax rate prevailing (in mills)?
   b. Suppose Springton needs to increase its budget by 18% in order to accommodate wage and cost increases. What would the new budget figure be?
   c. How much (in mills) will the property tax rate in Springton have to be increased in order to finance the new budget?

5. Mrs. Dunbar purchased a $6000 (U.S.) fur coat in Paris. Upon returning to the U.S., she will have to pay a 20% ad valorem duty for the coat. What amount will Mrs. Dunbar owe to customs?

CHAPTER 15
Payroll and payroll deductions

Businesses must keep accurate records to determine the amount of pay due each employee at the end of a pay period. For a person on a fixed salary, this is not very difficult to calculate, but for a person paid by the hour, the computations are more complex. The number of hours worked is found on the time punch cards used by most businesses. These cards show the time of arrival and time of departure for each day of the week. The hours worked are then recorded in the *payroll journal* or *register*. A portion of a payroll journal is shown below.

Hourly Payroll No. 26													Week Ending May 13, 19 X9									
Emp No.	Name	Marital Status	Inc Tax Ex.	**Hours by Day**							**Hours Week**		**Reg. Hrly Rate**		**Earnings**								
				S	M	T	W	T	F	S	Tot.	O.T.			Regular		Overtime			Total			
26	F. Barlowe	M	2		8	8	4	8	8	4	40	0	3	00	1 2 0	00	0	00	1	2 0	00	
27	T. Terence	M	4		7	9	9	9	8	4	46	6	3	10	1 2 4	10	2 7	90	1	5 1	90	
28	B. Capic	M	3		8	8	8	8	8	4	44	4	3	90	1 5 6	00	2 3	40	1	7 9	40	
29	S. Halidow	M	2		9	9	9	9		4	40	0	2	75	1 1 0	00	0	00	1	1 0	00	
30	J. Kuzmik	S	1		9	9	9	9	7	8	51	11	4	20	1 6 8	00	6 9	30	2	3 7	30	

Usually, an employee is paid a higher wage for any time worked over his normal work week, for example, forty hours. Because of this, the hours worked column is subdivided into two sections. In most cases, the employee is paid *time and a half* for overtime hours. This means he is paid $1\frac{1}{2}$ times his regular rate per hour. The two examples below illustrate the two methods of computing wages when overtime hours must be considered.

Example. Jim Cupp worked 42 hours at $3.20 per hour. If the wages are computed on the basis of a 40-hour regular work week with $1\frac{1}{2}$ overtime allowance, what are his total gross wages?

$$\begin{aligned}
\text{Total Wages} &= (\text{No. of Regular Hours} \times \text{Regular Hourly Rate}) \\
&\quad + (\text{Overtime Hours} \times 1\tfrac{1}{2} \text{ Regular Hourly Rate}) \\
&= (40 \text{ hr} \times \$3.20/\text{hr}) + [2 \text{ hr} \times 1\tfrac{1}{2}(\$3.20)] \\
&= \$128 + (2 \text{ hr} \times \$4.80) \\
&= \$128 + \$9.60 \\
&= \$137.60
\end{aligned}$$

$$\begin{aligned}
\text{Total Wages} &= (\text{No. of Total Hours} \times \text{Regular Hourly Rate}) \\
&\quad + (\text{Overtime Hours} \times \tfrac{1}{2} \text{ Regular Hourly Rate}) \\
&= (42 \text{ hr} \times \$3.20) + [2 \text{ hr} \times \tfrac{1}{2}(3.20)] \\
&= \$134.40 + (2 \text{ hr} \times \$1.60) \\
&= \$134.40 + \$3.20 \\
&= \$137.60
\end{aligned}$$

DEDUCTIONS

After the total earnings are recorded, there are certain deductions which must be made. The two most important deductions are Social Security payments and Federal income tax withholding.

Social Security

Under the Federal Insurance Contributions Act (FICA) employers are required to withhold certain amounts from the salary or wages of their employees to cover their Social Security tax obligations. The amount of Social Security tax withheld from the employee's pay is matched by an equal payment from the employer. The payments are used to finance the payment of Social Security benefits to those individuals qualifying for them.

TABLE 15.1

		Social Security Tax Rate Schedule			
YEAR	MAXIMUM INCOME SUBJECT TO TAX	EMPLOYER AND EMPLOYEE TAX (EACH) %	MAXIMUM TAX (EACH)	SELF-EMPLOYED TAX (%)	MAXIMUM TAX
1978	$17,700	6.05	$1,070.85	8.10	$1,433.70
1979	22,900	6.13	1,403.77	8.10	1,854.90
1980	25,900	6.13	1,587.67	8.10	2,097.90
1981	29,700	6.65	1,709.05	9.30	2,762.10
1982	31,800	6.70	2,130.60	9.35	2,973.30
1983	33,900	6.70	2,271.30	9.35	3,169.65
1984	36,000	6.70	2,412.00	9.35	3,366.00
1985	38,100	7.05	2,686.05	9.90	3,771.90
1986	40,200	7.15	2,874.30	10.00	4,020.00
1987	42,600	7.15	3,045.90	10.00	4,260.00

The Social Security tax is levied only up to a certain maximum amount of income which, under current law, will change each year. For example, the tax rate in 1979 was 6.13% for both the employer and employee and the maximum income subject to the tax was $22,900; thus, the maximum tax any employee paid was $1403.77, which was matched by an equal amount paid by the employer. An employee earning $25,000 in 1979 would still pay only $1403.77 in Social Security taxes (see Table 15.1).

Example. A salaried executive earns $28,000 a year in 1979. What amount of Social Security tax will he have to pay for the year? How much per week? How many weeks?

To find the total tax, remember that it is based on only the first $22,900 of income.

Total Tax = $22,900 × 6.13%
          = $1403.77

To find the tax per week, first find the employee's salary per week.

Salary per week = $28,000 ÷ 52 = $538.46

To find the tax per week, apply the tax rate to the salary per week.

Tax per Week = Salary per Week × Rate
             = $538.46 × 6.13%
             = $33.01

To find the number of weeks he must pay this $33.01, divide the total tax payable by the tax per week.

Number of Weeks = Total Tax ÷ Tax per Week
    42.5 weeks = $1403.77 ÷ $33.01

This means that for 42 weeks the $33.01 will be paid and for the 43rd week only $17.35 will be paid.

$1403.77 − (42 × $33.01) =
    $1403.77 − $1386.42 = $17.35

An employee earning less than $22,900 annually will pay the tax all year. To simplify the calculation of the tax, the government provides Social Security tax tables such as those following for various hourly, weekly, and monthly salaries. A sample of the 1978 tables (6.05% rate) is shown below.

Self-employed people pay the tax themselves but must use a different rate as shown in Table 15.1.

Federal Income Tax

In addition to Social Security contributions, an employer must withhold Federal income tax. The amount of Federal income tax withheld is dependent on a taxpayer's filing status and level of income, and the number of withholding allowances claimed. The number of withholding allowances is chosen by the employee. The tax withheld is calculated by using the tables provided by the Internal Revenue Service for this purpose. A portion of these tables is shown on page 170.

Example. Fred Barlow is married and earns $220 a week and claims two withholding allowances. What is the amount of Federal income tax that should be withheld from his salary

Social Security Employee Tax Table
6.05 percent employee tax deductions

Wages At least	But less than	Tax to be withheld	Wages At least	But less than	Tax to be withheld	Wages At least	But less than	Tax to be withheld	Wages At least	But less than	Tax to be withheld
$0.00	$0.09	$0.00	$12.81	$12.98	$.78	$25.71	$25.87	$1.56	$38.60	$38.77	$2.34
.09	.25	.01	12.98	13.15	.79	25.87	26.04	1.57	38.77	38.93	2.35
.25	.42	.02	13.15	13.31	.80	26.04	26.20	1.58	38.93	39.10	2.36
.42	.58	.03	13.31	13.48	.81	26.20	26.37	1.59	39.10	39.26	2.37
.58	.75	.04	13.48	13.64	.82	26.37	26.53	1.60	39.26	39.43	2.38
.75	.91	.05	13.64	13.81	.83	26.53	26.70	1.61	39.43	39.59	2.39
.91	1.08	.06	13.81	13.97	.84	26.70	26.86	1.62	39.59	39.76	2.40
1.08	1.24	.07	13.97	14.14	.85	26.86	27.03	1.63	39.76	39.92	2.41
1.24	1.41	.08	14.14	14.30	.86	27.03	27.20	1.64	39.92	40.09	2.42
1.41	1.58	.09	14.30	14.47	.87	27.20	27.36	1.65	40.09	40.25	2.43
1.58	1.74	.10	14.47	14.63	.88	27.36	27.53	1.66	40.25	40.42	2.44
1.74	1.91	.11	14.63	14.80	.89	27.53	27.69	1.67	40.42	40.58	2.45
1.91	2.07	.12	14.80	14.96	.90	27.69	27.86	1.68	40.58	40.75	2.46
2.07	2.24	.13	14.96	15.13	.91	27.86	28.02	1.69	40.75	40.91	2.47
2.24	2.40	.14	15.13	15.29	.92	28.02	28.19	1.70	40.91	41.08	2.48
2.40	2.57	.15	15.29	15.46	.93	28.19	28.35	1.71	41.08	41.24	2.49
2.57	2.73	.16	15.46	15.62	.94	28.35	28.52	1.72	41.24	41.41	2.50
2.73	2.90	.17	15.62	15.79	.95	28.52	28.68	1.73	41.41	41.58	2.51
2.90	3.06	.18	15.79	15.96	.96	28.68	28.85	1.74	41.58	41.74	2.52
3.06	3.23	.19	15.96	16.12	.97	28.85	29.01	1.75	41.74	41.91	2.53
3.23	3.39	.20	16.12	16.29	.98	29.01	29.18	1.76	41.91	42.07	2.54
3.39	3.56	.21	16.29	16.45	.99	29.18	29.34	1.77	42.07	42.24	2.55
3.56	3.72	.22	16.45	16.62	1.00	29.34	29.51	1.78	42.24	42.40	2.56
3.72	3.89	.23	16.62	16.78	1.01	29.51	29.67	1.79	42.40	42.57	2.57
3.89	4.05	.24	16.78	16.95	1.02	29.67	29.84	1.80	42.57	42.73	2.58
4.05	4.22	.25	16.95	17.11	1.03	29.84	30.00	1.81	42.73	42.90	2.59
4.22	4.39	.26	17.11	17.28	1.04	30.00	30.17	1.82	42.90	43.06	2.60
4.39	4.55	.27	17.28	17.44	1.05	30.17	30.34	1.83	43.06	43.23	2.61
4.55	4.72	.28	17.44	17.61	1.06	30.34	30.50	1.84	43.23	43.39	2.62
4.72	4.88	.29	17.61	17.77	1.07	30.50	30.67	1.85	43.39	43.56	2.63
4.88	5.05	.30	17.77	17.94	1.08	30.67	30.83	1.86	43.56	43.72	2.64
5.05	5.21	.31	17.94	18.10	1.09	30.83	31.00	1.87	43.72	43.89	2.65
5.21	5.38	.32	18.10	18.27	1.10	31.00	31.16	1.88	43.89	44.05	2.66
5.38	5.54	.33	18.27	18.43	1.11	31.16	31.33	1.89	44.05	44.22	2.67
5.54	5.71	.34	18.43	18.60	1.12	31.33	31.49	1.90	44.22	44.39	2.68
5.71	5.87	.35	18.60	18.77	1.13	31.49	31.66	1.91	44.39	44.55	2.69
5.87	6.04	.36	18.77	18.93	1.14	31.66	31.82	1.92	44.55	44.72	2.70
6.04	6.20	.37	18.93	19.10	1.15	31.82	31.99	1.93	44.72	44.88	2.71
6.20	6.37	.38	19.10	19.26	1.16	31.99	32.15	1.94	44.88	45.05	2.72
6.37	6.53	.39	19.26	19.43	1.17	32.15	32.32	1.95	45.05	45.21	2.73
6.53	6.70	.40	19.43	19.59	1.18	32.32	32.48	1.96	45.21	45.38	2.74
6.70	6.86	.41	19.59	19.76	1.19	32.48	32.65	1.97	45.38	45.54	2.75
6.86	7.03	.42	19.76	19.92	1.20	32.65	32.81	1.98	45.54	45.71	2.76
7.03	7.20	.43	19.92	20.09	1.21	32.81	32.98	1.99	45.71	45.87	2.77
7.20	7.36	.44	20.09	20.25	1.22	32.98	33.15	2.00	45.87	46.04	2.78
7.36	7.53	.45	20.25	20.42	1.23	33.15	33.31	2.01	46.04	46.20	2.79
7.53	7.69	.46	20.42	20.58	1.24	33.31	33.48	2.02	46.20	46.37	2.80
7.69	7.86	.47	20.58	20.75	1.25	33.48	33.64	2.03	46.37	46.53	2.81
7.86	8.02	.48	20.75	20.91	1.26	33.64	33.81	2.04	46.53	46.70	2.82
8.02	8.19	.49	20.91	21.08	1.27	33.81	33.97	2.05	46.70	46.86	2.83
8.19	8.35	.50	21.08	21.24	1.28	33.97	34.14	2.06	46.86	47.03	2.84
8.35	8.52	.51	21.24	21.41	1.29	34.14	34.30	2.07	47.03	47.20	2.85
8.52	8.68	.52	21.41	21.58	1.30	34.30	34.47	2.08	47.20	47.36	2.86
8.68	8.85	.53	21.58	21.74	1.31	34.47	34.63	2.09	47.36	47.53	2.87
8.85	9.01	.54	21.74	21.91	1.32	34.63	34.80	2.10	47.53	47.69	2.88
9.01	9.18	.55	21.91	22.07	1.33	34.80	34.96	2.11	47.69	47.86	2.89
9.18	9.34	.56	22.07	22.24	1.34	34.96	35.13	2.12	47.86	48.02	2.90
9.34	9.51	.57	22.24	22.40	1.35	35.13	35.29	2.13	48.02	48.19	2.91
9.51	9.67	.58	22.40	22.57	1.36	35.29	35.46	2.14	48.19	48.35	2.92
9.67	9.84	.59	22.57	22.73	1.37	35.46	35.62	2.15	48.35	48.52	2.93
9.84	10.00	.60	22.73	22.90	1.38	35.62	35.79	2.16	48.52	48.68	2.94
10.00	10.17	.61	22.90	23.06	1.39	35.79	35.96	2.17	48.68	48.85	2.95
10.17	10.34	.62	23.06	23.23	1.40	35.96	36.12	2.18	48.85	49.01	2.96
10.34	10.50	.63	23.23	23.39	1.41	36.12	36.29	2.19	49.01	49.18	2.97
10.50	10.67	.64	23.39	23.56	1.42	36.29	36.45	2.20	49.18	49.34	2.98
10.67	10.83	.65	23.56	23.72	1.43	36.45	36.62	2.21	49.34	49.51	2.99
10.83	11.00	.66	23.72	23.89	1.44	36.62	36.78	2.22	49.51	49.67	3.00
11.00	11.16	.67	23.89	24.05	1.45	36.78	36.95	2.23	49.67	49.84	3.01
11.16	11.33	.68	24.05	24.22	1.46	36.95	37.11	2.24	49.84	50.00	3.02
11.33	11.49	.69	24.22	24.39	1.47	37.11	37.28	2.25	50.00	50.17	3.03
11.49	11.66	.70	24.39	24.55	1.48	37.28	37.44	2.26	50.17	50.34	3.04
11.66	11.82	.71	24.55	24.72	1.49	37.44	37.61	2.27	50.34	50.50	3.05
11.82	11.99	.72	24.72	24.88	1.50	37.61	37.77	2.28	50.50	50.67	3.06
11.99	12.15	.73	24.88	25.05	1.51	37.77	37.94	2.29	50.67	50.83	3.07
12.15	12.32	.74	25.05	25.21	1.52	37.94	38.10	2.30	50.83	51.00	3.08
12.32	12.48	.75	25.21	25.38	1.53	38.10	38.27	2.31	51.00	51.16	3.09
12.48	12.65	.76	25.38	25.54	1.54	38.27	38.43	2.32	51.16	51.33	3.10
12.65	12.81	.77	25.54	25.71	1.55	38.43	38.60	2.33	51.33	51.49	3.11

Social Security Employee Tax Table
6.05 percent employee tax deductions

Wages At least	But less than	Tax to be withheld
$51.49	$51.66	$3.12
51.66	51.82	3.13
51.82	51.99	3.14
51.99	52.15	3.15
52.15	52.32	3.16
52.32	52.48	3.17
52.48	52.65	3.18
52.65	52.81	3.19
52.81	52.98	3.20
52.98	53.15	3.21
53.15	53.31	3.22
53.31	53.48	3.23
53.48	53.64	3.24
53.64	53.81	3.25
53.81	53.97	3.26
53.97	54.14	3.27
54.14	54.30	3.28
54.30	54.47	3.29
54.47	54.63	3.30
54.63	54.80	3.31
54.80	54.96	3.32
54.96	55.13	3.33
55.13	55.29	3.34
55.29	55.46	3.35
55.46	55.62	3.36
55.62	55.79	3.37
55.79	55.96	3.38
55.96	56.12	3.39
56.12	56.29	3.40
56.29	56.45	3.41
56.45	56.62	3.42
56.62	56.78	3.43
56.78	56.95	3.44
56.95	57.11	3.45
57.11	57.28	3.46
57.28	57.44	3.47
57.44	57.61	3.48
57.61	57.77	3.49
57.77	57.94	3.50
57.94	58.10	3.51
58.10	58.27	3.52
58.27	58.43	3.53
58.43	58.60	3.54
58.60	58.77	3.55
58.77	58.93	3.56
58.93	59.10	3.57
59.10	59.26	3.58
59.26	59.43	3.59
59.43	59.59	3.60
59.59	59.76	3.61
59.76	59.92	3.62
59.92	60.09	3.63
60.09	60.25	3.64
60.25	60.42	3.65
60.42	60.58	3.66
60.58	60.75	3.67
60.75	60.91	3.68
60.91	61.08	3.69
61.08	61.24	3.70
61.24	61.41	3.71
61.41	61.58	3.72
61.58	61.74	3.73
61.74	61.91	3.74
61.91	62.07	3.75
62.07	62.24	3.76
62.24	62.40	3.77
62.40	62.57	3.78
62.57	62.73	3.79
62.73	62.90	3.80
62.90	63.06	3.81
63.06	63.23	3.82
63.23	63.39	3.83
63.39	63.56	3.84
63.56	63.72	3.85
63.72	63.89	3.86
63.89	64.05	3.87
64.05	64.22	3.88
64.22	64.39	3.89

Wages At least	But less than	Tax to be withheld
$64.39	$64.55	$3.90
64.55	64.72	3.91
64.72	64.88	3.92
64.88	65.05	3.93
65.05	65.21	3.94
65.21	65.38	3.95
65.38	65.54	3.96
65.54	65.71	3.97
65.71	65.87	3.98
65.87	66.04	3.99
66.04	66.20	4.00
66.20	66.37	4.01
66.37	66.53	4.02
66.53	66.70	4.03
66.70	66.86	4.04
66.86	67.03	4.05
67.03	67.20	4.06
67.20	67.36	4.07
67.36	67.53	4.08
67.53	67.69	4.09
67.69	67.86	4.10
67.86	68.02	4.11
68.02	68.19	4.12
68.19	68.35	4.13
68.35	68.52	4.14
68.52	68.68	4.15
68.68	68.85	4.16
68.85	69.01	4.17
69.01	69.18	4.18
69.18	69.34	4.19
69.34	69.51	4.20
69.51	69.67	4.21
69.67	69.84	4.22
69.84	70.00	4.23
70.00	70.17	4.24
70.17	70.34	4.25
70.34	70.50	4.26
70.50	70.67	4.27
70.67	70.83	4.28
70.83	71.00	4.29
71.00	71.16	4.30
71.16	71.33	4.31
71.33	71.49	4.32
71.49	71.66	4.33
71.66	71.82	4.34
71.82	71.99	4.35
71.99	72.15	4.36
72.15	72.32	4.37
72.32	72.48	4.38
72.48	72.65	4.39
72.65	72.81	4.40
72.81	72.98	4.41
72.98	73.15	4.42
73.15	73.31	4.43
73.31	73.48	4.44
73.48	73.64	4.45
73.64	73.81	4.46
73.81	73.97	4.47
73.97	74.14	4.48
74.14	74.30	4.49
74.30	74.47	4.50
74.47	74.63	4.51
74.63	74.80	4.52
74.80	74.96	4.53
74.96	75.13	4.54
75.13	75.29	4.55
75.29	75.46	4.56
75.46	75.62	4.57
75.62	75.79	4.58
75.79	75.96	4.59
75.96	76.12	4.60
76.12	76.29	4.61
76.29	76.45	4.62
76.45	76.62	4.63
76.62	76.78	4.64
76.78	76.95	4.65
76.95	77.11	4.66
77.11	77.28	4.67

Wages At least	But less than	Tax to be withheld
$77.28	$77.44	$4.68
77.44	77.61	4.69
77.61	77.77	4.70
77.77	77.94	4.71
77.94	78.10	4.72
78.10	78.27	4.73
78.27	78.43	4.74
78.43	78.60	4.75
78.60	78.77	4.76
78.77	78.93	4.77
78.93	79.10	4.78
79.10	79.26	4.79
79.26	79.43	4.80
79.43	79.59	4.81
79.59	79.76	4.82
79.76	79.92	4.83
79.92	80.09	4.84
80.09	80.25	4.85
80.25	80.42	4.86
80.42	80.58	4.87
80.58	80.75	4.88
80.75	80.91	4.89
80.91	81.08	4.90
81.08	81.24	4.91
81.24	81.41	4.92
81.41	81.58	4.93
81.58	81.74	4.94
81.74	81.91	4.95
81.91	82.07	4.96
82.07	82.24	4.97
82.24	82.40	4.98
82.40	82.57	4.99
82.57	82.73	5.00
82.73	82.90	5.01
82.90	83.06	5.02
83.06	83.23	5.03
83.23	83.39	5.04
83.39	83.56	5.05
83.56	83.72	5.06
83.72	83.89	5.07
83.89	84.05	5.08
84.05	84.22	5.09
84.22	84.39	5.10
84.39	84.55	5.11
84.55	84.72	5.12
84.72	84.88	5.13
84.88	85.05	5.14
85.05	85.21	5.15
85.21	85.38	5.16
85.38	85.54	5.17
85.54	85.71	5.18
85.71	85.87	5.19
85.87	86.04	5.20
86.04	86.20	5.21
86.20	86.37	5.22
86.37	86.53	5.23
86.53	86.70	5.24
86.70	86.86	5.25
86.86	87.03	5.26
87.03	87.20	5.27
87.20	87.36	5.28
87.36	87.53	5.29
87.53	87.69	5.30
87.69	87.86	5.31
87.86	88.02	5.32
88.02	88.19	5.33
88.19	88.35	5.34
88.35	88.52	5.35
88.52	88.68	5.36
88.68	88.85	5.37
88.85	89.01	5.38
89.01	89.18	5.39
89.18	89.34	5.40
89.34	89.51	5.41
89.51	89.67	5.42
89.67	89.84	5.43
89.84	90.00	5.44
90.00	90.17	5.45

Wages At least	But less than	Tax to be withheld
$90.17	$90.34	$5.46
90.34	90.50	5.47
90.50	90.67	5.48
90.67	90.83	5.49
90.83	91.00	5.50
91.00	91.16	5.51
91.16	91.33	5.52
91.33	91.49	5.53
91.49	91.66	5.54
91.66	91.82	5.55
91.82	91.99	5.56
91.99	92.15	5.57
92.15	92.32	5.58
92.32	92.48	5.59
92.48	92.65	5.60
92.65	92.81	5.61
92.81	92.98	5.62
92.98	93.15	5.63
93.15	93.31	5.64
93.31	93.48	5.65
93.48	93.64	5.66
93.64	93.81	5.67
93.81	93.97	5.68
93.97	94.14	5.69
94.14	94.30	5.70
94.30	94.47	5.71
94.47	94.63	5.72
94.63	94.80	5.73
94.80	94.96	5.74
94.96	95.13	5.75
95.13	95.29	5.76
95.29	95.46	5.77
95.46	95.62	5.78
95.62	95.79	5.79
95.79	95.96	5.80
95.96	96.12	5.81
96.12	96.29	5.82
96.29	96.45	5.83
96.45	96.62	5.84
96.62	96.78	5.85
96.78	96.95	5.86
96.95	97.11	5.87
97.11	97.28	5.88
97.28	97.44	5.89
97.44	97.61	5.90
97.61	97.77	5.91
97.77	97.94	5.92
97.94	98.10	5.93
98.10	98.27	5.94
98.27	98.43	5.95
98.43	98.60	5.96
98.60	98.77	5.97
98.77	98.93	5.98
98.93	99.10	5.99
99.10	99.26	6.00
99.26	99.43	6.01
99.43	99.59	6.02
99.59	99.76	6.03
99.76	99.92	6.04
99.92	100.09	6.05

The multiples of the withholding for FICA on $100 are

Wage	Tax to be withheld
$100	$6.05
200	12.10
300	18.15
400	24.20
500	30.25
600	36.30
700	42.35
800	48.40
900	54.45
1,000	60.50

MARRIED Persons — WEEKLY Payroll Period

And the wages are—		And the number of withholding allowances claimed is—										
At least	But less than	0	1	2	3	4	5	6	7	8	9	10 or more
		The amount of income tax to be withheld shall be—										
$0	$48	$0	$0	$0	$0	$0	$0	$0	$0	$0	$0	$0
48	49	.10	0	0	0	0	0	0	0	0	0	0
49	50	.20	0	0	0	0	0	0	0	0	0	0
50	51	.40	0	0	0	0	0	0	0	0	0	0
51	52	.60	0	0	0	0	0	0	0	0	0	0
52	53	.80	0	0	0	0	0	0	0	0	0	0
53	54	.90	0	0	0	0	0	0	0	0	0	0
54	55	1.10	0	0	0	0	0	0	0	0	0	0
55	56	1.30	0	0	0	0	0	0	0	0	0	0
56	57	1.40	0	0	0	0	0	0	0	0	0	0
57	58	1.60	0	0	0	0	0	0	0	0	0	0
58	59	1.80	0	0	0	0	0	0	0	0	0	0
59	60	1.90	0	0	0	0	0	0	0	0	0	0
60	62	2.20	0	0	0	0	0	0	0	0	0	0
62	64	2.50	.10	0	0	0	0	0	0	0	0	0
64	66	2.90	.40	0	0	0	0	0	0	0	0	0
66	68	3.20	.80	0	0	0	0	0	0	0	0	0
68	70	3.60	1.10	0	0	0	0	0	0	0	0	0
70	72	3.90	1.40	0	0	0	0	0	0	0	0	0
72	74	4.20	1.80	0	0	0	0	0	0	0	0	0
74	76	4.60	2.10	0	0	0	0	0	0	0	0	0
76	78	4.90	2.50	0	0	0	0	0	0	0	0	0
78	80	5.30	2.80	.40	0	0	0	0	0	0	0	0
80	82	5.60	3.10	.70	0	0	0	0	0	0	0	0
82	84	5.90	3.50	1.00	0	0	0	0	0	0	0	0
84	86	6.30	3.80	1.40	0	0	0	0	0	0	0	0
86	88	6.60	4.20	1.70	0	0	0	0	0	0	0	0
88	90	7.00	4.50	2.10	0	0	0	0	0	0	0	0
90	92	7.30	4.80	2.40	0	0	0	0	0	0	0	0
92	94	7.60	5.20	2.70	.30	0	0	0	0	0	0	0
94	96	8.00	5.50	3.10	.60	0	0	0	0	0	0	0
96	98	8.30	5.90	3.40	1.00	0	0	0	0	0	0	0
98	100	8.70	6.20	3.80	1.30	0	0	0	0	0	0	0
100	105	9.40	6.80	4.30	1.90	0	0	0	0	0	0	0
105	110	10.40	7.70	5.20	2.70	.30	0	0	0	0	0	0
110	115	11.40	8.60	6.00	3.60	1.10	0	0	0	0	0	0
115	120	12.40	9.60	6.90	4.40	2.00	0	0	0	0	0	0
120	125	13.40	10.60	7.70	5.30	2.80	.40	0	0	0	0	0
125	130	14.40	11.60	8.70	6.10	3.70	1.20	0	0	0	0	0
130	135	15.40	12.60	9.70	7.00	4.50	2.10	0	0	0	0	0
135	140	16.40	13.60	10.70	7.80	5.40	2.90	.50	0	0	0	0
140	145	17.40	14.60	11.70	8.80	6.20	3.80	1.30	0	0	0	0
145	150	18.40	15.60	12.70	9.80	7.10	4.60	2.20	0	0	0	0
150	160	19.90	17.10	14.20	11.30	8.40	5.90	3.50	1.00	0	0	0
160	170	21.90	19.10	16.20	13.30	10.40	7.60	5.20	2.70	.30	0	0
170	180	23.90	21.10	18.20	15.30	12.40	9.50	6.90	4.40	2.00	0	0
180	190	25.60	23.10	20.20	17.30	14.40	11.50	8.60	6.10	3.70	1.20	0
190	200	27.30	24.80	22.20	19.30	16.40	13.50	10.60	7.80	5.40	2.90	.50
200	210	29.00	26.50	24.10	21.30	18.40	15.50	12.60	9.80	7.10	4.60	2.20
210	220	30.70	28.20	25.80	23.30	20.40	17.50	14.60	11.80	8.90	6.30	3.90
220	230	32.40	29.90	27.50	25.00	22.40	19.50	16.60	13.80	10.90	8.00	5.60
230	240	34.10	31.60	29.20	26.70	24.30	21.50	18.60	15.80	12.90	10.00	7.30
240	250	35.80	33.30	30.90	28.40	26.00	23.50	20.60	17.80	14.90	12.00	9.10
250	260	37.50	35.00	32.60	30.10	27.70	25.20	22.60	19.80	16.90	14.00	11.10
260	270	39.20	36.70	34.30	31.80	29.40	26.90	24.50	21.80	18.90	16.00	13.10
270	280	41.70	38.40	36.00	33.50	31.10	28.60	26.20	23.70	20.90	18.00	15.10
280	290	44.20	40.60	37.70	35.20	32.80	30.30	27.90	25.40	22.90	20.00	17.10
290	300	46.70	43.10	39.50	36.90	34.50	32.00	29.60	27.10	24.70	22.00	19.10
300	310	49.20	45.60	42.00	38.60	36.20	33.70	31.30	28.80	26.40	23.90	21.10
310	320	51.70	48.10	44.50	40.90	37.90	35.40	33.00	30.50	28.10	25.60	23.10

(Continued on next page)

by the Ball Manufacturing Company? We turn to the Federal income tax weekly withholding table for married taxpayers and find, in the row for those earning at least $220 but less than $230, the amount to be withheld if two withholding allowances are claimed. It is $27.50.

Other Deductions

In addition to the deductions for Federal income tax and Social Security contributions there are often other deductions for a wide variety of purposes such as medical insurance, savings bonds, union dues, and other programs to which employees contribute. Because of their varied nature, these deductions have not been included in the examples and problems below.

Once all deductions are computed, they too are recorded in the payroll journal, and the net amount to be paid is found by subtracting these deductions from total wages. A completed payroll journal is shown below.

Hourly Payroll No. 26   Week Ending *May 13*, 19 *X9*   Paid *May 16*, 19 *X9*

Emp. No.	Name	Marital Status	Inc. Tax	Hours by Day S M T W T F S	Hours Work Tot OT	Reg. Hrly Rate	Earnings Regular	Over-time	Total	Deductions Soc. Sec.	Inc. Tax	Other	Paid Net Amount	Ck. No.
26	F. Barlowe	M	2	8 8 4 8 8 4	40 0	3 00	120 00	0 00	120 00	7 26	5 00		107 74	
27	T. Terence	M	4	7 9 9 9 8 4	46 6	3 10	124 00	27 90	151 90	9 19	5 50		136 21	
28	B. Capic	M	3	8 8 8 8 8 4	44 4	3 90	156 00	23 40	179 40	10 85	11 50		157 05	
29	S. Halidow	M	2	9 9 9 9 4	40 0	2 75	110 00	0 00	110 00	6 66	3 50		99 84	
30	J. Kuzmik	S	1	9 9 9 9 7 8	51 11	4 20	168 00	69 30	237 30	14 36	36 80		186 14	

PAY DISTRIBUTION

Most employees today are paid by check, but for those employees paid in cash, a *change tally* sheet is prepared. A portion of one is shown below. The columns of this

Change Tally

Name	Net Wages Due	$20	$10	$5	$2	$1	50¢	25¢	10¢	5¢	1¢
F. Barlowe	101 04	5					1				4
T. Terence	130 11	6	1						1		1
B. Capic	150 79	7	1					1	1		4
S. Halidow	93 12	4	1		1	1			1		2
J. Kuzmik	190 01	9	1								1
Total	665 07	31	4		1	2	1	1	2	0	12

Change Slip

Denomination	No.	Amount			
$20	3/	6	2	0	00
$10	4		4	0	00
$5	—				
$2	/			2	00
$1	2			2	00
50¢	/				50
25¢	/				25
10¢	2				20
5¢	—				
1¢	/2				12
	Total	6	6	5	07

change tally are added up in order to request the bank to provide money in the required denominations. This request is made on a *change slip*. Payment is made in the largest currency denomination possible.

ASSIGNMENT 26 PAYROLLS AND PAYROLL DEDUCTIONS

Assume the Easy Paint Company computes wages on a 40 hour regular time, and time and a half for overtime basis and all workers are married. Fill in the blank spaces where applicable in payroll journals below.

A.

Hourly Payroll No. 26   Week Ending June 31, 19 x9

Emp No.	Name	Marital Status	Inc Tax Ex.	S	M	T	W	T	F	S	Tot.	O.T.	Reg. Hrly Rate	Regular	Overtime	Total
1	C. Field	M	6		4	8	8	8	4	4			2 75			
2	W. Crenshaw	M	2		8	8	8	8	8	8			3 10			
3	F. Kapper	M	2	4	4	8	8	9	8				3 10			
4	T. Moore	M	4		9	9	8	8	8	4			2 90			
5	L. Mattle	M	4	2	9	8	8	8	8	4			2 80			
6	S. Stemmel	M	2		9	8	9	8	9	8			2 85			
7	C. Idler	M	1	3	9	9	9	6	4	3			2 75			
8	H. Doolittle	M	3	8	6	8	4						3 40			
9	F. Jones	M	2		10	10		8	8	8			3 60			
10	A. Eipstan	M	3		10	6	6	10	10	8			2 60			

B.

Hourly Payroll No. 34   Week Ending Sept. 16, 19 x9

Emp No.	Name	Marital Status	Inc Tax Ex.	S	M	T	W	T	F	S	Tot.	O.T.	Reg. Hrly Rate	Regular	Overtime	Total
1	J. McCormick	M	4		4	4	4	10	10	10			4 25			
2	B. Rice	M	3		7	7	7	4	10				3 85			
3	D. Mathews	M	5		4	4	4	4	4				2 50			
4	E. Tragle	M	6		8	8	8	8	8	4			3 10			
5	G. Hilanny	M	2		7	8	8	8	7	4			3 30			
6	I. Isaac	M	2	4	8	8	8	8	8	4			3 90			
7	K. Brassen	M	2		9	9	9	9	9				4 00			
8	M. Peule	M	3		9	8	8	9	4	8			3 40			
9	N. Fitzgerald	M	2		10	8	8	10	8	4			2 90			
10	V. Nagle	M	1	4		10	10	10	6				2 70			

C.

Emp No	Name	Inc Tax Ex	S	M	T	W	T	F	S	Tot	OT	Reg Hrly Rate	Regular	Overtime	Total	Soc Sec	Inc Tax	Other	Net Amount	Ck No
1	L. Levenson	2	8	9	8	9	8	9				4 60								1001
2	J. Harper	3	9	2	8	8	8	8				3 60								1002
3	B. O'Conner	2		8	4	8	8	4	4			2 25								1003
4	A. Swinger	2	3	9	9	9	10		3			3 40								1004
5	E. Reed	4		6	6	10	10	8	4			2 80								1005
6	D. Lewis	3		8	8	8	8	8				2 85								1006
7	T. Hitchcock	2		8		6	8	9				3 10								1007
8	C. Oliver	1	4	8	8	4	8	9				2 90								1008
9	K. Young	4	10	10			8	8	8			2 75								1009
10	M. Wolfe	2	9	9	8	8	8	4				3 10								1010

D.

Emp No	Name	Inc Tax Ex	S	M	T	W	T	F	S	Tot	OT	Reg Hrly Rate	Regular	Overtime	Total	Soc Sec	Inc Tax	Other	Net Amount	Ck No
1	R. Ohr	3	1	7	7	10	4					4 50								2031
2	T. Holmes	4	9	9	9	9	9					5 90								2032
3	E. Lara	2		9	8	8	9	4	8			3 10								2033
4	H. Swartz	1	8	10	10	8	8		4			4 00								2034
5	G. Regan	0		4	10	4	10	4	10			2 50								2035
6	W. Hertz	0		10	10	10		6	4			3 40								2036
7	V. Yates	3	8	8	8	8	8	4				3 85								2037
8	S. Jenkins	2		4	4	4	4	4				2 90								2038
9	N. Hahn	3	4	8	8	8	8	8	4			4 25								2039
10	O. Roberts	2		8	7	8	8	1	4			2 70								2040

PART THREE

Simple and Compound Interest

CHAPTER 16
Simple interest

There are many times when an individual or business may find it necessary to engage in a transaction on a credit basis. *Credit* is the extending of money or goods for immediate use in exchange for a promise to repay all or part of the amount owed by some specific date. If the repayment period is less than a year, the credit is said to be *short term*. If the repayment period is more than a year, the credit is said to be *long term*. The charge or fee for the use of this service, or, more specifically, for the use of money, is called *interest*. The *principal* is the amount of money borrowed or the value of the goods purchased on credit.

Interest is computed on the basis of a specific percent of the principal for a specific period of time. The basic factors that must be known to compute interest (I) are the principal (P), the rate (r), and the time (T). This results in the following simple interest equation:

$$I = P \times r \times T$$

The interest is equal to the principal times the rate times the time.

Example. What is the interest charged on a $1000 loan at 6% for one year?

$$I = P \times r \times T$$
$$= \$1000 \times .06 \times 1$$
$$= \$60$$

Example. What is the interest charged on a $700 loan at 5% interest for three years?

$$I = P \times r \times T$$
$$= \$700 \times .05 \times 3$$
$$= \$105$$

Often the period of the loan is less than a year. It is quite common for a loan to be issued for 30-, 60-, or 90-day periods. In this case, the equation stays the same but T must be expressed in terms of a fraction of a year. In other words, the number of days of the loan must be placed over the number of days in a year. In Federal Reserve and Federal government transactions, the number of days of the loan is placed over 365. The amount of interest computed using a 365-day basis is called *exact* or *actual interest*.

Example. Find the exact interest on a $1000 loan at 4% interest for 73 days.

$$I = P \times r \times T$$

$$= \$1000 \times .04 \times \frac{73}{365}$$

$$= \$40.00 \times \frac{1}{5}$$

$$= \$8.00$$

Most banks and businesses place the number of days of the loan over 360. The amount of interest computed using a 360-day basis is called *ordinary interest.*

Example. Compute the ordinary interest on a loan of $900 at 6% interest for 90 days.

$$I = P \times r \times T$$

$$= \$900 \times .06 \times \frac{90}{360}$$

$$= \$54 \times \frac{1}{4}$$

$$= \$13.50$$

If the time period of the loan is given in months, the number of months of the loan is placed over 12 and the same equation is used.

Example. Compute the interest on a loan of $1200 at 5% interest for six months.

$$I = P \times r \times T$$

$$= \$1200 \times .05 \times \frac{6}{12}$$

$$= \$60 \times \frac{1}{2}$$

$$= \$30$$

60 DAY-6% SHORTCUT

If the terms of a loan are 6% for 60 days, the equation would look as follows:

$$I = P \times .06 \times \frac{1}{6}$$

$$I = P \times .01$$

In other words, whenever these terms are given, the principal times .01 will give you the interest amount. As was pointed out in the discussion of decimals, this simply involves moving the decimal point in the principal two places to the left.

Example. What will be the interest at 6% for 60 days on the following loans?

$1000 = $10.00 $23,400 = $234.00
 $275 = $2.75 $19.95 = $.1995 or $.20

Keeping this in mind, we can use the concept of aliquot parts to find the interest amount on time periods other than 60 days. The first step is to find the interest for 60 days at 6% by the process above. Then the time period given must be expressed as a fraction of 60 (see Table 16.1). The resulting fraction reduced to lowest terms is then multiplied by the interest found for 60 days. It should be remembered that this process holds true only for a 6% interest rate.

TABLE 16.1

Fractional Parts of 60

$30 \text{ days} = \frac{30}{60} \text{ or } \frac{1}{2} \text{ of 60 days}$

$20 \text{ days} = \frac{20}{60} \text{ or } \frac{1}{3} \text{ of 60 days}$

$15 \text{ days} = \frac{15}{60} \text{ or } \frac{1}{4} \text{ of 60 days}$

$12 \text{ days} = \frac{12}{60} \text{ or } \frac{1}{5} \text{ of 60 days}$

$10 \text{ days} = \frac{10}{60} \text{ or } \frac{1}{6} \text{ of 60 days}$

$6 \text{ days} = \frac{6}{60} \text{ or } \frac{1}{10} \text{ of 60 days}$

$5 \text{ days} = \frac{5}{60} \text{ or } \frac{1}{12} \text{ of 60 days}$

$4 \text{ days} = \frac{4}{60} \text{ or } \frac{1}{15} \text{ of 60 days}$

$3 \text{ days} = \frac{3}{60} \text{ or } \frac{1}{20} \text{ of 60 days}$

$2 \text{ days} = \frac{2}{60} \text{ or } \frac{1}{30} \text{ of 60 days}$

Example. Find the interest amounts of the following:

$600 at 6% for 30 days
6% for 60 days = $6.00

$30 \text{ days} = \frac{1}{2} \text{ of 60 days}$

$\$6.00 \times \frac{1}{2} = \$3.00$

$1000 at 6% for 45 days
6% for 60 days = $10.00

$30 \text{ days} = \frac{1}{2} \text{ of 60 days}$ $15 \text{ days} = \frac{1}{4} \text{ of 60 days}$

$\$10.00 \times \frac{1}{2} = \$5.00$ $\$10.00 \times \frac{1}{4} = \$2.50$

$\$5.00 + \$2.50 = \$7.50$

$4000 at 6% for 3 years (ordinary)
6% for 60 days = $40.00
3 yr = 3 × 360 days = 1080 days
1080 days = 18 × 60 days
$40.00 × 18 = $720

Using this same idea, we can find the interest amount for 60 days at rates other than 6%. In this case, we first find the interest at 6% and then express the given interest as a fraction of 6%. The resulting fraction is then multiplied by the interest found at 6%.

Example. Find the interest amounts of the following:

$500 at 3% for 60 days
$500 at 6% for 60 days = $5.00

$$3\% = \frac{.03}{.06} \text{ of } 6\% = \frac{1}{2} \text{ of } 6\%$$

$$\frac{1}{2} \times \$5.00 = \$2.50$$

$1000 at 10% for 60 days
$1000 at 6% for 60 days = $10.00

$$\$1000 \text{ at } 4\% \text{ for } 60 \text{ days} = \frac{4}{6} \times \$10.00$$

$$= \frac{2}{3} \times \$10.00$$

$$= \quad \$\ 6.67$$
$$\overline{10\%} \quad = \quad \overline{\$16.67}$$

    Finally we can find the interest if the rate and the time can be expressed in terms of 60 days = 6% by simply combining the methods above.

Example. Find the interest on a $900 loan at 3% for 20 days.

6% for 60 days   = $9.00

$$6\% \text{ for } 20 \text{ days} = \frac{1}{3} \times \$9.00 = \$3.00$$

$$3\% \text{ for } 20 \text{ days} = \frac{1}{2} \times \$3.00 = \$1.50$$

ASSIGNMENT 27 SIMPLE INTEREST

A. Find the simple interest, given the information below.

	PRINCIPAL	RATE	TIME	INTEREST
a.	$500	3%	3 yr	
1.	$400	8%	1 yr	
2.	$750	$7\frac{1}{2}\%$	2 yr	
3.	$1000	6%	3 yr	
4.	$1200	5%	3 yr	
5.	$650	7%	2 yr	
6.	$920	$8\frac{1}{2}\%$	4 yr	
7.	$2500	6%	8 yr	
8.	$40,000	7%	10 yr	
9.	$1280	8%	7 yr	
10.	$5500	5%	8 yr	

B. Given the information below, find each of the *ordinary* interest amounts.

	PRINCIPAL	RATE	TIME	INTEREST
a.	$1800	3%	60 da	
1.	$600	$6\frac{1}{2}\%$	180 da	
2.	$2400	7%	90 da	
3.	$3500	5%	120 da	
4.	$800	6%	30 da	
5.	$10,000	$7\frac{1}{2}\%$	60 da	

C. Given the information below, find each of the *exact* interest amounts.

	PRINCIPAL	RATE	TIME	INTEREST
a.	$700	4%	73 da	
1.	$500	$7\frac{1}{2}\%$	5 da	
2.	$1200	6%	260 da	
3.	$4500	8%	100 da	
4.	$300	7%	225 da	
5.	$3800	5%	95 da	

D. Using the 60 day-6% shortcut, compute the interest on the following.

	PRINCIPAL	RATE/YR	TIME	INTEREST
a.	$4000	4%	80 da	
1.	$350	6%	60 da	
2.	$1975	6%	60 da	
3.	$800	6%	120 da	
4.	$15,420	6%	60 da	
5.	$1550	6%	90 da	
6.	$8250	6%	20 da	
7.	$275	6%	180 da	
8.	$14,500	4%	60 da	
9.	$995	3%	60 da	
10.	$7200	8%	60 da	
11.	$430	6%	45 da	
12.	$72,100	6%	60 da	
13.	$3000	4%	90 da	
14.	$22,500	3%	180 da	
15.	$94,150	8%	75 da	

E. Solve each of the following problems. Assume "banker's year" of 360 days unless otherwise instructed.

1. Jackson Talbot needed $4600 to start an appliance repair shop. The Small Business Administration, a Federal lending agency, agreed to lend Mr. Talbot this amount at a rate of 7% simple interest for five years. What is the total amount Mr. Talbot had to repay?

2. Raymond Sling decided to borrow $480 at 4% for 60 days in order to pay his property tax on time. If he had not borrowed the money, he would have had to pay a 6% penalty in addition to the $480. How much did he save by borrowing the money?

3. Ninety days ago, Jean Marian signed a 5% 120-day note. The amount of the note was $5100. How much money will she save in interest if she repays the note now?

4. The Clark Company borrows $3400 for 25 days from the First National Bank at $7\frac{1}{2}$%. What amount will it owe in interest at the end of that period?

5. Tom Warren borrowed $1600 at $6\frac{3}{4}$% for one year. What amount of interest did he owe at the end of that period?

6. Jim took out a 90-day loan of $300 in order to buy his fiancee an engagement ring. At the end of his borrowing period, he owed $5.63 in interest. What was the interest rate applicable to this loan?

7. What is the *exact* interest computed on a $4800 loan at 7% for 120 days?

8. Mr. Nelson borrowed $22,000 at 6% for a 5-year period. What was the interest charged at the end of his borrowing period?

9. The Blakes are planning to buy a boat for which they will need to take out a loan of $14,000. One finance company offers terms of 6% interest over 1 year. The other offers 5% interest over a two-year period. Since the Blakes need two years to repay the loan and interest, they accept the latter offer. How much interest could they have saved by choosing to repay the loan in one year instead of two years?

10. Mr. Joyce wants to borrow $2000 over a 60-day period at 6.25%. Would he save any money if the interest were computed using the exact method rather than the ordinary method? If so, how much?

CHAPTER 17
Debt and credit instruments

A credit or debt instrument is anything that proves the existence of a debt. It shows the terms of the agreement, the amount of the loan, the interest rate, the date due, and the borrower's signature. One of the most common debt instruments is the promissory note. A *promissory note* is a written and signed promise to pay a stated sum of money to another party on demand at some specific future date. The borrower is called the *maker* of the note. The recipient of the note is called the *payee*. The *face value* of the note is the amount to be paid. The *maturity value* is the face value plus the interest due. The *sum* is the total amount to be paid when the note is due. A promissory note may be interest bearing or non-interest bearing. If the words "with interest" appear on the note, the instrument is interest bearing. If there is no stated interest on an interest bearing note, the legal rate of interest may be charged. One must also be careful to observe whether the interest is stated per year, per month, or per day. A copy of a promissory note is shown below.

$ _____ 3,000.00 _____   Centerville, State   Sept. 17,   19 X9

_____ Three Months _____   *after date* __I__ *promise to pay*

to the order of _____ Thomas P. Peterson _____

_____ Three thousand and 00/XXX - *Dollars*

Payable at _____ Second Federal Bank of Centerville _____

With interest at _____ 6% per year _____

No. __95__   Due _December 17,_ 19 X9   *Stephen A. Barlowe*

In this case the face value is $3000. The maturity value is $3045 ($3000 face value + $45 interest). The maker is Stephen A. Barlowe and the payee is Thomas P. Peterson.

Another common debt instrument is the trade acceptance. The *trade acceptance* is similar to the promissory note, with one difference. While a note is sometimes issued

<table>
<tr><td rowspan="8">TRADE ACCEPTANCE</td><td>No. _____ 74 _____</td><td>Franklin, State</td><td>June 26, __ 19 X9</td></tr>
</table>

No. ___74___	Franklin, State		June 26, __ 19 _X9_
To	Timberlake Manufacturing Company,	Timberlake, State	
On	Sept. 26, 19X9 _____ pay to the order of _____ Ourselves _____		
	One Thousand Five Hundred and 00/XXX ____ DOLLARS ___$1,500.00___		
			00 —

Accepted at ___Timberlake, June 28___

Payable at ___Union Bank___

Bank location ___Scarton, State___   Dodd Machinery Incorporated

Buyer's signature ___Timberlake Manufacturing Co.___

By agent ___John L. Kane___   By ___Thomas Dodd___

for payment of an account at some time *after* the account was opened, a trade acceptance is issued at the time of purchase.

The procedure connected with a trade acceptance is also different. When one company sells merchandise to another, it may include a trade acceptance with the goods and invoice. When the buyer accepts the goods and signs the trade acceptance form, it, in effect, becomes a non-interest bearing note that the seller may, if he or she wishes, borrow against at a bank.

The trade acceptance shown above was issued by Dodd Machinery Corporation when it made a shipment of merchandise to Timberlake Manufacturing Company on June 26. The merchandise was released to Timberlake Manufacturing Company when an official of Timberlake signed the trade acceptance on June 28. The acceptence on June 28 became, for practical purposes, a non-interest bearing loan for $1500 given by Dodd Machinery to Timberlake. The time of a trade acceptance begins with the date of acceptance, not the date of issue. For example, a 90-day trade acceptance dated June 10 and accepted on June 20 becomes due 90 days from June 20.

COMPUTING THE NUMBER OF DAYS OR DATE DUE

One problem with debt instruments is computing the number of days between the date a note was issued and the date it becomes due. The interest is computed on the actual days between the two dates. Usually, the issue date is not charged interest (not counted in actual days), but the due date is.

Example. For interest purposes, how many actual days are there between June 10 and July 26?

    30 days in June
  − 10 days already gone by in June
    20 days to be used for interest in June
    26 days to be used for interest in July
    46 actual days

Example. How many actual days between September 3 and November 19?

30	days in September
− 3	days already gone by in September
27	days to be used for interest in September
31	days to be used for interest in October
19	days to be used for interest in November
77	actual days

Many times, the date issued and the number of actual days of the note are known, but the due date must be computed. The procedure here is similar to finding the number of days.

TABLE 17.1

Number of Day of Each Calendar Date

Mo. Day	Jan.	Feb.	March	April	May	June	July	Aug.	Sept.	Oct.	Nov.	Dec.
1	1	32	60	91	121	152	182	213	244	274	305	335
2	2	33	61	92	122	153	183	214	245	275	306	336
3	3	34	62	93	123	154	184	215	246	276	307	337
4	4	35	63	94	124	155	185	216	247	277	308	338
5	5	36	64	95	125	156	186	217	248	278	309	339
6	6	37	65	96	126	157	187	218	249	279	310	340
7	7	38	66	97	127	158	188	219	250	280	311	341
8	8	39	67	98	128	159	189	220	251	281	312	342
9	9	40	68	99	129	160	190	221	252	282	313	343
10	10	41	69	100	130	161	191	222	253	283	314	344
11	11	42	70	101	131	162	192	223	254	284	315	345
12	12	43	71	102	132	163	193	224	255	285	316	346
13	13	44	72	103	133	164	194	225	256	286	317	347
14	14	45	73	104	134	165	195	226	257	287	318	348
15	15	46	74	105	135	166	196	227	258	288	319	349
16	16	47	75	106	136	167	197	228	259	289	320	350
17	17	48	76	107	137	168	198	229	260	290	321	351
18	18	49	77	108	138	169	199	230	261	291	322	352
19	19	50	78	109	139	170	200	231	262	292	323	353
20	20	51	79	110	140	171	201	232	263	293	324	354
21	21	52	80	111	141	172	202	233	264	294	325	355
22	22	53	81	112	142	173	203	234	265	295	326	356
23	23	54	82	113	143	174	204	235	266	296	327	357
24	24	55	83	114	144	175	205	236	267	297	328	358
25	25	56	84	115	145	176	206	237	268	298	329	359
26	26	57	85	116	146	177	207	238	269	299	330	360
27	27	58	86	117	147	178	208	239	270	300	331	361
28	28	59	87	118	148	179	209	240	271	301	332	362
29	29	—	88	119	149	180	210	241	272	302	333	363
30	30	—	89	120	150	181	211	242	273	303	334	364
31	31	—	90	—	151	—	212	243	—	304	—	365

For Leap Year, one day must be added to each number of days after February 28.

Example. What is the due date on a 60-day note issued March 19?

31 days in March	60 days of note
− 19 March days gone by	− 12 days left in March
12 days left in March	48
	− 30 days in April
	18 due date in May

Because the note is for 60 days, and 42 days takes us to the end of April, we need 18 days in May. Thus, the due date is May 18.

This procedure can be time consuming to a banker who has many notes to compute. For this reason, a table such as Table 17.1 may be used.

To find the number of days using the table, find the number that corresponds to both the issue date and the due date. The difference between these corresponding numbers is the number of days.

Example. How many actual days between June 16 and August 18?

August 18 = 230
June 16   = 167
          63

To compute the due date, find the number that corresponds to the issue date and add the length of the note. Then simply find the day that corresponds to this new number.

Example. Find the due date of a 90-day note issued on September 26.

September 26 = 269
Length of note = 90 days
              359 = December 25

A. *Without* using the table, find the number of days between the dates given below.

	ISSUED	DUE	DAYS		ISSUED	DUE	DAYS
a.	Jan. 9	Feb. 8		**b.**	Aug. 12	Dec. 23	
1.	March 16	April 3		**2.**	June 4	Aug. 6	
3.	Nov. 23	Dec. 25		**4.**	Feb. 27	April 30	
5.	May 19	July 4		**6.**	April 16	Nov. 4	
7.	Jan. 6	July 19		**8.**	July 29	Sept. 2	
9.	March 19	Nov. 29		**10.**	Oct. 5	Dec. 31	

B. *Without* using the table, find the date due on the following notes.

	ISSUED	DAYS	DUE		ISSUED	DAYS	DUE
a.	June 9	60		**b.**	April 16	30	
1.	Jan. 6	90		**2.**	March 12	45	
3.	July 26	120		**4.**	Sept. 16	60	
5.	Oct. 26	30		**6.**	Feb. 6	60	
7.	May 22	90		**8.**	June 14	120	
9.	Aug. 21	45		**10.**	Jan. 29	75	

C. Using the table, find the number of days between the following dates.

	ISSUED	DUE	DAYS
a.	Oct. 14	Dec. 26	
1.	Feb. 16	June 30	
2.	March 3	July 12	
3.	April 26	Nov. 17	
4.	Aug. 2	Nov. 4	
5.	Jun. 3	Oct. 19	

D. Using the table, find the due date of the following notes.

	ISSUED	DAYS	DUE
a.	March 8	30	
1.	Oct. 2	60	
2.	June 13	90	
3.	April 14	120	
4.	Aug. 29	45	
5.	May 21	75	

E. Given the following information, fill in the blanks.

	ISSUE DATE	DUE DATE	NO. OF DAYS	FACE VALUE	INTEREST RATE	MATURITY VALUE
a.	May 7		30	$ 3000	6%/yr	
1.	June 12	Aug. 11		1500	4%/yr	
2.	Oct. 9		60	2750	3%/yr	
3.	April 4	July 3		875	8%/yr	
4.	Oct. 29		30	15,500	6%/yr	
5.	May 21	Sept. 18		20,000	5%/yr	

F. Solve each of the following problems.

1. On December 17, Dr. Richards signed a trade acceptance for new medical equipment. The terms of the trade acceptance were $6\frac{1}{2}\%$ and 120 days. On February 28, Dr. Richards paid the entire amount of the trade acceptance, which was $8570. How much money did he save by paying early?

2. If Douglas Rampart agrees to the terms of a note offered to him by the Friendly Finance Association, he will have to repay a principal of $7550 in 97 days, plus interest computed at 7% simple. Mr. Rampart signs the note on March 2. What is the maturity date and the amount of interest due?

3. Sam's men's store has three invoices which offer a cash discount on the terms shown. Sam can borrow money from his bank at 12% per year. How much will Sam save by borrowing money to pay these invoices within the cash discount period? (Assume that they can be paid the same day he borrows the money.)

INVOICE AMOUNT	TERMS	AMOUNT OF CASH DISCOUNT	TIME OF LOAN (DAYS)	AMOUNT OF INTEREST ON LOAN	AMOUNT OF SAVINGS
$1467.50	2/30, net/90		$60 = 90 - 30$		
$ 950.25	3/15, net/30				
$2005.00	3/10, net/120				

CHAPTER 18
Interest tables

When the interest on a large number of loans is to be computed, as in the case of banks or businesses, an interest table can be of great value. *Interest tables* show the amount of interest on a specific principal, given a certain interest rate and length of time. With the use of a table, the banker saves time and effort.

The tables are computed on principals of any amount, but the most common are based on multiples of ten. Table 18.1 is based on loans of $100. In practice a more complete table giving an entry for 1 to 360 days and more interest rate intervals would be used.

To find the interest on a loan of $100, first find the number of days of the loan in the time column. Move across the row until you reach the column that gives the interest rate of the loan. The number at this intersection of time and interest rate is the amount of interest.

Example. Find the interest on a $100 loan at $4\frac{1}{2}\%$ for 12 days.

First, find 12 days in the time column. Move across this row until you reach the $4\frac{1}{2}\%$ column. The interest is .1500 or $.15.

Other loan amounts can be computed by expressing them in terms of 100. This can be done by moving the decimal point in the loan amount two places to the left. Given the time and interest rate, the interest on a $100 loan can be multiplied by this figure to obtain interest on amounts other than $100.

$$\left.\begin{array}{l} \$86 \text{ loan} = .86 \\ \$116 \text{ loan} = 1.16 \\ \$2031 \text{ loan} = 20.31 \end{array}\right\} \times \text{Amount in Table} = \text{Interest}$$

Example. Find the interest on a 26-day loan of $900 at $5\frac{1}{2}\%$.

From the table, a $100 loan at $5\frac{1}{2}\%$ for 26 days yields an interest amount of $.3972. The loan of $900 is nine times that amount:

$$\begin{array}{r} \$\ .3972 \\ \times \qquad 9 \\ \hline \$3.5748 \end{array} = \text{interest on } \$900$$

TABLE 18.1

					Simple Interest					
DAYS	4½%	5%	5½%	6%	6½%	7%	7½%	8%	8½%	9%
1	.0125	.0139	.0153	.0167	.0181	.0194	.0208	.0222	.0236	.0250
2	.0250	.0278	.0306	.0333	.0361	.0389	.0417	.0444	.0472	.0500
3	.0375	.0417	.0458	.0500	.0542	.0583	.0625	.0667	.0708	.0750
4	.0500	.0556	.0611	.0667	.0722	.0778	.0833	.0889	.0944	.1000
5	.0625	.0694	.0764	.0833	.0903	.0972	.1042	.1111	.1181	.1250
6	.0750	.0833	.0917	.1000	.1083	.1167	.1250	.1333	.1417	.1500
7	.0875	.0972	.1069	.1167	.1264	.1361	.1458	.1556	.1653	.1750
8	.1000	.1111	.1222	.1333	.1444	.1556	.1667	.1778	.1889	.2000
9	.1125	.1250	.1375	.1500	.1625	.1750	.1875	.2000	.2125	.2250
10	.1250	.1389	.1528	.1667	.1806	.1944	.2083	.2222	.2361	.2500
11	.1375	.1528	.1681	.1833	.1986	.2139	.2292	.2444	.2597	.2750
12	.1500	.1667	.1833	.2000	.2167	.2333	.2500	.2667	.2833	.3000
13	.1625	.1806	.1986	.2167	.2347	.2528	.2708	.2889	.3069	.3250
14	.1750	.1944	.2139	.2333	.2528	.2722	.2917	.3111	.3306	.3500
15	.1875	.2083	.2292	.2500	.2708	.2917	.3125	.3333	.3542	.3750
16	.2000	.2222	.2444	.2667	.2889	.3111	.3333	.3556	.3778	.4000
17	.2125	.2361	.2597	.2833	.3069	.3306	.3542	.3778	.4014	.4250
18	.2250	.2500	.2750	.3000	.3250	.3500	.3750	.4000	.4250	.4500
19	.2375	.2639	.2903	.3167	.3431	.3694	.3958	.4222	.4486	.4750
20	.2500	.2778	.3056	.3333	.3611	.3889	.4167	.4444	.4722	.5000
21	.2625	.2917	.3208	.3500	.3792	.4083	.4375	.4667	.4958	.5250
22	.2750	.3056	.3361	.3667	.3972	.4278	.4583	.4889	.5194	.5500
23	.2875	.3194	.3514	.3833	.4153	.4472	.4792	.5111	.5431	.5750
24	.3000	.3333	.3667	.4000	.4333	.4667	.5000	.5333	.5667	.6000
25	.3125	.3472	.3819	.4167	.4514	.4861	.5208	.5555	.5903	.6250
26	.3250	.3611	.3972	.4333	.4694	.5056	.5417	.5778	.6139	.6500
27	.3375	.3750	.4125	.4500	.4875	.5250	.5625	.6000	.6375	.6750
28	.3500	.3889	.4278	.4667	.5056	.5444	.5833	.6222	.6611	.7000
29	.3625	.4028	.4431	.4833	.5236	.5639	.6042	.6444	.6847	.7250
30	.3750	.4167	.4583	.5000	.5417	.5833	.6250	.6667	.7083	.7500
60	.7500	.8333	.9167	1.0000	1.0833	1.1667	1.2500	1.3333	1.4167	1.5000
90	1.1250	1.2500	1.3750	1.5000	1.6250	1.7500	1.8750	2.0000	2.1250	2.2500
120	1.5000	1.6667	1.8333	2.0000	2.1667	2.3333	2.5000	2.6670	2.8333	3.0000
150	1.8750	2.0833	2.2917	2.5000	2.7083	2.9160	3.1250	3.3330	3.5417	3.7500
180	2.2500	2.5000	2.7500	3.0000	3.2500	3.5070	3.7500	4.0000	4.2500	4.5000

Example. Find the interest on a 12-day loan of $2960 at $4\frac{1}{2}\%$.

$.1500$ = interest on a $100 loan for 12 days

$\times\quad 29.6$
$\overline{9000}$
$1\ 3500$
$\underline{3\ 000}$
$\overline{\$4.44000} = \$4.40$ = interest on a $2960 loan for 12 days

Example. Find the interest on a 24-day loan of $6350 at $8\frac{1}{2}\%$.

$.5667$ = Interest on a 24-day loan of $6350 at $8\frac{1}{2}\%$

$\times\quad 63.5$
$\overline{28335}$
17001
$\underline{34002}$
$\overline{35.98545} = \$35.99$ = interest on a $6350 loan for 24 days

A. From the Simple Interest Table, find the interest due on a $100 loan if the rate and time are given as the following.

a. 6% for 20 days
2. $4\frac{1}{2}$% for 29 days
4. $8\frac{1}{2}$% for 15 days
6. $6\frac{1}{2}$% for 23 days
8. 5% for 4 days
10. $5\frac{1}{2}$% for 26 days

1. 5% for 12 days
3. 7% for 5 days
5. 9% for 120 days
7. $7\frac{1}{2}$% for 22 days
9. 8% for 18 days
11. 7% for 60 days

B. From the Simple Interest Table, find the interest due on the following loans.

	PRINCIPAL	RATE	DAYS	INTEREST
a.	$8100	$7\frac{1}{2}$%	12	
1.	$92	$8\frac{1}{2}$%	14	
2.	$50	5%	18	
3.	$125	6%	26	
4.	$300	7%	6	
5.	$525	9%	10	
6.	$1160	8%	5	
7.	$263	$8\frac{1}{2}$%	17	
8.	$496	$6\frac{1}{2}$%	21	
9.	$959	$7\frac{1}{2}$%	25	
10.	$2306	7%	29	

C. From the Simple Interest Table, compute the interest on the following loans.

	ISSUED	DUE	DAYS	PRINCIPAL	RATE	INTEREST
a.	Sept. 26	Oct. 19		$925	7%	
1.	Aug. 12	Aug. 18		$100	$8\frac{1}{2}$%	
2.	Jan. 3	Jan. 9		$85	9%	
3.	March 1	March 13		$2000	$7\frac{1}{2}$%	
4.	July 30	Aug. 29		$550	5%	
5.	Nov. 19	Nov. 27		$792	$5\frac{1}{2}$%	
6.	Dec. 24	Jan. 22		$3420	6%	
7.	April 26	May 10		$11,200	7%	
8.	Feb. 18	Feb. 28		$9090	$6\frac{1}{2}$%	
9.	Oct. 28	Mar. 16		$57,755	8%	
10.	Sept. 20	Oct. 15		$8200	$4\frac{1}{2}$%	

D. Solve the following problems.

1. Mrs. Harris obtained a loan of $850 for 90 days on September 2. What date is the loan due? If the interest rate is $7\frac{1}{2}$%, what amount of interest does she owe at the end of the borrowing period?

2. John Hendricks has to repay a loan of $1700 at $6\frac{1}{2}$% interest in 120 days. What *total* amount will he owe at the end of that period?

3. Ms. Powell needs to borrow $2500 and has a choice of two bank loan offers. First Industrial Bank offers a 90-day borrowing period at 7%, while Second Union Bank offers 120 days to repay the loan at 6%. Which offer should she take? Why?

4. The Martinson Company borrows $9500 at $7\frac{1}{2}\%$ for 60 days. The due date for repayment is January 18.

   a. When was the loan issued?
   b. What amount of interest is due on January 18?

5. Gary borrows $450 at $6\frac{1}{2}\%$ for a period of 60 days. However, he is able to repay the loan and computed interest at the end of 30 days. a) What total amount does Gary repay at this time? b) If he had waited until the end of 60 days to repay the loan and interest, how much more interest would be owed for the loan?

CHAPTER 19
Bank discounts

It is common for banks to collect interest on loans in advance. This is done by deducting the interest amount of the loan from the maturity value at the time the loan is issued. When the interest is deducted on the day the money is borrowed, it is known as a *discount* and the process is known as *discounting*. The major difference between discount and interest, then, is that the charge for borrowing is paid at a different time.

Example. Thomas Crown borrowed $5000 for 120 days discounted at 6%. What was the amount of discount and what amount did he actually receive?

Using the 60 day-6% method, the discount would be $100.

$5000 for 60 days @ 6% = $50
$5000 for 120 days @ 6% = 2 × $50 = $100

To discount the loan, this $100 must be subtracted from the maturity value. Since no interest is to be paid on the due date, the maturity value is equal to the face value. Thus Mr. Crown receives $4900. The amount actually received is called the *proceeds*.

Maturity Value − Discount = Proceeds
$5000 − $100 = $4900

Mr. Crown receives $4900 but must repay $5000.

A comparison can be made between discount and interest with regard to rates. If the loan in our example is discounted, Mr. Crown is paying $100 for the use of $4900. If the loan had been transacted using simple interest, Mr. Crown's $100 would have paid for the use of $5000. Thus, the rate of discount is higher than the simple interest rate. Another example of discounting is given below.

Example. Find the proceeds on a $490 loan for 60 days discounted at 3%.

$490 for 60 days @ 6% = $4.90

$490 for 60 days @ 3% = $\frac{1}{2}$ × $4.90 = $2.45

$490 − $2.45 = $487.55 proceeds

DISCOUNTING OF COMMERCIAL PAPER

If an individual is the holder of notes, drafts, trade acceptances, or other credit instruments, he may use them to raise needed cash instead of obtaining a loan on his own note. The procedure simply involves selling these instruments to a willing buyer. In most cases, the buyer is a bank. The bank discounts these purchases based on the time it must hold the instrument to maturity. This is known as the *discounting of commercial paper* and can be applied to both non-interest-bearing (such as an account receivable) and interest-bearing credit instruments.

NON-INTEREST-BEARING INSTRUMENTS

To discount a non-interest bearing commercial instrument involves three basic steps. First, the number of days the bank holds the note must be determined. This is done by finding the number of days between the date of discount and the maturity date. Second, based on the number of days, the specific discount rate, and the maturity value of the instrument to be discounted, the amount of discount can be determined. Third, this amount must be subtracted from the maturity value, which leaves the proceeds or the amount actually received for the sale of the instruments. Since the instruments are non-interest bearing in this case, the only charge involved is the discount in the sale of the instruments after they were originally issued.

Example. Fred Johnston decided to sell non-interest-bearing trade acceptances totaling $1500 due December 21. On December 1, a bank agreed to purchase them at a 6% discount. What amount of cash did Mr. Johnston receive?

Proceeds = Maturity Value

$$- \left(\text{Maturity Value} \times \text{Discount Rate} \times \frac{\text{Days to Maturity}}{360} \right)$$

$$\text{Proceeds} = \$1500 - \left(\$1500 \times .06 \times \frac{20}{360} \right)$$

$$= \$1500 - \left(\$90 \times \frac{1}{18} \right)$$

$$= \$1500 - \$5$$
$$= \$1495$$

We can also make use of the 60 day-6% shortcut in this type of problem.

December 21
December 1
$\overline{20}$ days

$1500 for 60 days @ 6% = $15

$1500 for 20 days @ 6% = $15 $\times \dfrac{1}{3}$ = $5 discount

$1500 − $5 = $1495 proceeds

The procedure here is similar to the non-interest-bearing method. However, in all cases, the purchaser must take into account how much he would receive when the note is due. In the case of a non-interest-bearing note, this was equal to the face value. If the note is interest-bearing, this is not the case. Thus, to discount an interest-bearing note, the purchaser must first compute what he would receive when the note matures. The remaining steps are the same as those used for non-interest-bearing discounting.

Example. What is the amount of proceeds if a 90 day-3% note with a face value of $2000 and maturity date of March 21 is discounted on March 1 at a rate of 6%?

Proceeds = Maturity Value

$$- \left(\text{Maturity Value} \times \text{Discount Rate} \times \frac{\text{Days to Maturity}}{360} \right)$$

Maturity Value = Face Value + Interest

Interest = PRT

$$= \$2000 \times 3\% \times \frac{90}{360}$$

$$= \$60 \times \frac{1}{4}$$

$$= \$15$$

Maturity Value = $2000 + $15
$$= \$2015$$

$$\text{Proceeds} = \$2015 - \left(\$2015 \times .06 \times \frac{20}{360} \right)$$

$$= \$2015 - \$6.72$$
$$= \$2008.28$$

Again, the 60 day-6% shortcut can be applied.

$2000 for 60 days at 6% = $20
$2000 for 60 days at 3% = $10
$2000 for 30 days at 3% = $ 5
$2000 for 90 days at 3% = $15

Maturity Value = $2000 + $15 = $2015

March 21
March 1
20 days to be held

$2015 for 20 days at 6%
$2015 for 60 days at 6% = $20.15

$$\$20.15 \times \frac{1}{3} = \$6.72 = \text{discount}$$

$2015 − $6.72 = $2008.28 = proceeds

ASSIGNMENT 30 BANK DISCOUNTS

A. Given the following information, find the amount of discount and the proceeds on the following loans.

a. Amount of loan: $3000
Time of loan: 120 days
Discount rate: 6%
Discount:
Proceeds:

1. Amount of loan: $200
Time of loan: 60 days
Discount rate: 6%
Discount:
Proceeds:

2. Amount of loan: $375
Time of loan: 4 months
Discount rate: 9%
Discount:
Proceeds:

3. Amount of loan: $455
Time of loan: 90 days
Discount rate: 4%
Discount:
Proceeds:

4. Amount of loan: $775
Time of loan: 45 days
Discount rate: 2%
Discount:
Proceeds:

5. Amount of loan: $1152
Time of loan: 135 days
Discount rate: 6%
Discount:
Proceeds:

B. The following are non-interest-bearing notes. Given the discount date and the date due, find the proceeds and amount of discount.

a. Amount of note: $44,000
Discount date: June 3
Date due: June 13
Discount rate: 3%
Discount:
Proceeds:

1. Amount of note: $250
Discount date: April 6
Date Due: June 5
Discount rate: 4%
Discount:
Proceeds:

2. Amount of note: $590
Discount date: June 18
Date due: July 28
Discount rate: 2%
Discount:
Proceeds:

C. The following are interest-bearing notes. Given the following information, find the maturity value, the discount, and the proceeds.

a. 60 day-6% note discounted October 3
Maturity date: October 23
Discount rate: 3%
Face value: $2000
Maturity value:
Discount:
Proceeds:

1. $3500 face value with due date of October 23 was discounted on September 23
Terms of the note: 90 days @ 3%
Discount rate: 6%
Maturity value:
Discount:
Proceeds:

2. Discount date: May 16
   Maturity date: May 26
   120-day note @ 6% with face value of $9000
   Discount rate: 6%
   Maturity value:
   Discount:
   Proceeds:

D. Solve the following problems, using the formulas learned in this chapter.

1. Mr. Murray borrowed $10,500 for 90 days discounted at $7\frac{1}{2}\%$.

   a. What was the amount of the discount?
   b. What amount did he actually receive?

2. Daniel Blake sold $3600 worth of non-interest-bearing notes due May 16 to the Garfield State Bank on April 28 at a 7% discount. What were the proceeds received from this sale?

3. Mr. Herrold sells a 60-day 8% note with face value of $5000 and maturity date of June 3 on May 14. If a 5% discount is allowed, what are the proceeds of Mr. Herrold's sale?

4. Robert Stevens receives $9005.80 from the sale of a non-interest-bearing note with a maturity date of November 6 discounted at 8%. If the date of sale is October 25, what is the face value of the note?

CHAPTER 20
Interest and installment payments

Often interest is charged monthly and is computed on the basis of the unpaid balance. This method is commonly used by small loan agencies and by retailers who offer installment plan purchases. The procedure is simple. If a monthly interest rate is given, it is simply applied to the unpaid balance at the end of the month until the debt is repaid.

Example. Donald Franklin borrowed $500 at 1% per month on the unpaid balance. He agreed to make $40 payments each month on the principal, plus the interest payment. How much interest will he pay in 3 months?

MONTH	INTEREST	PRINCIPAL PAYMENT	TOTAL	BALANCE
				$500
1st	$500 × .01 = $ 5.00	$ 40	$ 45.00	460
2nd	460 × .01 = 4.60	$ 40	$ 44.60	420
3rd	420 × .01 = 4.20	$ 40	$ 44.20	380
	$13.80	$120	$133.80	

The above example demonstrates the basic approach of applying the interest rate to the unpaid balance. The usual procedure, however, is to keep the total monthly payment constant and have it include both the interest and principal payment. Perhaps the easiest way to understand this method is to apply it to the following example.

Example. Assume the same information given in the first example, except that the $40 payment includes the interest payment. How much interest will be paid in 3 months?

MONTH	INTEREST	PRINCIPAL PAYMENT	TOTAL	BALANCE
				$500.00
1st	$500 × .01 = $ 5.00	$ 35.00	$ 40.00	$465.00
2nd	$465 × .01 = $ 4.65	$ 35.35	$ 40.00	$429.65
3rd	$429.65 × .01 = $ 4.30	$ 35.70	$ 40.00	$393.95
	$13.95	$106.05	$120.00	

Under the constant payment method, as the monthly interest payment declines, the principal payment rises. In installment payments, either the principal payment or the total payment may be held constant.

CHARGE ACCOUNTS

Charge accounts are one of the most common forms of consumer credit and are one of the cheaper forms of credit available to the consumer, if managed correctly. Charge accounts may be classified into two categories: (1) regular and (2) revolving charge accounts.

Regular Charge Accounts are a convenience to customers, require payment within a short period, usually 25 to 30 days, and carry no finance charges.

Most stores have introduced a form of charge account which permits extended repayment terms. This is actually a form of consumer loan. Most *revolving charge accounts* are 30-day accounts with optional repayment plans. The word "revolving" comes from the practice that each account has some limit ($200, $300, or $400, for example) on the total amount that may be owed at any one time. As long as the outstanding balance in the account is below the limit, the customer may charge additional merchandise until the credit limit is reached. With these revolving accounts the customer usually has the following two repayment options:

1.   He may pay his bill in full within some fixed period, usually 25 to 30 days from the date of the bill, without incurring any finance charge. This way, the account operates exactly like a regular charge account.

2.   He may pay the minimum amount requested on the statement. This minimum payment may vary, but is often computed as 10% of the unpaid balance. Alternatively, the customer may pay an amount larger than the minimum amount, thereby reducing future finance charges.

The interest rates charged may vary from 1% to $1\frac{1}{2}$% per month, equivalent to an annual interest rate of 12% to 18% respectively. The method of computing the outstanding finance charge is restricted by the Federal Truth in Lending Act. A copy of this act is given to you at the time an account is opened and should be read carefully. In general, interest is not charged on purchases of the current month, so that the revolving charge account customer has the same 25 to 30 day period to pay for his purchases without a finance charge as the regular charge account customer.

Example. Richard Swenson's revolving charge account balance on his September statement from Goodie's Department Store was $165.50. During September, he bought two articles valued at $35.30 and $10.95. On September 15, he made a payment of $30.00. Goodie's requires a minimum payment of 10% and adds a finance charge of $1\frac{1}{2}$% on the previous balance less payments made this month.
(1)   Did Mr. Swenson satisfy the minimum payment?
(2)   What was his finance charge for September?
(3)   What was his new balance on his October statement?

Solution (1):
10% of $165.50 = $16.55, so his payment was greater than the minimum payment.

Solution (2):
$$\begin{aligned} \$165.50 &= \text{previous balance} \\ -\quad 30.00 &= \text{this month's payment} \\ \hline \$135.50 &= \text{unpaid balance} \end{aligned}$$

$135.50 \times 1\frac{1}{2}\% = \$2.0325 = \$2.03 = \text{finance charge}$

Solution (3):

$165.50 = previous month's balance

$\left.\begin{matrix} 35.30 \\ 10.95 \end{matrix}\right\}$ = current month's purchases

2.03 = finance charge
_____
$213.78

− 30.00 = payment
_____
$183.78 = new balance on October statement

CREDIT CARDS

Credit cards are used by more than 400 million consumers today. From a credit point of view they are similar to charge accounts. There are three general categories of credit cards.

1. The travel-entertainment card issued by private companies such as American Express and Diners Club upon which no finance charge is made. Payment, however, is expected in full within a specified number of days and extended payment facilities are not provided.

2. Company-issued cards, such as Sears or Exxon, usable at specified outlets and having repayment terms similar to revolving charge accounts.

3. Bank-issued credit cards such as Visa and Master Charge which are usable at numerous stores and service establishments on terms also similar to those of revolving charge accounts. In addition, the bank-issued credit cards permit the borrowing of cash directly, in which case there is usually no interest-free period before interest is charged. The calculation of finance charges and new balances is similar to that for charge accounts, though details may vary from card to card.

In general, for short periods of time (up to, say, three months) charge accounts and credit cards are a relatively cheap source of consumer credit. For longer periods of time bank loans may be cheaper. It is now easier to compare the various forms of credit because of the Truth-in-Lending Act, which requires every lender to state the simple interest equivalent of the credit which it offers.

FINDING THE RATE

Before the passage of Federal legislation in 1968, loan or finance companies could advertise loans without stating an interest rate. For example, they would sometimes state that one could borrow a certain amount and would quote only the dollar amount of the periodic payments and the number of payments required to pay off the loan. When faced with such a situation, the interest rate on the unpaid balance can be computed quite simply. The method of solution may be seen most clearly if we use an example.

Example. A finance company offers loans of $500 to be repaid in ten monthly payments of $56. What is the rate of interest on the unpaid balance?

The first step is to find the total amount of interest charged. This is found by multiplying the amount of the payments times the number of payments and subtracting the original principal.

Interest Charged = (Number of Payments × Amount of Each Payment) − Principal
$$= (10 \times \$56) - \$500$$
$$= \$560 - \$500$$
$$= \$60$$

Having computed the amount of interest, we can compute the approximate rate by multiplying the interest charged by 24 (2 × the number of annual payments) and dividing the result by the principal times one more than the number of payments.

$$\text{Simple Interest Rate Equivalent} = \frac{24 \times \text{Total Interest Charged}}{\text{Principal} \times (\text{No. of Payments} + 1)}$$

$$= \frac{24 \times \$60}{500 \times 11}$$

$$= \frac{\$1,440}{\$5,500}$$

$$= 26.2\%$$

Although this rate may seem high, the small loan maximum rates are usually established by state law and may, in fact, be high. The high rate may be justified by the risk of issuing such loans on little, if any, security provided by the borrower. Because of such high rates, one must be careful when entering into such an agreement. Before a consumer enters into any agreement, he should shop around to be sure he is paying the least amount of interest possible. Generally, banks charge less interest than other installment lenders. An individual must also be sure he knows if the interest is given on a yearly or monthly basis; 2% is less than 6%, but if it is 2% per month and 6% per year, the difference is costly.

AMORTIZATION OF MORTGAGES

One of the many types of loans employing equal monthly payments is a home mortgage. Each installment or periodic payment made includes both a payment on the principal and an interest payment. This process of gradually eliminating the principal and its

TABLE 20.1

Monthly Payments Required to Amortize a $1,000 Loan					
Time	5%	5½%	6%	6½%	7%	7½%
5 yr	18.88	19.11	19.34	19.57	19.80	20.03
10	10.61	10.86	11.11	11.36	11.61	11.86
15	7.91	8.18	8.44	8.72	8.99	9.26
20	6.60	6.88	7.17	7.46	7.75	8.04
25	5.85	6.15	6.45	6.76	7.07	7.38

interest through equal payment intervals is known as *amortization*. To save time in calculating the amount of monthly payment, finance institutions make use of tables such as Table 20.1.

Given the time of the loan and interest rate per year, the monthly payment can be found. Other principals can be computed by this table, if they are expressed in terms of $1000. To express any number in terms of $1000, simply move the decimal point three places to the left.

Example. Find the monthly payment on a $2000 principal at 5% for 5 years.

2.000 times the monthly payment for $1000

$2 \times \$18.88 = \$37.76$.

Assuming the same terms, find the payment on a $500 principal.

.500 times the monthly payment for $1000

$.5 \times \$18.88 = \$9.44$.

Once the monthly payments are found, the company usually records all the pertinent information on a *loan payment schedule*.

Example. A $7000 loan is issued for 10 years at 6%. Fill out a loan payment schedule for the first three payments.

From the amortization table, a $1000 loan with these terms would require $11.11 monthly payments. For $7000, then, monthly payments of $77.77 would be required.

MONTHLY PAYMENT NO.	MONTHLY INSTALLMENT	PAYMENT ON INTEREST	PAYMENT ON PRINCIPAL	UNPAID BALANCE
				$7000.00
1	$77.77	$35.00	$42.77	6957.23
2	77.77	34.79	42.98	6914.25
3	77.77	34.57	43.20	6871.05

Since 6% a year is charged, $\frac{1}{2}$% is charged per month (6% ÷ 12). The interest for the first month is $7000 × .005, which equals $35. The second interest payment is then computed on the basis of the $6957.23 balance. The third interest payment is then computed on the basis of the second balance, and so forth.

A. Compute the total payments for the first five monthly periods if the following information is given and the constant principal payment method is used. The interest rates given here and in subsequent sections are *annual* rates, unless otherwise specified.

1. $1000 principal at 4%; the principal payment is $25 for each monthly period

1st = (a)
2nd =
3rd =
4th =
5th =

2. $7500 at 3%; the principal payment is $30 for each monthly period

1st =
2nd =
3rd = (b)
4th =
5th =

B. Compute the principal payments for the first five monthly periods if the following information is given and the constant total payment method is used.

1. $500 principal at 6%; total payment is $40 per month

1st = (a)
2nd =
3rd =
4th =
5th =

2. $2500 principal at 4%; total payment is $50 per month

1st =
2nd =
3rd = (b)
4th =
5th =

C. Given the following information, compute the rate of interest on the unpaid balance.

a. $8000 principal; 36 monthly payments of $300

1. $500 principal; 3 payments of $170

2. $1000 principal; 12 monthly payments of $86

D. Ralph Jackson borrowed $2000 at an interest rate of 5%. He agreed to make total monthly payments of $40. Complete the loan table below for the first five months of Mr. Jackson's loan.

PERIOD	MONTHLY PAYMENT	PAYMENT ON INTEREST	PAYMENT ON PRINCIPAL	UNPAID BALANCE
1	$40			
2	40			
3	40			
4	40			
5	40			

E. Given the following principal amounts and annual interest rates, match them correctly with the proper first-month interest payment.

1. $7400; 6% _____
2. $5800; $6\frac{1}{2}$% _____
3. $6450; 7% _____
4. $8100; $5\frac{1}{2}$% _____
5. $4900; $7\frac{1}{2}$% _____

a. $37.62
b. $30.63
c. $31.32
d. $37.00
e. $37.12

F. Solve the following problems.

1. Mrs. Boyle has a revolving charge account with the Dinwiddie Department Store. Her February balance there totaled $239.88, and she had charged one item at $35.99 during that month. If Dinwiddie demands a 15% minimum payment and places a 1.25% finance charge on the balance remaining after payments,

   a. What is the minimum payment required of Mrs. Boyle?
   b. What is the amount of the finance charge for February?

2. The Cranes have a limit of $450 on their revolving charge account at Roberts' Department Store. Their balance for the month of May is shown to be $278.00. They would like to charge a $235 sewing machine to their account, but first, some payment must be made or they will exceed their $450 limit.

   a. If the Cranes pay the minimum amount required (10% of the balance), will that payment sufficiently reduce their account balance so that they can charge the sewing machine? If not, how much more than the minimum amount must be paid?
   b. Roberts' computes a 1.5% finance charge on the remaining balance after payments made. What will be the amount of the finance charge for the Cranes' account?

3. Mr. Conway owns a business and often uses his Quikcharge credit card for various items. During the month of March he made the following Quikcharge purchases:

DATE	ITEM	AMOUNT
3/4	Business lunch	$12.50
3/12	Motel room (out of town meeting)	$25.00
3/12	Dinner at motel	$10.65
3/16	Business dinner	$26.90
3/17	Car rental	$37.50
3/26	Entertaining clients	$44.75
		TOTAL

   Assume that Mr. Conway's previous Quikcharge balance was $0. If he pays the full March account balance by April 30, there is no finance charge applicable. If he does not do this, any remainder will be subject to a 1% monthly finance charge.

   a. Mr. Conway decides to pay 75% of his March balance on April 20. What amount will he pay at that time?
   b. The remaining 25% of his account balance is subject to the above finance charge. If Mr. Conway will pay the rest of his March balance and the finance charge computed for the month of May by May 31, what will be the total amount due Quikcharge?

4. The Waltons have a mortgage of $27,500 on their new house. This will be repaid over 15 years at 6%. What is the monthly payment required if interest is included?

5. Using the above information, complete the loan payment schedule below for the Waltons' first three mortgage payments.

MONTH	INSTALLMENT PAYMENT	PAYMENT ON INTEREST	PAYMENT ON PRINCIPAL	UNPAID BALANCE
				$27,500
1	$232.10	_____	_____	_____
2	$232.10	_____	_____	_____
3	$232.10	_____	_____	_____

6. Mrs. Edwards has taken a loan of $650 from the Cromwell Finance Company. She makes nine monthly payments of $80 each. What is the rate of interest on the unpaid balance?

CHAPTER 21
Compound interest

In a savings account at a bank, the computation of interest is slightly more complicated. In this case, the bank pays interest to the depositor for the use of his money. Periodically, this interest is added to the principal and then earns interest itself. This method is known as the compound interest method or simply *compound interest*. The mechanics involved are illustrated in the following example.

Example. Compute the compound interest on the principal sum $5000 for three years at 3% interest compounded annually.

First, compute the simple interest for the first year at 3% employing the simple interest formula (see p. 177).

1st year: $I = P \times r \times T$
$$= \$5000 \times .03 \times 1$$
$$= \$150$$

This amount of interest is then added to the principal so that the principal now equals $5150 and the interest is computed for the second year.

2nd year: $I = P \times r \times T$
$$= (\$5000 + \$150) \times .03 \times 1 = \$5150 \times .03 \times 1$$
$$= \$154.50$$

Again, this new interest is added to the balance at the beginning of the year, so that the new principal is $5304.50. This new sum is the basis for the interest for the third year.

3rd year: $I = P \times r \times T$
$$= (\$5150 + \$154.50) \times 03 \times 1 = \$5304.50 \times .03 \times 1$$
$$= \$159.14$$

The balance at the end of three years is thus $5304.50 + $159.14, or a total of $5463.64. To find the total amount of compound interest, the original deposit is subtracted from the final balance.

Compound Amount = Final Balance − Original Deposit
$$= \$5463.64 - \$5000$$
$$= \$463.64$$

To compute compound interest this way is tedious, especially for a large number of years. There is a simple formula available, however, that can be used to shorten the calculation of compound interest. Given the rate of interest (r) and the number of years that interest is accumulated (n), the annual compounded amount (A) of a principal (P) is found by the following formula:

Compounded Amount = Principal(1 + Interest Rate)$^{\text{Number of Years}}$
$$A = P(1 + r)^n$$

Example. Employing the formula given above, find the compounded amount on $5000 for three years at 3% compounded annually.

$$
\begin{aligned}
A &= P(1 + r)^n \\
&= \$5000\,(1 + .03)^3 \\
&= \$5000 \times 1.093 \\
&= \$5465
\end{aligned}
$$

This result can be verified by the previous example. The small difference is due to using only three decimal places in the table.

Frequently banks will calculate the compound interest more than once a year. Interest may be compounded semiannually, quarterly, or even daily. To find the compounded amount (A) when interest is compounded i times a year, the following formula may be employed:

$$A = P\left(1 + \frac{r}{i}\right)^{ni}$$

Example. Find the compounded amount on $100 for two years at 8% compounded quarterly.

$$A = \$100\left(1 + \frac{.08}{4}\right)^{2 \times 4}$$

$$= \$100(1 + .02)^8 = \$100 \times 1.17165$$
$$= \$117.17$$

To compute compound interest quarterly is cumbersome, even when the number of years is small, and tables have been developed to facilitate the calculation. These tables show the amount $1.00 will grow if compounded at various interest rates and a various number of times. The table, in fact, provides the answer to the part of the compound interest equation shown below.

$$\left(1 + \frac{r}{i}\right)^{ni}$$

This number from the table must then be multiplied by the principal to arrive at the compounded amount. An example of a compound interest table is given in Table 21.1.

Example. Using the table, find the interest on $500 for three years at 12% compounded quarterly.

TABLE 21.1

Amount to which $1.00 Will Accumulate at Compound Interest

NUMBER OF PERIODS (N)	INTEREST RATE PER PERIOD							
	3%	4%	5%	6%	7%	8%	10%	12%
1	1.030	1.040	1.050	1.060	1.070	1.080	1.100	1.120
2	1.061	1.082	1.103	1.124	1.145	1.166	1.210	1.254
3	1.093	1.125	1.158	1.191	1.225	1.260	1.331	1.405
4	1.126	1.170	1.216	1.262	1.311	1.360	1.464	1.574
5	1.159	1.217	1.276	1.338	1.403	1.469	1.611	1.762
6	1.194	1.265	1.340	1.419	1.501	1.587	1.772	1.974
7	1.230	1.316	1.407	1.504	1.606	1.714	1.949	2.211
8	1.267	1.369	1.477	1.594	1.718	1.851	2.144	2.476
9	1.305	1.423	1.551	1.689	1.838	1.999	2.358	2.773
10	1.344	1.480	1.629	1.791	1.967	2.159	2.594	3.106
11	1.384	1.539	1.710	1.898	2.105	2.332	2.853	3.479
12	1.426	1.601	1.796	2.012	2.252	2.518	3.138	3.896
13	1.469	1.665	1.886	2.133	2.410	2.720	3.452	4.363
14	1.513	1.732	1.980	2.261	2.579	2.937	3.797	4.887
15	1.558	1.801	2.079	2.397	2.759	3.172	4.177	5.474
16	1.605	1.873	2.183	2.540	2.952	3.426	4.595	6.130
17	1.653	1.948	2.292	2.693	3.159	3.700	5.054	6.866
18	1.702	2.026	2.407	2.854	3.380	3.996	5.560	7.690
19	1.754	2.107	2.527	3.026	3.617	4.316	6.116	8.613
20	1.806	2.191	2.653	3.207	3.870	4.661	6.727	9.646
21	1.860	2.279	2.786	3.400	4.141	5.034	7.400	10.804
22	1.916	2.370	2.925	3.604	4.430	5.437	8.140	12.100
23	1.974	2.465	3.072	3.820	4.741	5.871	8.954	13.552
24	2.033	2.563	3.225	4.049	5.072	6.341	9.850	15.179
25	2.094	2.666	3.386	4.292	5.427	6.848	10.835	17.000
30	2.427	3.243	4.322	5.743	7.612	10.063	17.449	29.960
35	2.814	3.946	5.516	7.686	10.677	14.785	28.102	52.799
40	3.262	4.801	7.040	10.286	14.974	21.725	45.259	93.051
45	3.782	5.841	8.985	13.765	21.002	31.920	72.890	163.987
50	4.384	7.107	11.467	18.420	29.457	46.902	117.391	289.001

Three years compounded quarterly means that the interest will be calculated 12 times (3 × 4). Looking down the period column, we first find the "12" row. We now follow this row across until we reach the column headed 3% (12% ÷ 4). The figure here is 1.426. If we multiply this by $500, we obtain the balance or compounded amount at the end of three years.

$$A = \$500\left(1 + \frac{.12}{4}\right)^{3 \times 4} = \$500(1 + .03)^{12}$$

Compounded Amount = Deposit × Table Figure
$$= \$500 \times 1.426$$
$$= \$713$$

If we subtract the original deposit or amount from the compounded amount, we obtain the amount of interest accumulated.

$$\text{Compound Interest} = \text{Compounded Amount} - \text{Original Amount}$$
$$= \$713 - \$500.00$$
$$= \$213$$

Example. Find the compound interest on $750 for two years at 6% interest compounded semiannually.

$$A = \$750\left(1 + \frac{.06}{2}\right)^{2 \times 2} = \$750(1 + .03)^4$$

$$\text{Compounded Amount} = \text{Deposit} \times \text{Table Figure}$$
$$= \$750 \times 1.126$$
$$= \$844.500 = \$844.50$$

$$\text{Compound Interest} = \text{Compounded Amount} - \text{Original Amount}$$
$$= \$844.50 - \$750.00$$
$$= \$94.50$$

PRESENT VALUE

A concept closely related to compound interest is *present value*. If an individual is to receive $1.00 at some future date, he is worse off than if he receives it today. If the individual were to have $1.00 today, he could invest it at the current rate of interest and have more than $1.00 at some future date. In other words, the present value of a future claim to money is worth something less than its future value. If the interest rate is 10%, $1.00 received today and invested at 10% would be worth $1.21 two years from now. By the same reasoning, $1.21 to be received two years from now is worth only $1.00 today, and $1.00 received two years from now is worth something less than $1.00 today. If the interest rate is 10%, $1.00 received two years from now is worth only $.83 today, since $.83 at 10% compound interest is worth $1.00 in two years (check this for yourself). The present value of $1.00 to be received at some future date can also be found by using a table similar to Table 21.2.

The use of this table is similar to that of a compound interest table. Given the rate of interest and the number of years before $1.00 will be received, the present value of the future $1.00 may be found. To find the present value of a future sum of money given the rate of interest, locate in the table the present value of $1.00 received a number of years hence (n) and multiply the future sum by this number.

Example. Mr. Rogers expects to receive $1000 in five years. If the current interest rate is 4% compounded annually, what is the present value of the $1000?

First, find the present value of $1.00 from the table, $n = 5$, $i = .04$. This amount is .8219. The present value is then equal to this figure times the expected amount.

$$\text{Present Value} = \text{Table Figure} \times \text{Expected Amount}$$
$$= .8219 \times \$1000$$
$$= \$821.9 = \$821.90$$

TABLE 21.2

Present Value of $1.00

NUMBER OF PERIODS (N)	INTEREST RATE PER PERIOD							
	3%	4%	5%	6%	7%	8%	10%	12%
1	.9709	.9615	.9524	.9434	.9346	.9259	.9091	.8929
2	.9426	.9246	.9070	.8900	.8734	.8573	.8264	.7972
3	.9151	.8890	.8638	.8396	.8163	.7938	.7513	.7118
4	.8885	.8548	.8227	.7921	.7629	.7350	.6830	.6355
5	.8626	.8219	.7835	.7473	.7130	.6806	.6209	.5674
6	.8375	.7903	.7462	.7050	.6663	.6302	.5645	.5066
7	.8131	.7599	.7107	.6651	.6227	.5835	.5132	.4523
8	.7894	.7307	.6768	.6274	.5820	.5403	.4665	.4039
9	.7664	.7026	.6446	.5919	.5439	.5002	.4241	.3606
10	.7441	.6756	.6139	.5584	.5083	.4632	.3855	.3220
11	.7224	.6496	.5847	.5268	.4751	.4289	.3505	.2875
12	.7014	.6246	.5568	.4970	.4440	.3971	.3186	.2567
13	.6810	.6006	.5303	.4688	.4150	.3677	.2897	.2292
14	.6611	.5775	.5051	.4423	.3878	.3405	.2633	.2046
15	.6419	.5553	.4810	.4173	.3624	.3152	.2394	.1827
16	.6232	.5339	.4581	.3936	.3387	.2919	.2176	.1631
17	.6050	.5134	.4363	.3714	.3166	.2703	.1978	.1456
18	.5874	.4936	.4155	.3503	.2959	.2502	.1799	.1300
19	.5703	.4746	.3957	.3305	.2765	.2317	.1635	.1161
20	.5537	.4564	.3769	.3118	.2584	.2145	.1486	.1037
21	.5375	.4388	.3589	.2942	.2415	.1987	.1351	.0926
22	.5219	.4220	.3418	.2775	.2257	.1839	.1228	.0826
23	.5067	.4057	.3256	.2618	.2109	.1703	.1117	.0738
24	.4919	.3901	.3101	.2470	.1971	.1577	.1015	.0659
25	.4776	.3751	.2953	.2330	.1842	.1460	.0923	.0588
30	.4120	.3083	.2314	.1741	.1314	.0994	.0573	.0334
35	.3554	.2534	.1813	.1301	.0937	.0676	.0356	.0189
40	.3066	.2083	.1420	.0972	.0668	.0460	.0221	.0107
45	.2644	.1712	.1113	.0727	.0476	.0313	.0137	.0061
50	.2281	.1407	.0872	.0543	.0339	.0213	.0085	.0035

The same procedure can be used to determine the value of the expected future money payment next year. The calculation is the same except that the date receivable (*n*) will be four years instead of five years.

Example. Mr. Harris expects to receive $1000 in five years. If the current rate of interest is 12% compounded quarterly, what is the present value of $1000?

$$r = \frac{.12}{4} = .03 \qquad n = 5 \times 4 = 20$$

Using the above values of *r* and *n*, find the present value of $1.00 from the table. This amount is .5537. The present value is equal to this number times the expected future amount.

Present Value = .5537 × $1000 = $553.70

In the case of compound interest, we know the principal (or deposit) and want to find the future sum. In the case of the present value, just the opposite is true. We know the future amount and want to find its present value. The relationship between the present value (P) and the future value (R_n) is a simple one which we can derive directly from the formula for compound interest.

$$\text{Present Value} = P = \frac{R_n}{\left(1 \times \dfrac{r}{i}\right)^{ni}}$$

$$\text{Future Value} = R_n = P\left(1 + \frac{r}{i}\right)^{ni}$$

This association, as was discussed in Chapter 1, is called a *reciprocal relationship*. Therefore, there is a simple relationship between the Compound Interest Table and the Present Value of $1.00 Table. The present value factor is simply the reciprocal of the compound interest factor, and vice versa:

$$\text{Present Value Factor} = \frac{1}{\text{Compound Interest Factor}}$$

$$\text{Compound Interest Factor} = \frac{1}{\text{Present Value Factor}}$$

As a consequence of this reciprocal relationship, if we know the present value factor, we can find the compound interest factor by dividing 1 by the present value factor. The opposite is true if we are trying to find the present value factor. If only one table is available, that table can be used to find either amount.

A. Without using a table, compute the compounded amount and the compound interest for each of the following.

    a. $1000 for one year at 5% compounded semiannually
    1. $500 for two years at 4% compounded annually
    2. $2000 for one year at 8% compounded quarterly
    3. $3500 for two years at 3% compounded semiannually
    4. $750 for three years at 6% compounded semiannually
    5. $1250 for three years at 5% compounded annually

B. With the use of the Compound Interest Table, compute the compounded amount and the compound interest for each of the following.

    a. $500 for three years at 6% compounded semiannually
    2. $800 for three years at 8% compounded quarterly
    3. $2000 for six years at 10% compounded semiannually
    4. $3900 for five years at 10% compounded annually
    5. $1780 for two years at 36% compounded monthly

C. For each of the following problems, compute the compound interest and the simple interest. Compare the results by finding how much more can be earned by compound interest.

    a. $1000 for five years at 12% compounded quarterly and at simple interest
    1. $2500 for two years at 6% compounded semiannually and at simple interest
    2. $10,000 for four years at 5% compounded annually and at simple interest
    3. $7500 for five years at 6% compounded semiannually and at simple interest
    4. $8750 for one year at 12% compounded quarterly and at simple interest
    5. $14,300 for six years at 3% compounded annually and at simple interest

D. Solve each of the following problems.

    a. Danson Corporation deposits $10,000 a month in an account that pays 12% a year compounded quarterly. How much will Danson have in its account at the end of the year?

    1. Mr. Jackson deposited $20,000 at a rate of 3% compounded annually. How much can he expect to have earned in 20 years? How much more is this earning than if he had deposited the money in an account paying only simple interest?

    2. If Mr. Bruce borrows $5000 at 3% a year for six years and reinvests this money for the same length of time at 12% compounded quarterly, how much profit will he make on this type of financing?

    3. On a certain account of $5000, the Union Bank has paid interest of 6% compounded annually for nine years. How much interest has the bank paid?

4. Dr. Regis deposits $600 in a savings account that pays an interest rate of 6% compounded semiannually. What is the total amount Dr. Regis has in this account at the end of the first full year?

5. The Lawry Company deposits $6300 a month into a savings account that earns 10% interest compounded semiannually. At the end of twelve months, what is the total amount in this account?

6. Five years ago, at Mineral Savings Bank, Ms. Miller placed $7500 for her daughter's education in a savings account which pays 12% interest compounded quarterly. What is the current total value of the account?

7. The Bayard Company deposited $42,000 in a savings account at Gateway Bank, which has remained "untouched" while earning interest compounded semiannually. Now, exactly four years after the deposit was made, the account totals $57,498. What rate of interest (compounded semiannually) did Gateway Bank pay to Bayard's savings account?

A. Find the present value for each set of information given below.

	AMOUNT	EXPECTED IN	RATE	COMPOUNDED	PRESENT VALUE
a.	$ 1000	5 yr	3%	annually	
1.	500	3	6	semiannually	
2.	750	2	4	annually	
3.	1100	3	8	annually	
4.	1750	4	10	semiannually	
5.	2500	6	6	annually	
6.	2900	5	7	annually	
7.	11,700	7	12	quarterly	
8.	23,300	9	8	semiannually	
9.	31,050	10	6	annually	
10.	17,000	1	36	monthly	

B. Solve each of the following problems.

1. Mr. Timmons has calculated that by purchasing a piece of land he can expect a profit of $20,000 five years from now. If he had this money now, he could earn at least 6% compounded annually. What is the present value of the $20,000?

2. Miss Smith is considering an investment which would bring her $50,000 in ten years. If she could invest her money for ten years at 6% (compounded semiannually), what is the present value of the $50,000 she would receive? What would be its present value if it were received in 20 years?

CHAPTER 22
Rates of return

One of the most difficult tasks that confronts a businessman is to discover all his potential investment opportunities and then to evaluate which among them is the most profitable. The evaluation of alternative investment opportunities is especially difficult when they have different amounts of annual returns over different periods of time. For example, for a small machine shop, which is a better investment: to buy a drilling machine for $100, which will increase profits $20 a year for six years; or to purchase a machine for $125, which will increase profits $50 a year for three years?

In order to solve this type of problem, we must reduce the investment alternatives to some common measure in order to compare and evaluate them. There are three widely used methods for comparing investment opportunities: the payback period, the present value, and the internal rate of return.

THE PAYBACK PERIOD

The most widely used yardstick employed by businessmen to judge the relative attractiveness of alternative investment opportunities is the *payback period*. This method asks in how many years (p) will the additional cost savings or additional profits (R) pay back the cost of the investment (C). This may be stated in the form of a simple equation:

$$p = \frac{C}{R}$$

p = number of years to recover cost of investment (payback period)
C = cost of the investment
R = annual return on investment after taxes

In our previous example of the two drilling machines, the payback period of the first machine is five years and the payback period of the second initially more costly investment is $2\frac{1}{2}$ years.

Drilling machine I	Drilling machine II
$C = \$100$	$C = \$125$
$R = \$20$	$R = \$50$
$p = \dfrac{100}{20} = 5$ years	$p = \dfrac{125}{50} = 2\frac{1}{2}$ years

By this measure the investment costing $125 appears to be the superior choice. This rough-and-ready measure of comparing investments has three important short-comings.

1. It does not take into account the economic life of the investment. If the $100 drilling machine lasted 50 years instead of, say, only 10 years, it still would not change the length of the payback period, although if it lasted longer, it would increase the total profit over the life of the machine.

2. The formula assumes that the return (R) is uniform over the economic life of the investment, which is seldom true.

3. The payback period ignores the fact that future dollars are worth less than present dollars; one can always earn interest on present dollars.

To take account of the objections to the payback period, another type of rate of return has been devised which takes into account the lost interest incurred while waiting for an investment alternative to produce profits. This is the discounted rate of return which has two variant forms: *present value* and *internal rate of return*.

PRESENT VALUE OF INVESTMENT ALTERNATIVES

We have already seen in Chapter 21 that $1.00 to be received in five years has a present value less than $1.00 received next year because one can earn four years' interest before receiving $1.00 payable in five years. The formula for computing the present value (P) of any future receipt of money n years from now (R_n) is simply

$$P = \frac{R_n}{(1 + r)^n}$$

$P =$ present value of future receipt
$R_n =$ future receipt received n years from now
$r =$ rate of interest

For example, if the rate of interest is 6% compounded annually, the present value of $50 received three years from now is

$$P = \frac{R_n}{(1 + r)^n} = \frac{\$50}{(1 + .06)^3}$$

Looking up the value of $(1 + .06)^3$ in Table 21.2, we find it equal to .8396; therefore,

$$P = \$50 \times \frac{1}{(1 + .06)^3} = \$50 \times .8396 = \$41.98$$

We may now apply this principle of discounting to an investment that produces a stream of profits or cost savings annually over its life (R_n) and finally when its economic life is over is sold for scrap for an amount (S). The present value of the income stream produced by an investment is expressed by simply applying the discount formula to the net profits received each year (substituting R_n for V in the discount formula) and summing the result:

$$P = \frac{R_1}{(r+1)} + \frac{R_2}{(r+2)^2} + \frac{R_3}{(r+3)^3} - \cdots - \frac{R_n}{(1+r)^n} + \frac{S}{(1+r)^n}$$

P = present value
r = cost of capital (rate of interest)
R_i = net profits from investment in year i, $i = 1, 2, 3, \ldots, n$
S = scrap value

Applying this method to our drilling machine example, we get the following results, assuming a rate of interest of 6% and no scrap value (S):

$R_i = \$20$
$i = 1, 2, \ldots, 6$
$r = .06$
$S = 0$

$$P = \frac{\$20}{(1+.06)} + \frac{\$20}{(1+.06)^2} + \frac{\$20}{(1+.06)^3} + \frac{\$20}{(1+.06)^4} + \frac{\$20}{(1+.06)^5} + \frac{\$20}{(1+.06)^6}$$

$$+ \frac{0}{(1+.06)^6}$$

Using a discount table to find the present values of R_i by obtaining the values of

$\dfrac{1}{(1+.06)^n}$ we obtain

$$P = (20 \times .943) + (20 \times .890) + (20 \times .840) + (20 \times .792) + (20 \times .747)$$
$$+ (20 \times .705) + (0 \times .705)$$
$$= \$98.34$$

Here we see that the present value of the income stream produced by the drilling machine costing $100 is less than its original cost. The investment is therefore not worth making, since one could earn more money holding cash and investing it at the rate of interest of 6%.

The present value of the drilling machine costing $125 is calculated exactly the same way.

$R_i = \$50$
$i = 1, 2, 3$
$r = .06$
$S = 0$

$$P = \frac{\$50}{(1+.06)} + \frac{\$50}{(1+.06)^2} + \frac{\$50}{(1+.06)^3} + \frac{0}{(1+.06)^3}$$

$$P = \$133.65$$

The present value of the second drilling machine is $133.65, which is clearly higher than the first drilling machine and more than the cost of $125 for the machine, so that it would pay to make the investment. One could obtain a higher yield by investing one's money in the machine than investing it at the current rate of interest. The conclusion arrived at by this analysis is that drilling machine II is sufficiently profitable to make an investment in it.

THE INTERNAL RATE OF RETURN

The internal rate of return is similar to the present value method of evaluating investment alternatives. The present value method assumes a given rate of interest and computes the present value of the stream of income that the investment produces by discounting it. The internal rate of return, however, asks a different question. It sets the present value of the stream of income equal to the cost of the investment, and asks what rate of discount will make the discounted stream of annual income from the investment just equal to the cost of the investment. This method has the advantage that it is not necessary to presume a rate of interest that may not, in fact, prevail over the life of the investment. The formula for the internal rate of return is

$$C = P' = \frac{R_1}{(1 + r)} + \frac{R_2}{(1 + r)^2} + \cdots + \frac{R_n}{(1 + r)^n} + \frac{S}{(1 + r)^n}$$

C = cost of investment
P' = present value of net annual income produced by investment
R_i = net annual income produced by investment, $i = 1, 2, 3, \ldots, n$
r = rate of discount necessary to make $C = P'$
S = scrap value of investment

Applying this investment alternative to our two examples, we obtain the following results.

Internal Rate of Return of Investment Alternative I

First let us try the rate of interest of 6% as the rate of discount.

$R_n = \$20$
$i = 1, 2, 3, \ldots, 6$
$r = .06$
$S = 0$

$$P = \frac{\$20}{(1 + .06)} + \frac{\$20}{(1 + .06)^2} + \frac{\$20}{(1 + .06)^3} + \frac{\$20}{(1 + .06)^4} + \frac{\$20}{(1 + .06)^5}$$
$$+ \frac{\$20}{(1 + .06)^6} + \frac{0}{(1 + .06)^6}$$

Employing Table 21.2,

$P = (18.86) + (17.80) + (16.80) + (15.84) + (14.94) + (14.10) + (0)$
$P = \$98.34$

The answer, $98.34, is below the cost of the investment, so we try a lower rate of discount of 5%.

$$P = \frac{\$20}{(1+.05)} + \frac{\$20}{(1+.05)^2} + \frac{\$20}{(1+.05)^3} + \frac{\$20}{(1+.05)^4} + \frac{\$20}{(1+.05)^5}$$

$$+ \frac{\$20}{(1+.05)^6} + \frac{0}{(1+.05)^6}$$

Again employing Table 21.2 to simplify the calculations, we find:

$$P = 19.04 + 18.14 + 17.28 + 16.46 + 15.68 + 14.92 + 0$$
$$P = \$101.52$$

A rate of discount of 5% almost makes the present value of all the future annual returns from drilling machine I equal to its cost of acquisition. The true value of the internal rate of return must lie between 5 and 6%. To find this more precisely, we interpolate, using the method more fully explained in Chapter 33, and obtain:

$$\frac{101.52 - 100.00}{101.52 - 98.34} = \frac{x}{6.0 - 5.0}$$

$$\frac{1.52}{3.18} = \frac{x}{1.0}$$

$$3.18x = 1.52$$
$$x = .48$$

The internal rate of return, therefore, is equal to 5.48% or 5.5%.

Internal Rate of Return of Investment Alternative II

Applying the internal rate of return formula, we find that

$$C = \$125$$
$$R_i = \$50$$
$$i = 1, 2, 3$$
$$S = 0$$

$$\$125 = \frac{\$50}{(1+r)} + \frac{\$50}{(1+r)^2} + \frac{\$50}{(1+r)^3} + \frac{0}{(1+r)^3}$$

Trying a rate of interest of 10% and employing discount tables to facilitate the calculation, we obtain

$$C = \frac{\$50}{(1+.10)} + \frac{\$50}{(1+.10)^2} + \frac{\$50}{(1+.10)^3} + \frac{0}{(1+.10)^3}$$

$$C = \$124.43$$

This figure is slightly less than the $125 cost of drilling machine II, so we try 9%. We get the following result.

$$C = \frac{\$50}{(1+.09)} + \frac{\$50}{(1+.09)^2} + \frac{\$50}{(1+.09)^3} + \frac{0}{(1+.09)^3}$$

$$C = \$126.65$$

Clearly, the rate of interest that will make the present value of the income stream generated by investment II just equal to the cost of $125 of the drilling machine will lie between 9 and 10%. Interpolating between these two values we obtain the following results:

$$\frac{125.65 - 125.00}{125.65 - 124.43} = \frac{x}{10.0 - 9.0}$$

$$\frac{1.65}{2.22} = \frac{x}{1.0}$$

$$x = .74$$

The answer is then 9.74% or rounded to 9.7%.

It is obvious that an internal rate of return of 9.7% for investment alternative II is superior to a 5.5% yield for investment alternative I. As long as the cost of capital is below 9.7%, investment alternative II will be a profitable investment. If the cost of capital to the firm should rise above 9.7%, neither of the investments will be profitable compared to investing the money at the going rate of interest, so that neither investment alternative should be undertaken.

Also, all three methods showed the superiority of investment alternative II. In general, one should expect all three methods to yield similar results, especially if the life of the investment prospect is long and the rate of return on the investments high. The exact choice of methods will depend on how precise an answer one requires. For example, the payback period method may be employed to weed out the least attractive investment opportunities and the more precise methods may be applied in choosing among the remaining alternatives.

A. Given the following alternative investments, use the payback period method to determine which alternative Malcolm Manufacturing should invest in.

	INVESTMENT I	INVESTMENT II
a.	Drill press costing $200 increases revenue $25/yr	Drill press costing $210 increases revenue $30 yr
1.	Turret lathe costing $850 increases revenue $80/yr	Turret lathe costing $975 increases revenue $90 yr
2.	Assembly system costing $8000 increases revenue $3600/yr	Assembly system costing $7200 increases revenue $3300/yr
3.	Cut-out press costing $450 increases revenue $8/yr	Cut-out press costing $5500 increases revenue $9/yr
4.	High-lift storage machine costing $5700 increases revenue $200/yr	High-lift storage machine costing $6000 increases revenue $220/yr
5.	Conveyor belt apparatus costing $9600 increases revenue $1200/yr	Conveyor belt apparatus costing $10,200 increases revenue $1300/yr

B. Given the following information, decide between the alternative investments using the present value system. Assume there is no scrap value.

	INVESTMENT I				INVESTMENT II			
	COST	INCREASED REVENUE/YR	INTEREST	ESTIMATED LIFE	COST	INCREASED REVENUE/YR	INTEREST	ESTIMATED LIFE
a.	$ 700	$300	6%	5 yr	$ 650	$250	6%	6 yr
1.	300	60	4	3	400	60	4	5
2.	1000	450	5	4	1100	500	5	6

C. With the information given below, decide between the alternative investments using the internal rate of return method.

	COST	INCREASED REVENUE/YR	LIFE
Investment I	$200	$30	4 yr
Investment II	250	40	5

D. Solve each of the following problems.

1. If the current interest rate is 6%, what is the present value of $650 received five years from now?

2. A manager for Travis Housewares has recommended that the company should not invest in a new multimold converter. If the converter costs $2200 and will increase revenue by $700 for four years, do you agree or disagree with the manager's suggestion, assuming an interest rate of 5%. (Use either present value method or internal rate of return to justify your answer)

3. Jenson's Knitwear has the opportunity to purchase a two-year-old mechanized loom at a cost of $1500. If the original life of the loom was seven years and the machine will increase revenue $600 per year for the remaining years of its life, what is the internal rate of return?

4. Teakwood Gifts, Inc. must decide between two types of wood planers. The first planer costs $200 and will increase revenue $75 per year for three years. The second planer costs $180 and will increase revenue $50 per year for five years. If the current interest rate is 6%, in which planer should Teakwood invest?

CHAPTER 23
Annuities

People accumulate funds to provide retirement income, to send their children to school, to buy a house, to make regular investments, or to retire a debt. The question is posed, how much must be invested to achieve a given objective and how fast will these sums grow. An *annuity* is a fixed sum of money that is paid at regular fixed intervals. These periodic payments can be annual, semiannual, or made at any other interval provided that they are consistent. There are several important uses of annuities in business related to installment payments, insurance premiums, investment opportunities, and sinking funds.

The main classes of annuities are annuities certain and contingent annuities. *Annuities certain* have a specified number of payments, beginning and ending on specified dates, for example, when one is guaranteed to receive monthly payments for five full years beginning in January 19X4 and ending December 19X9. *Contingent annuities* run for an uncertain length of time depending on some event, such as when insurance companies agree to pay a certain sum to an individual until his death or recovery or some other specified happening.

Annuities can be further classified according to when the payments are made. *Ordinary annuities* have the payments paid at the end of each interval, while *annuities due* have payments made at the beginning of each interval.

ORDINARY ANNUITIES

The amount of an ordinary annuity is calculated in a manner similar to the calculation of compound interest. The total sum of the payments and interest due at the end of the annuity is called the *amount*.

Example. Find the amount of an ordinary annuity of $100 at 4% compound interest if invested at the end of the year each year for three years.

Solution 1.

$100.00 = investment at the end of the 1st year
+   4.00 = interest for the 2nd year

$104.00 = value of investment at end of 2nd year
+ 100.00 = invested at the end of 2nd year

   204.00 = value of investment at end of 2nd year
+   8.16 = interest for the 3rd year

   212.16 = value of investment at end of 3rd year
+ 100.00 = invested at the end of 3rd year

$312.16 = value of investment at end of 3rd year or the amount of the annuity

Since this is nothing more than compound interest, Table 21.1 can be used to solve this example.

TABLE 23.1

Amount to which $1.00 Received per End of Each Period Will Accumulate

NUMBER OF PERIODS (N)	INTEREST RATE PER PERIOD							
	3%	4%	5%	6%	7%	8%	10%	12%
1	1.000	1.000	1.000	1.000	1.000	1.000	1.000	1.000
2	2.030	2.040	2.050	2.060	2.070	2.080	2.100	2.120
3	3.091	3.122	3.153	3.184	3.215	3.246	3.310	3.374
4	4.184	4.246	4.310	4.375	4.440	4.506	4.641	4.779
5	5.309	5.416	5.526	5.637	5.751	5.867	6.105	6.353
6	6.468	6.633	6.802	6.975	7.153	7.336	7.716	8.115
7	7.662	7.898	8.142	8.394	8.654	8.923	9.487	10.089
8	8.892	9.214	9.549	9.897	10.260	10.637	11.436	12.300
9	10.159	10.583	11.027	11.491	11.978	12.488	13.579	14.776
10	11.464	12.006	12.578	13.181	13.816	14.487	15.937	17.549
11	12.808	13.486	14.207	14.972	15.784	16.645	18.531	20.655
12	14.192	15.026	15.917	16.870	17.888	18.977	21.384	24.133
13	15.618	16.627	17.713	18.882	20.141	21.495	24.523	28.029
14	17.086	18.292	19.599	21.015	22.550	24.215	27.975	32.393
15	18.599	20.024	21.579	23.276	25.129	27.152	31.772	37.280
16	20.157	21.825	23.657	25.673	27.888	30.324	35.950	42.753
17	21.762	23.698	25.840	28.213	30.840	33.750	40.545	48.884
18	23.414	25.645	28.132	30.906	33.999	37.450	45.599	55.750
19	25.117	27.671	30.539	33.760	37.379	41.446	51.159	63.440
20	26.870	29.778	33.066	36.786	40.995	45.762	57.275	72.052
21	28.676	31.969	35.719	39.993	44.865	50.423	64.002	81.699
22	30.537	34.248	38.505	43.392	49.006	55.457	71.403	92.502
23	32.453	36.618	41.430	46.996	53.436	60.893	79.543	104.603
24	34.426	39.083	44.502	50.816	58.177	66.765	88.497	118.155
25	36.459	41.646	47.727	54.865	63.249	73.106	98.347	133.334
30	47.575	56.085	66.439	79.058	94.461	113.283	164.494	241.332
35	60.462	73.652	90.320	111.435	138.237	172.317	271.024	431.663
40	75.401	95.026	120.800	154.762	199.635	259.057	442.593	767.088
45	92.720	121.029	159.700	212.744	285.749	386.506	718.905	1358.224
50	112.797	152.667	209.348	290.336	406.529	573.770	1163.909	2400.008

Solution 2. Since the first $100 was invested at the end of the first year, the investment does not earn interest for the full three years of the annuity, but only for the last two years. The second $100 only earns interest for the last year. The final $100 does not earn any interest. With this information, we can use the compound interest table.

$100 at the end of 1st year (4% for 2 years) = $108.16
$100 at the end of 2nd year (4% for 1 year) = $104.00
$100 at the end of 3rd year (4% for 0 years) = $100.00
                                                —————
                                                $312.16

Although these methods are not complex, tables have been constructed to make the calculations easier. Such a table is Table 23.1, which is derived for $1.00. To find amounts of annuities for investments other than $1.00, multiply the table figure by the amount of the investment. If the payments are made semiannually, double the years and halve the rate. If the payments are quarterly, take four times the years and one-fourth the rate. The following examples illustrate the use of Table 23.1.

Example. Find the value of a $200 annuity at 3% for eight years annually.

Value Amount of Annuity = Table Figure × Annuity Amount
                       = 8.892 × $200
                       = $1778.40

Example. Find the value of a $525 annuity at 8% compounded semiannually for three years. Since it is calculated semiannually, the interest is 4% (8% ÷ 2) for six periods (2 × 3).

Value Amount of Annuity = Table Figure × Annuity Amount
                       = 6.633 × $525
                       = $3482.32

ANNUITIES DUE

There is a close relationship between the value or cost of ordinary annuities and annuities due. The value of an annuity due may be found by finding the ordinary annuity for one period more than the period of the annuity due and then subtracting the amount of one annuity payment.

Annuity Due = (Ordinary Annuity for Period + 1) − 1 Annuity Due Payment

Example. Find the final value of a $200 annual annuity due at 4% for 6 years.

Annuity due = (Ordinary Annuity for Period + 1) − 1 Annuity Due Payment
            = ($200 at 4% for 6 + 1 periods) − $200
            = ($200 × 7.898) − $200
            = $1579.60 − $200
            = $1379.60

Example. Find the final value of a $550 semiannual annuity due at 6% for 3 years.

$$\text{Annuity due} = (\$550 \text{ at } 3\% \text{ for } 6 + 1 \text{ periods}) - \$550$$
$$= (\$550 \times 7.662) - \$550$$
$$= \$4214.10 - \$550$$
$$= \$3664.10$$

PRESENT VALUE

The final question to be considered is the present value of an annuity. The present value of an annuity is related to the present value of a future payment, as explained in Chapter 21. This relationship is used mainly when one wants to find what amount, at

TABLE 23.2

Present Value of $1.00 per Period

NUMBER OF PERIODS (N)	INTEREST RATE PER PERIOD							
	3%	4%	5%	6%	7%	8%	10%	12%
1	0.971	0.962	0.952	0.943	0.935	0.926	0.909	0.893
2	1.913	1.886	1.859	1.833	1.808	1.783	1.736	1.690
3	2.829	2.775	2.723	2.673	2.624	2.577	2.487	2.402
4	3.717	3.630	3.546	3.465	3.387	3.312	3.170	3.037
5	4.580	4.452	4.329	4.212	4.100	3.993	3.791	3.605
6	5.417	5.242	5.076	4.917	4.767	4.623	4.355	4.111
7	6.230	6.002	5.786	5.582	5.389	5.206	4.868	4.564
8	7.020	6.733	6.463	6.210	5.971	5.747	5.335	4.968
9	7.786	7.435	7.108	6.802	6.515	6.247	5.759	5.328
10	8.530	8.111	7.722	7.360	7.024	6.710	6.144	5.650
11	9.253	8.760	8.306	7.887	7.499	7.139	6.495	5.938
12	9.954	9.385	8.863	8.384	7.943	7.536	6.814	6.194
13	10.635	9.986	9.394	8.853	8.358	7.904	7.103	6.424
14	11.296	10.563	9.899	9.295	8.745	8.244	7.367	6.628
15	11.938	11.118	10.380	9.712	9.108	8.559	7.606	6.811
16	12.561	11.652	10.838	10.106	9.447	8.851	7.824	6.974
17	13.166	12.166	11.274	10.477	9.763	9.122	8.022	7.120
18	13.754	12.659	11.690	10.828	10.059	9.372	8.201	7.250
19	14.324	13.134	12.085	11.158	10.336	9.604	8.365	7.366
20	14.877	13.590	12.462	11.470	10.594	9.818	8.514	7.469
21	15.415	14.029	12.821	11.764	10.836	10.017	8.649	7.562
22	15.937	14.451	13.163	12.042	11.061	10.201	8.772	7.645
23	16.444	14.857	13.489	12.303	11.272	10.371	8.883	7.718
24	16.936	15.247	13.799	12.550	11.469	10.529	8.985	7.784
25	17.413	15.622	14.094	12.783	11.654	10.675	9.077	7.843
30	19.600	17.292	15.372	13.765	12.409	11.258	9.427	8.055
35	21.487	18.665	16.374	14.498	12.948	11.655	9.644	8.176
40	23.115	19.793	17.159	15.046	13.332	11.925	9.779	8.244
45	24.519	20.720	17.774	15.456	13.606	12.108	9.863	8.283
50	25.730	21.482	18.256	15.762	13.801	12.233	9.915	8.305

a given interest rate, must be invested now to yield a periodic fixed annuity for a specified time. As in Chapter 21, tables are available for the present value of an annuity for $1.00. Table 23.2 is such a table and to find the present value, multiply the table figure by the value of the annuity.

Example. What amount must be invested now at 8% to yield an annuity of $2000 semiannually for 3 years?

Semiannually for 3 years means 6 annuity payments. From the table, using 4% (.08 ÷ 2) and 6 periods, we find the figure 5.242. If we multiply this figure by the anticipated yield, $2000, we obtain the present value.

Present Value = Table Figure × Anticipated Yield
= 5.242 × $2000
= $10,484

A. *Without* using the table, find the final value of the following ordinary annuities and annuities due.

   a. Annual ordinary annuity of $500 at 8% compound interest for three years
   1. Annual ordinary annuity of $1000 at 5% compound interest for four years
   2. Semiannual ordinary annuity of $100 at 6% compound interest for two years
   3. Annual annuity due of $400 at 7% compound interest for three years
   4. Semiannual annuity due of $500 at 6% compound interest for one year
   5. Annual annuity due of $1000 at 8% compound interest for six years

B. Using the table, find the final value of the following ordinary annuities and annuities due.

   a. Annual annuity due of $1000 at 5% compound interest for six years
   1. Semiannual annuity due of $500 at 8% compound interest for five years
   2. Semiannual ordinary annuity of $11,000 at 6% compound interest for three years
   3. Annual ordinary annuity of $22,500 at 7% compound interest for nine years
   4. Annual annuity due of $13,000 at 5% compound interest for ten years
   5. Semiannual ordinary annuity of $17,500 at 6% compound interest for four years

C. Solve the following problems.

   a. Mr. Jasper must pay an annual ordinary annuity of $500 at 6% for five years. What is the difference in the value of the annuity he would have to pay if the annuity were an annual annuity due?

   1. Jefferson Manufacturing Co. decided to deposit $10,000 at the end of each year for five years at an interest rate of 6%. What amount of money will they have at the end of the five-year period?

   2. Mr. Sanford took out a $2000 installment loan upon which he must pay $100 principal at the beginning of each year for 20 years, plus 6% interest on the unpaid balance. What is the total amount of money he will have paid at the end of 20 years? (Hint: the total amount paid in an installment loan with the principal constant is equal to an annuity due for the same period of time.)

   3. Tillson Textiles expansion plans reveal that they will need $5,000 a year for the next 10 years. If the present interest rate is 5%, what amount must be invested now to yield the needed $5000 a year?

   4. What amount must be invested now at 12% to yield an annuity of $500 quarterly for three years?

   5. Mr. Rogers wants to provide $10,000 for his son's education when he enters college ten years from now. How much must he save semiannually to achieve this objective if he can invest at 8%?

6. Miss Heinz invested $5,000 in a mutual fund. After six years this had increased to $30,000, at which time she wished to convert this sum to an annuity making equal semiannual payments over ten years. What would the amount of these payments be at an interest rate of 6%

CHAPTER 24
Insurance

The basic idea of insurance is to pay certain fixed small amounts of money periodically to eliminate the possibility of large future loss due to some unforeseen and uncertain event. The payments made to the insurance companies are known as *premiums*. These premiums are established after careful analysis of statistical data concerning the probability of losses due to the potential risks. The premiums are also dependent on the amount of risk accepted by the insurance company. Determining the amount of risk can be a highly complex decision. For example, in the insurance against the loss of life, such things as age, health, and occupation may affect the possibility of death in a certain period. The possibility of property loss by fire may be affected by location, construction, and age of the property.

A full discussion of insurance is not possible here. We can, however, examine the two basic types of insurance in general use.

LIFE INSURANCE

An individual wishing to take out a life insurance policy can choose from any of the following types of contracts.

Term Policy or Pure Insurance. This is a policy that is issued for a limited time. Payment is made only if the insured dies during the term of the policy. In the event that the insured lives, the policy is terminated at the end of the protection period and the insured receives nothing. This type of policy provides the maximum amount of insurance per dollar of premium. It is pure insurance in that it contains no element of savings, as in other "permanent" types of insurance.

Straight Policy. The premiums on this type of policy must be paid every year until the death of the insured. At that time, the value of the policy is paid to a person called the beneficiary, who is designated by the insured when he takes out the policy.

Limited Payment Life. This policy requires premiums to be paid for a specified number of years or until the insured dies if this happens before the premium payment period ends.

Endowment Policy. This type of policy either pays if the insured dies during the term of the policy or pays the insured the same amount at the end of a specified term if he survives.

Premiums differ from contract to contract and from company to company. Hypothetical premium schedules are given in Table 24.1.

TABLE 24.1

Premiums per $1,000 of Insurance

Age Nearest Birthday	5-YEAR RENEWABLE TERM		10-YEAR TERM		ORDINARY LIFE		LIFE PAID-UP AT 65		Age Nearest Birthday
	Annual	Monthly	Annual	Monthly	Annual	Monthly	Annual	Monthly	
20	$4.44	$.39	$4.37	$.39	$13.09	$1.16	$14.24	$1.26	20
21	4.47	.39	4.41	.39	13.44	1.19	14.66	1.29	21
22	4.48	.40	4.43	.39	13.78	1.22	15.09	1.33	22
23	4.52	.40	4.47	.39	14.15	1.25	15.55	1.37	23
24	4.57	.40	4.51	.40	14.53	1.28	16.04	1.42	24
25	4.60	.41	4.57	.40	14.93	1.32	16.55	1.46	25
26	4.65	.41	4.64	.41	15.35	1.36	17.09	1.51	26
27	4.71	.42	4.70	.42	15.78	1.39	17.67	1.56	27
28	4.79	.42	4.80	.42	16.25	1.44	18.29	1.62	28
29	4.86	.43	4.90	.43	16.72	1.48	18.94	1.67	29
30	4.95	.44	5.04	.45	17.23	1.52	19.62	1.73	30
31	5.05	.45	5.19	.46	17.77	1.57	20.35	1.80	31
32	5.19	.46	5.38	.48	18.33	1.62	21.14	1.87	32
33	5.35	.47	5.60	.49	18.92	1.67	21.98	1.94	33
34	5.55	.49	5.87	.52	19.54	1.73	22.87	2.02	34
35	5.79	.51	6.15	.54	20.19	1.78	23.81	2.10	35
36	6.06	.54	6.47	.57	20.88	1.84	24.84	2.19	36
37	6.40	.57	6.85	.61	21.60	1.91	25.94	2.29	37
38	6.76	.60	7.28	.64	22.36	1.98	27.13	2.40	38
39	7.17	.63	7.69	.68	23.16	2.05	28.40	2.51	39
40	7.61	.67	8.12	.72	24.01	2.12	29.77	2.63	40
41	8.09	.71	8.58	.76	24.91	2.20	31.26	2.76	41
42	8.63	.76	9.11	.80	25.84	2.28	32.87	2.90	42
43	9.19	.81	9.71	.86	26.82	2.37	34.63	3.06	43
44	9.82	.87	10.35	.91	27.88	2.46	36.55	3.23	44
45	10.52	.93	11.07	.98	28.98	2.56	38.65	3.41	45
46	11.30	1.00	11.88	1.05	30.15	2.66	40.97	3.62	46
47	12.16	1.07	12.80	1.13	31.39	2.77	43.53	3.85	47
48	13.11	1.16	13.81	1.22	32.71	2.89	46.40	4.10	48
49	14.17	1.25	14.93	1.32	34.10	3.01	49.60	4.38	49
50	15.34	1.35	16.20	1.43	35.59	3.14	53.22	4.70	50
51	16.61	1.47	17.37	1.53	37.17	3.28	57.31	5.06	51
52	17.92	1.58	18.65	1.65	38.85	3.43	62.02	5.48	52
53	19.28	1.70	20.07	1.77	40.63	3.59	67.47	5.96	53
54	20.80	1.84	21.61	1.91	42.55	3.76	73.88	6.53	54
55	22.49	1.99	23.31	2.06	44.57	3.94	81.50	7.20	55
56	21.28	1.88	22.65	2.00	43.95	3.88	87.44	7.72	56
57	22.91	2.02	24.43	2.16	45.92	4.06	98.36	8.69	57
58	24.70	2.18	26.37	2.33	48.00	4.24	112.32	9.92	58
59	26.63	2.35	28.47	2.51	50.21	4.44	130.86	11.56	59
60	28.76	2.54	30.76	2.72	52.55	4.64	156.75	13.85	60

TABLE 24.1 (*cont.*)

Premiums per $1,000 of Insurance—continued

Age Nearest Birthday	20-PAY LIFE Annual	20-PAY LIFE Monthly	ENDOWMENT AT AGE 65 Annual	ENDOWMENT AT AGE 65 Monthly	20-YEAR ENDOWMENT Annual	20-YEAR ENDOWMENT Monthly	Age Nearest Birthday
20	$21.93	$1.94	$17.04	$1.51	$43.46	$3.84	20
21	22.37	1.98	17.56	1.55	43.48	3.84	21
22	22.82	2.02	18.12	1.60	43.51	3.84	22
23	23.28	2.06	18.71	1.65	43.54	3.85	23
24	23.74	2.10	19.32	1.71	43.59	3.85	24
25	24.23	2.14	19.98	1.76	43.62	3.85	25
26	24.73	2.18	20.67	1.83	43.68	3.86	26
27	25.24	2.23	21.40	1.89	43.74	3.86	27
28	25.78	2.28	22.18	1.96	43.80	3.87	28
29	26.32	2.32	23.00	2.03	43.88	3.88	29
30	26.89	2.38	23.87	2.11	43.97	3.88	30
31	27.48	2.43	24.80	2.19	44.09	3.89	31
32	28.09	2.48	25.81	2.28	44.20	3.90	32
33	28.72	2.54	26.86	2.37	44.35	3.92	33
34	29.37	2.59	28.00	2.47	44.51	3.93	34
35	30.06	2.66	29.22	2.58	44.70	3.95	35
36	30.75	2.72	30.53	2.70	44.91	3.97	36
37	31.50	2.78	31.93	2.82	45.15	3.99	37
38	32.26	2.85	33.45	2.95	45.43	4.01	38
39	33.07	2.92	35.09	3.10	45.72	4.04	39
40	33.90	2.99	36.86	3.26	46.07	4.07	40
41	34.79	3.07	38.77	3.42	46.46	4.10	41
42	35.69	3.15	40.86	3.61	46.88	4.14	42
43	36.63	3.24	43.12	3.81	47.32	4.18	43
44	37.62	3.32	45.62	4.03	47.82	4.22	44
45	38.65	3.41	48.36	4.27	48.36	4.27	45
46	39.73	3.51	51.39	4.54	48.96	4.32	46
47	40.85	3.61	54.75	4.84	49.60	4.38	47
48	42.06	3.72	58.51	5.17	50.31	4.44	48
49	43.29	3.82	62.74	5.54	51.10	4.51	49
50	44.62	3.94	67.52	5.96	51.95	4.59	50
51	46.02	4.06	72.98	6.45	52.91	4.67	51
52	47.50	4.20	79.26	7.00	53.95	4.77	52
53	49.07	4.33	86.57	7.65	55.08	4.87	53
54	50.75	4.48	95.18	8.41	56.34	4.98	54
55	52.54	4.64	105.49	9.32	57.72	5.10	55
56	51.43	4.54	113.74	10.05	55.96	4.94	56
57	53.09	4.69	128.62	11.36	57.24	5.06	57
58	54.85	4.84	147.72	13.05	58.63	5.18	58
59	56.72	5.01	173.19	15.30	60.15	5.31	59
60	58.71	5.19	208.90	18.45	61.79	5.46	60

The premiums on life insurance policies can be paid annually, semiannually, quarterly, or even monthly. Because of lower bookkeeping costs, it is cheaper to pay the premium annually. The premium table given here is for $1000 worth of insurance. The premium for amounts other than $1000 can be computed by dividing the desired amount by 1000 and multiplying this result by the premium given for $1000 worth of the same insurance. In equation form, this is

$$\text{Premium} = \frac{\text{Desired Amount of Insurance}}{1000} \times \text{Premium Given for \$1000.}$$

Example. Find the annual premium on $7000 worth of 20-payment life insurance issued at age 35.

$$\text{Premium} = \frac{7000}{1000} \times \$30.06$$

$$= 7 \times \$30.06$$
$$= \$210.42$$

If the annual premium is known and a table is unavailable, a close approximation of semiannual, quarterly, and monthly premiums can be found by a schedule similar to the one in Table 24.2.

TABLE 24.2

Periodic Premium Schedule	
Period	Multiply Annual Premium by
Semiannual	.51
Quarterly	.26
Monthly	.087

Example. What is the semiannual, quarterly, and monthly premium on $1000 worth of straight life insurance issued at age 15 with an annual premium of $15.78?

$$\text{Semiannual} = \$15.78 \times .51$$
$$= \$8.05$$
$$\text{Quarterly} = \$15.78 \times .26$$
$$= \$4.10$$
$$\text{Monthly} = \$15.78 \times .087$$
$$= \$1.37$$

TABLE 24.3

Cash Surrender and Loan Value for Policies Issued at Age 35 for $1,000

End of policy year	CASH SURRENDER AND LOAN VALUE			
	Term	Straight	20-payment	20-year Endowment
3		$ 25	$ 50	$ 95
5	No Cash Surrender	40	100	200
10	or Loan Value	120	250	450
15		200	400	720
20		300	575	1,000

Most insurance companies make it possible to cash in the policy during its term. The amount received, if an individual turns in his policy, is called the *cash surrender value*. An individual can also borrow an amount of money against his policy, known as the *loan value* of the policy. Usually an interest charge is placed on such loans. In many cases, the cash surrender value and the loan value are the same. A hypothetical value schedule is given in Table 24.3. The procedure for calculating amounts other than $1000 is the same as explained previously.

Example. Mr. Fredericks decides to cash in a 20-year endowment policy after 10 years. If the face value of the policy is $10,000, how much cash does Mr. Fredericks receive?

From the table, a $1000 policy would be worth $450.

$$\text{Cash value} = \frac{\$10,000}{\$1000} \times \$450$$

$$= 10 \times \$450$$
$$= \$4500$$

FIRE INSURANCE

Premiums on fire insurance policies are usually quoted as so many cents for $100 worth of insurance. If the amount is greater, as is the usual case, simply divide the desired amount by $100 and multiply this result by the cost per $100. In equation form, this is

$$\text{Premium} = \frac{\text{Desired Amount}}{100} \times \text{Cost of \$100 Worth of Insurance}$$

Example. Find the yearly premium of $17,000 worth of fire insurance at a rate of $.26 per $100 worth of insurance.

$$\text{Premium} = \frac{\$17,000}{100} \times \$.26$$

$$= 170 \times \$.26$$
$$= \$44.20$$

Premiums for fire insurance policies are paid on a yearly basis; however, discounts are given if the premium is paid for more than one year at a time. These discounts are similar to the hypothetical schedule given in Table 24.4.

TABLE 24.4

Insurance Rates for Periods Greater Than 1 Year	
Period	Rate
2 yr	1.85 times the yearly premium
3	2.70
4	3.55
5	4.40

Many times a policy must be canceled by the insured before a full year expires. In this case, the amount of the premium for the unused insurance is returned to the insured. The amount retained by the company can be found by the Standard Short Rate Table given in Table 24.5. If the policy is canceled by the insurer, the amount returned is simply the premium times the number of days the insurance was in force divided by 365.

TABLE 24.5

Standard Short-Rate Table for Computing Premiums for Terms Less Than 1 Year

Days in force	%	Days in force	%	Days in force	%
1	5	92– 94	36	215–218	68
2	6	95– 98	37	219–223	69
3– 4	7	99–102	38	224–228	70
5– 6	8	103–105	39	229–232	71
7– 8	9	106–109	40	233–237	72
9–10	10	110–113	41	238–241	73
11–12	11	114–116	42	242–246 (8 mos.)	74
13–14	12	117–120 (4 mos.)	43	247–250	75
15–16	13	121–124	44	251–255	76
17–18	14	125–127	45	256–260	77
19–20	15	128–131	46	261–264	78
21–22	16	132–135	47	265–269	79
23–25	17	136–138	48	270–273 (9 mos.)	80
26–29	18	139–142	49	274–278	81
30–32 (1 mo.)	19	143–146	50	279–282	82
33–36	20	147–149	51	283–287	83
37–40	21	150–153 (5 mos.)	52	288–291	84
41–43	22	154–156	53	292–296	85
44–47	23	157–160	54	297–301	86
48–51	24	161–164	55	302–305 (10 mos.)	87
52–54	25	165–167	56	306–310	88
55–58	26	168–171	57	311–314	89
59–62 (2 mos.)	27	172–175	58	315–319	90
63–65	28	176–178	59	320–323	91
66–69	29	179–182 (6 mos.)	60	324–328	92
70–73	30	183–187	61	329–332	93
74–76	31	188–191	62	333–337 (11 mos.)	94
77–80	32	192–196	63	338–342	95
81–83	33	197–200	64	343–346	96
84–87	34	201–205	65	347–351	97
88–91 (3 mos.)	35	206–209	66	352–355	98
		210–214 (7 mos.)	67	356–360	99
				361–365 (12 mos.)	100

Example. How much money was returned to a policyholder who canceled a fire insurance policy after 48 days? The yearly premium had been $33.40.

From the table, the amount retained by the company for 48 days of coverage is 24% of the premium.

$$\text{Amount Retained} = .24 \times \$33.40$$
$$= \$8.02$$
$$\text{Amount Returned} = \$33.40 - \$8.02$$
$$= \$25.38$$

Fire insurance policies are of two basic types: ordinary and 80% coinsurance. *Ordinary fire insurance* policies cover 100% of any loss up to the face value of the policy. Naturally, if the loss is greater than the amount of the policy, only the face value will be paid.

Example. Mr. Kingston's paintings and furniture are valued at $25,000. If he carries $20,000 worth of ordinary fire insurance, how much will he be paid if he suffers a fire loss of $15,000? of $20,000? of $22,500?

The policy will cover any loss up to $20,000. Thus, if the loss were $15,000, he would be paid $15,000. If it were $20,000, he would be paid $20,000. If it were $22,500, however, he would receive only the face value of the policy: $20,000.

The second type of policy is one that contains an *80% coinsurance clause*. An individual can obtain a policy for smaller premiums if this clause is included. In essence, with the inclusion of this 80% clause, the insurance company agrees to pay only a fraction of the loss and the insured must bear the rest. This fraction is determined from the value of the property and the face value of the policy. The denominator of this fraction is equal to 80% of the value of the property. The numerator is the face value of the policy itself. The resulting fraction is what part of any fire loss, up to the face value of the policy, the company must pay.

$$\text{Insurance Paid Under 80\% Clause} = \frac{\text{Face Value of Policy}}{80\% \text{ Property Value}} \times \text{Loss}$$

Example. Mr. Donaldson's house and furniture are valued at $60,000. If they are insured for $36,000, 80% coinsurance, what amount would the company pay if a fire caused $24,000 worth of damages?

$$\text{Insurance Paid} = \frac{\text{Face Value of Policy}}{80\% \text{ Property Value}} \times \text{Loss}$$

$$= \frac{\$36,000}{.80 \times \$60,000} \times \$24,000$$

$$= \frac{\$36,000}{\$48,000} \times \$24,000$$

$$= \frac{3}{4} \times \$24,000$$

$$= \$18,000$$

A. Using the sample premium schedule, compute the annual total premium for each of the policy contracts below.

	POLICY	AGE AT ISSUE	TYPE OF PAYMENTS	FACE VALUE	TOTAL ANNUAL PREMIUM
a.	10-year term	30	Annual	$20,000	
1.	Straight life	25	Semiannual	$1,000	
2.	20-year endowment	40	Quarterly	$15,000	
3.	20-payment life	20	Semiannual	$4,000	
4.	5-year term	35	Annual	$8,000	
5.	Straight life	50	Quarterly	$25,000	
6.	20-year endowment	45	Annual	$11,000	
7.	Straight life	20	Semiannual	$2,000	
8.	20-payment life	25	Annual	$10,000	
9.	20-payment life	30	Quarterly	$30,000	
10.	20-year endowment	40	Semiannual	$17,000	

B. Given the annual premium payments, find the semiannual, quarterly, and monthly premiums for the policy contracts below.

	POLICY	TOTAL ANNUAL PREMIUM	SEMIANNUAL	QUARTERLY	MONTHLY
a.	20-payment life	$42.60			
1.	10-year term	$12.10			
2.	5-year term	$9.56			
3.	Straight life	$37.15			
4.	20-year endowment	$53.17			
5.	20-payment life	$550.15			

C. Solve the following problems employing the appropriate tables in the text.

1. Mr. Donaldson cashed in a 20-payment life policy issued at age 35 after 15 years. If the face value were $20,000, how much did Mr. Donaldson receive?

2. At age 35, Mr. Wilson took out a 20-year endowment policy. In ten years, he plans to cash it in. If the face value of the policy is $10,000, how much more will he receive than he will have paid?

3. Mr. Benton, age 40, has decided to take out a 20-payment life policy. How much will Mr. Benton save a year by paying annually instead of semiannually or quarterly?

4. At age 35, Tom Hendricks took out a 20-year endowment policy. After 15 years he wanted to borrow money on his policy. If the face value were $5000, how much could he borrow?

ASSIGNMENT 37 FIRE INSURANCE

A. Given the information below, find the total premium due.

	AMOUNT OF INSURANCE	COST PER $100	PAYMENT PERIOD	PREMIUM PAYMENT
a.	$10,000	$.24	3 yr	
1.	$17,000	$.32	2	
2.	$24,000	$.16	1	
3.	$27,000	$.41	3	
4.	$30,000	$.36	4	
5.	$37,000	$.22	5	
6.	$41,000	$.19	3	
7.	$12,000	$.43	4	
8.	$15,000	$.26	1	
9.	$20,000	$.29	2	
10.	$22,000	$.31	5	

B. Given the information below, compute the amount of premium refunded.

	ANNUAL PREMIUM	NO. OF DAYS COVERAGE IN EFFECT BEFORE CANCELLATION	AMOUNT REFUNDED
a.	$36.40	36	
1.	$41.50	41	
2.	$16.90	54	
3.	$54.35	17	
4.	$28.45	73	
5.	$33.15	216	
6.	$57.00	91	
7.	$47.88	240	
8.	$18.80	68	
9.	$36.39	29	
10.	$40.40	14	

C. Given the information below, compute the amount paid by the insurance company for each fire loss.

	TYPE OF POLICY	FACE VALUE OF POLICY	VALUE OF PROPERTY	AMOUNT OF LOSS FROM FIRE	AMOUNT PAID BY COMPANY
a.	80% coinsurance	$20,000	$26,000	$18,000	
1.	Ordinary	$15,000	$20,000	$17,000	
2.	Ordinary	$17,500	$17,500	$15,000	
3.	80% coinsurance	$20,000	$25,000	$18,000	
4.	80% coinsurance	$25,000	$50,000	$24,000	
5.	Ordinary	$30,000	$50,000	$37,000	
6.	80% coinsurance	$32,000	$43,000	$40,000	
7.	80% coinsurance	$24,000	$26,000	$20,000	
8.	Ordinary	$25,000	$30,000	$25,000	
9.	Ordinary	$20,000	$25,000	$21,500	
10.	80% coinsurance	$30,000	$35,000	$25,000	

CHAPTER 25
Stocks and bonds

Companies require large amounts of money to finance their operations. One way they can acquire this money is by issuing securities, which are of two main types. First, they can issue *stock*, a certificate which, upon purchase, makes the buyer a fractional owner of the company. How much the buyer owns depends on the number of shares of stock purchased. Second, the company can borrow by issuing *bonds*, which are promissory notes issued at a fixed rate of interest that offer some security that the debt will be paid. Thus, in the case of stocks, the purchaser becomes an owner; while in the case of bonds, the purchaser becomes a creditor.

STOCKS

In many cases stocks have a value printed on them. This value is known as the *par value*, but does not necessarily mean that the price will be the same in the market. Usually, the par value and market value are different. Stocks without this value stated are called *no par value* stocks.

Stocks can be divided into two major categories: preferred and common. *Preferred stockholders* are usually entitled to special dividend privileges. A *dividend* is a part of total profits for the year that the directors of a company distribute to the stockholders. Usually, preferred stock is guaranteed to receive a fixed percent of par value per year if the company makes a profit. After the preferred dividend is paid, any profit remaining after the company decides on the amount needed for reinvestment is divided and distributed to the *common stockholders*. Thus, the dividend for preferred stock is dependent basically on the stated percent and par value, while the dividend for common stock is dependent on the level of profit for the year. Common stockholders have the right to vote for the directors of the corporation. Preferred stock can also be divided into two classes. If the stock guarantees that the company in future years will pay any dividends that they were unable to pay due to a low profit level, the preferred stock is called *cumulative*. If, however, no provision is made to pay dividends after the year in which they should be distributed, the preferred stock is *noncumulative*.

Example. Malcolm Manufacturing's portion of net profit for 19X9 to be distributed to stockholders was $13,500. If they had 10,000 shares outstanding of preferred 4% stock with a par value of $20, how much would be distributed as dividends to both the preferred and common stockholders?

Since the preferred dividend is based on the par value, we must compute 4% of $20.

$$\begin{aligned}\text{Preferred Dividend} &= \% \times \text{Par Value}\\ &= .04 \times \$20\\ &= \$.80/\text{share}\end{aligned}$$

To compute the total distributed to preferred stockholders, multiply the dividend per share times the number of shares.

$$\begin{aligned}\text{Preferred Dividend} &= 10{,}000 \times \$.80\\ &= \$8{,}000\end{aligned}$$

Since the remaining profit after preferred dividends are paid belongs to the common stockholders, we must subtract as follows.

$$\begin{aligned}\text{Common Dividend} &= \text{Distributed Profit} - \text{Preferred Dividend}\\ &= \$13{,}500 - \$8{,}000\\ &= \$5{,}500\end{aligned}$$

Purchasing and Selling Stock

Since buyers do not usually know who the sellers are, and vice versa, stockbrokers facilitate buying and selling. *Stockbrokers* are agents who handle transactions involving stock. Central trading exchanges are set up in large cities across the country. The best

19X9 High.	Low.	Stocks and Div. In Dollars.	Sls. 100s.	First.	High.	Low.	Last.	Net Chge.
29⅜	18	DentsplyInt 1	5	22¼	22⅝	22¼	22⅝	+ ⅜
18	13⅝	DenRGr 1.10	7	14⅞	14⅞	14¾	14¾	— ⅜
62¼	34	Dereco pf A	1	37¼	37¼	37¼	37¼	— ⅛
31¼	12½	DeSotoInc .40	14	18	18¼	18	18¼	+ ⅜
23½	17⅛	DetEdis 1.40	116	18	18⅛	18	18⅛	+ ⅛
85½	70¼	Det Ed pf5.50	1	73	73	73	73	....
16¾	8¾	Det Steel	4	12⅞	13	12⅞	12⅞	....
32⅜	15⅝	Dexter .24	7	16½	16¾	16½	16¾	+ ⅛
15	8⅛	DialFinan .40	3	11	11	10⅞	10⅞	— ⅛
42⅞	28¼	DiamIntl 1.80	54	35⅛	35⅞	35⅛	35⅞	+1⅛
20⅜	11⅞	Diam Sham 1	205	18⅛	18⅜	18	18¼	+ ⅛
17½	13¼	DiaS pf D1.20	7	15	15¼	15	15¼	+ ⅛
24⅞	8	Dictaphon .48	47	11⅜	11⅝	11⅛	11½	....
72¾	48⅞	Diebold 48b	6	59¼	59⅞	59¼	59⅞	+ ⅛
20	10	DiGiorgio .60	4	12⅜	12½	12⅜	12½	+ ⅛
26⅞	8⅞	Dillinghm .40	72	11⅞	12⅜	11½	12⅜	+ ¼
49	25	Dilling pf A 2	3	27½	27½	27¼	27¼	— ¼
17	13	Dillon Co .64	7	14⅞	15¼	14¾	15¼	+ ⅜
158	89⅞	Disney .30b	187	104	108½	103½	108½	+5¾
23⅝	6⅞	DiversInd .36	148	9	9¾	8¾	9⅝	+ ⅝
31¼	18⅛	DivMtg 1.54e	68	22½	22⅞	22¼	22⅞	+ ⅜
20⅛	13	DrPepper .30	47	17⅞	18⅜	17⅞	18⅛	+ ¼
62	45	DomeMin .80	8	58¼	58¼	57½	57⅝	—1⅛
13⅜	7	DomFnd .97e	11	8¾	8¾	8¾	8¾	....
25¼	13½	Donnelley .44	21	16	16¼	16	16⅛	— ⅛
28⅛	11⅛	Doric Cp .32	12	15⅜	15⅝	15⅜	15½	+ ⅛
19⅝	8	Dorr Oliver	7	10⅜	10⅝	10¼	10⅝	....
46⅜	30½	Dover Cp .70	1	37¼	37¼	37¼	37¼	+ ⅛
73⅞	58⅝	DowChm 2.60	334	69⅜	69½	69	69⅜	— ⅛
36½	23	DravoCp 1.40	6	27⅛	27⅛	27	27	— ¼
30½	22	DressInd 1.40	112	30⅛	30⅞	30⅛	30¼	+ ¼
35¾	28¾	Dressr pf2.20	67	34¼	34½	34⅛	34⅜	+ ⅛
32½	25	Dressr pf B2	8	31	31½	31	31½	+ ¾
32	13	Dreyfus Cp 1	6	18⅜	18½	18⅜	18½	+ ⅛
29½	20⅛	DukePw 1.40	39	21⅝	21⅝	21⅜	21½	— ⅛
59⅜	41⅝	DunBrad 1.20	83	45½	46⅞	45⅜	46¼	+ ⅝
35½	21¼	Duplan .60t	73	27¼	27⅜	26¾	26¾	— ½
128	92½	duPont 3.75e	115	119¾	121¾	119¾	121	+ ½
67¾	60½	duPont pf4.50	7	64¾	65	64¾	65	+ ½
54¼	48	duPont pf3.50	3	50	50⅛	50	50⅛	....
25⅞	20⅛	Duq Lt 1.66	48	21½	21½	21⅛	21⅛	— ¼
29	24½	DuqLt 4pf 2	2480	26½	26½	25¾	26½	+1
16¾	7⅝	Dymo Ind	4	11	11	10⅞	10⅞	— ⅛
11¾	4⅞	DynaAm .20p	69	5⅞	6	5⅞	6	....

known is the New York Stock Exchange. A consolidated record of daily transactions of these exchanges appears in most newspapers. A part of such a record is shown above. Moving across the columns from left to right, we are given the high and low of the stock for the year; the name of the stock and the current annual dividend in dollars per share; sales for the day in 100s; the opening, high, low, and closing price for the day; and the net change from yesterday's closing price. The prices are quoted as mixed fractions. The whole number is the dollar amount, while the fraction represents the cents.

$$14\frac{1}{4} = \$14.25$$

$$38\frac{1}{8} = \$38.125$$

$$72\frac{7}{8} = \$72.875$$

Also, dollar values are usually expressed in "points," with one point equal to one dollar when referring to stock. Thus, $14.25 is "14 and one-quarter points."

The final area of concern in buying or selling stock is the charge paid to the broker by the buyer or seller. Since 1975, there are no fixed commission schedules; each broker and seller must agree beforehand on the commission. This fee or commission is usually computed by the broker according to a commission schedule such as the one given in Table 25.1.

TABLE 25.1

Transactions Involving Units of 100 Shares	
VALUE OF TOTAL TRANSACTION	COMMISSION
Under $300	10%
$300–$1000	2% plus $6
$1001–$5000	1% plus $14
$5001–$10,000	$\frac{1}{2}$% plus $38
$10,000 and above	$\frac{1}{10}$% plus $78

Notice that this schedule is for transactions involving units of 100 shares. If the number of shares is a multiple of 100, the order is called a *round lot order*. Any other order is called an *odd lot order*.

100, 500, or 12,000 shares are round lot orders
52, 106, or 13,420 shares are odd lot orders

When commission rates on round lot orders are to be found, the steps are as follows:

Step 1. Find the total cost of the transaction.
Step 2. Look up the appropriate commission in the above table and apply it.

Example. Find the commission on 800 shares of stock bought at $10\frac{1}{4}$.

Step 1.   Total cost of 800 shares $= 800 \times \$10.25$

Total cost $= \$8200$

Step 2.   From the table we find that the commission for a transaction with a total cost of $8200 is equal to $\frac{1}{2}\% + \$38$.

$$\text{Commission} = \frac{1}{2}\%(\$8200) + \$38$$

$$= .005(\$8200) + \$38$$
$$= \$41 + \$38$$
$$= \$79$$

Odd lot commissions are found in exactly the same manner as round lots. However, an odd lot differential may be added to the price of the stock in the case of a purchase, or subtracted from the price of the stock in the case of a sale. When an odd lot differential is charged it is $\frac{1}{8}$ point.

Example. Find the commission on the purchase of 85 shares of stock bought at $10\frac{1}{4}$ where an odd lot differential is charged.

Step 1.   Total cost $= 85$ shares $\times (\$10.25 + \$.125$ odd lot differential)
$$= 85 \text{ shares} \times (\$10.375)$$
$$= \$881.875$$

Step 2.   Commission $= 2\%(\$881.875) + \$6$
$$= \$17.6375 + \$6$$
$$= \$23.64$$

Often an order will be a combination of round lots and odd lots.

182 shares $= 100$ shares round lot $+ 82$ shares odd lot
750 shares $= 700$ shares round lot $+ 50$ shares odd lot

In such cases the total cost of the round lot and the odd lot must be calculated separately and then added together.

Example. Find the commission on the purchase of 885 shares of stock bought at $10\frac{1}{4}$ where an odd lot differential is charged.

Step 1.   800 shares $\times \$10.25 = \$\ 8200$
85 shares $\times \$10.375 = \$\ \ \ 881.875$
Total cost $= \overline{\$10081.875}$

Step 2.   Commission $= \dfrac{1}{10}\%(\$10081.875) + \$78$

$$= \$10.08 + \$78$$
$$= \$88.08$$

Stock Transfer Taxes

There is a Security and Exchange Commission (SEC) fee of \$.01 for each \$500 of market price or fraction thereof; the broker withholds this from the proceeds due the seller of the stock. In addition, some states tax the transfer of stock. The stock transfer tax in New York is given below.

Shares selling at	Tax per share
Less than \$5	$\$.01\frac{1}{4}$
\$5 but less than \$10	$.02\frac{1}{4}$
\$10 but less than \$20	$.03\frac{1}{4}$
\$20 or more	.05

Example. John Roberts sold 220 shares of Gifford Corporation stock at \$14.

$$\text{Market Price} = 220 \times 14 = \$3080$$

$$\$3080 \div \$500 = 6\frac{4}{25} = 6 \text{ \$500 units of market value}$$

$$\text{SEC Fee} = 6 \times \$.01 = \$.06$$

$$\text{N.Y. State Tax} = 220 \times .03\frac{1}{4} = \$7.15$$

BONDS

Bonds are long-term loans. When they are secured by a mortgage on some or all of the assets of the firm issuing them, they are called *mortgage bonds. Debentures* are bonds that are backed only by the general credit of the company issuing them. Bonds are issued with a face or *par value* in multiples of \$100 and most frequently in multiples of \$1000. Bonds specify a fixed rate of interest to be paid on the par value by the issuer;

19X9 High.	Low.	Stocks and Div. In Dollars.	Sls. 100s.	First.	High.	Low.	Last.	Net Chge.
		CORPORATION BONDS						
		A—B						
79	78¾	Abbott Lab 6¼s93	20	78⅞	78⅞	78⅞	+ ⅛	
103¾	101¼	AddresMult 9⅜s,5	13	103½	103	103½	+ ⅝
74	59⅞	Air Red cv3⅞s87	35	65⅜	64⅞	64⅞	+ ⅛
79⅛	65	Allegh L cv4s81	10	69	69	69	.....
76⅜	66	Allied Ch 5.20s91	5	70	70	70	+ ⅞
77¼	73⅞	Allied Ch 3½s78	5	75½	75½	75½	.....
80	58	Allied Str cv4½s92	2	67	67	67	.....
85½	47	AlliedSup cv5¾s87	60	59½	57½	57½	—2¼
105½	99½	Alcoa 9s95	12	104⅜	104¼	104¼	— ¾
83¾	73	Alcoa 6s92	6	79½	79½	79½	+2½
102	75	Alcoa cv5¼s91	47	86¼	85¼	85¼	+ ⅛
74¼	65	Alcoa 4¼s82	5	67	67	67	.....
104¼	99	Alum Can 9½s95	33	102½	102⅛	102½	+1½
75½	64	Amer Esna cv5s92	7	68	68	68	.....
.....	.....	Am Airlin 11s88	54	103	101½	101½	.....
109½	66	AmAirlin cv5½s91	7	80	80	80	+ ¾
79½	46	AmAirlin cv4¼s92	70	62	60½	62	+1½
101½	56	Am Airlin cv4s90	9	71½	71½	71½	+ ½
105	99	Am Brands 8⅞s75	67	104	103	104	.....
69	65⅜	Am Brands 4⅝s90	60	65⅝	65⅝	65⅝	— ⅛
94	57	Am Bdcst cv5s93	15	79	78	79	+ ½
84⅛	71	Am Can 6s97	15	80	79	80	.....
62	37	AmExprt cv5¼s93	2	49	49	49	— ½
61½	50	Am FP 5s2030	24	55¾	55	55	.....
97½	63	Am Hoist cv4¾s92	1	69½	69½	69½	— ⅜
69	62½	Am Sug 5.30s93	3	66⅛	66⅛	66⅛	.....
.....	.....	AmSug 5.30s93reg	3	66⅛	66⅛	66⅛	.....
103¼	95⅜	AmTT 8¾s2000xw	666	103	102⅞	103	— ⅛

this is called the *coupon rate*. In the case of *bearer bonds*, there are a number of coupons attached to the bond, each of which calls for the payment of a specified amount of interest on a fixed date, generally every 6 months. On each of these dates the bondholder presents one coupon to his bank or the agent named in the bond for collection. If the bond is a *registered bond*, the owner's name is listed with the issuing company or its trustee, and the interest is paid automatically to the registered owner.

Each corporate bond issue is distinguished by the name of the company issuing it, the rate of interest, and the date of maturity when the bond is to be paid off in full at its par value. For example, Alcoa bonds paying 6% interest and due to be paid off in 1992 are listed as "Alcoa 6s 92."

The market value of bonds differs from their face or par value, depending on changes in the market rate of interest and the risk of default (the issuer not being able to repay the principal or pay the interest) on the bond. Bond prices are quoted as percentages of par value. For example, Alcoa 6s 92 quoted at 85 cost $850 (85% × $1000) before commissions and taxes; if they were quoted at 107, they would cost $1070 (107% × $1000).

When a bond is sold between the dates of interest payments, it is sold at the market price plus *accrued* interest. This is known as the *settlement sum*. The accrued interest is calculated from the last interest date to the day before the *date of settlement* which is four *business days* following the date of sale. Saturdays, Sundays and legal holidays are not business days so that the actual date of settlement may be as much as a week later than the date of sale. When one or more full months intervene between the last interest date and the settlement date they are counted as consisting of 30 days each.

Example. A $1000 bond bearing 7% interest payable November 1 and May 1 is sold on Thursday, July 14, at 103 plus accrued interest. Calculate the settlement sum before commissions.

103% × $1000 = $1030 = Market Price

The settlement date is July 20 (Saturday and Sunday are not business days) so there are 78 days accrued interest (May 1 to July 1 = 60 days, plus July 1 to July 19 = 18 days).

$\frac{78}{360} \times \$70 = \$15.17 = $ Accrued Interest

$1030 + $15.17 = $1045.17 = Settlement Sum

Commission and Taxes

Commission rates on the sale of bonds are negotiated with the selling broker. Typical commission rates might be like those given below.

Commission Rates on Bonds

Price	Commission per bond
Selling under $500 (50)	$2.00
At least $500 (50) and above	$5.00

In addition to the commission, there is a Security and Exchange Commission transaction tax of $\frac{1}{500}$ of 1% of the sales price, or $.01 for each $500 or fraction thereof.

Example. An investor buys 20 American Airlines $4\frac{1}{4}$s 92 at 81. Using the commission rates given above, calculate the total commission. From the schedule the commission on a bond selling at over $500 is $5.00.

$$\text{Total Commission} = \$5.00 \times 20 = \$100.00.$$

Example. Find the transaction tax on the sale of 75 Alcoa 6s 92 selling at 85. Transaction Tax $= 75 \times \$850 \times .00002 = \$1.28$

Computing the Yield on Bonds

The coupon rate of interest of a bond is based on its par value. Since the market value of a bond is usually different from its par value, the rate of return usually differs from the fixed rate stated on the bond. The *current yield* is found by the following formula.

$$\text{Current Yield} = \frac{\text{Annual Interest}}{\text{Market Value of the Bond}}$$

Example. Find the current yield on Alcoa 6s 92 selling for 85.

$$\text{Current Yield} = \frac{\$60}{\$850} = 7.06\%$$

Yield to Maturity

In the previous example the Alcoa bond sold at a discount from par, so that the current yield is not an accurate indication of the total rate of return since the buyer upon maturity will receive $1000, not $850. To take account of the fact that one may purchase a bond above or below its par value, investors compute what is called the *yield to maturity*. Normally this is found by the use of bond tables but it may be calculated approximately by the formula below.

$$\text{Yield to Maturity} = \frac{\text{Annual Interest} + \text{Annual Premium Amortization}}{\text{Average Principal Invested}}$$

Assume that the Alcoa bonds in the preceding example matured in exactly 10 years and that we wish to calculate the yield to maturity. The discount of $150($1000 − $850) divided by 10 years gives an annual premium amortization of $15. The annual interest is $60. The average principal invested is obtained by averaging the cost price and the face value at maturity. In this case it is $850 + 1000 divided by 2, or $925. Employing the formula above:

$$\text{Yield to Maturity} = \frac{\$60 + \$15}{\$925} = 8.11\%$$

The yield to maturity of 8.11% is more than the current yield of 7.06%. For the sake of simplicity, the brokerage charge is customarily omitted from the computation of yield to maturity since it is such a small part of the purchase price.

The formula for computing the yield to maturity when a bond is bought at a premium is

$$\text{Yield to Maturity} = \frac{\text{Annual Interest} - \text{Annual Premium Amortization}}{\text{Average Principal Invested}}$$

If the price of the Alcoa bonds had been 110, the yield to maturity would be less than the current yield, since upon maturity a purchaser would receive only $1000. The premium paid would be $100, and this divided by 10 years would give an annual premium amortization of $10.

The annual interest is still $60. The average principal investment is ($1100 + $1000) divided by 2, or $1050.

$$\text{Yield to Maturity} = \frac{\$60 - \$10}{\$1050} = 4.76\%$$

The yield in this case is less than the current yield because of the premium above par value paid for the bond.

ASSIGNMENT 38 STOCKS AND BONDS

A. Solve each of the following problems. Use the sample charges given in this chapter where appropriate.

a. John Harris bought 220 shares of Allegheny Ludlum Corporation at 24. What was his total cost? (Remember the odd lot differential on the 20 shares.)

1. Ronald Palmer purchased 80 shares of J. C. Penney common stock at 54. What was the total cost of this purchase?

2. Elkin Industries' Board of Directors decided to distribute $17,000 to its stockholders. If they have 5000 shares of 5% preferred stock at $80 par outstanding and 10,000 shares of common stock, how will this amount be distributed between each class of stock?

3. The Porter Company has $400,000 of 7% cumulative preferred stock, $100 par outstanding. In 1969, the company paid only a 2% dividend. In 1970, it paid a 6% dividend. In 1971, all the firm's profits amounting to $70,000 were distributed. How much was available for dividends for the common stock?

4. John Harris sold 200 shares of Porter Company common stock at 38. What were his net proceeds after commissions and taxes?

5. Don Jenkins sold 600 shares of TWA common stock for 42, which he had purchased two years ago at 32. What is his net gain after commissions and taxes?

B. Solve each of the following problems.

a. Find the yield to maturity of a bond bought at 90, paying 7% interest, maturing in ten years.

1. Ralph Candor purchased six National Cash Register bonds at $80\frac{1}{2}$. What is his total cost including commissions?

2. American Export 5s 93 are currently selling at 85. What is their current yield?

3. Sue Grayson must decide whether to buy Ludlum Corporation bonds paying 5% interest and maturing in ten years at 65 or Grayson Corporation 9% bonds maturing in five years at 100. Which of the bonds has the higher yield to maturity?

4. Jack Carson sold five Andy Gard bonds at 82. What were his net proceeds after commissions and taxes?

5. Paul Smith purchased through his broker 4 $1000 bonds bearing interest at 6%, payable semiannually on January 1 and July 1. The purchase price was 80. The settlement date was Friday, March 5. What was the total cost of the purchase including the accrued interest?

CHAPTER 26
Sinking funds

A fund consisting of equal periodic deposits at compound interest that is allowed to accumulate for the purpose of providing a specific sum of money is called a *sinking fund*. Frequently, businesses will finance their expansion by issuing bonds. To make sure there is enough money available to pay off the bonds at maturity, many firms set aside a certain sum of money each year to repay the bond when it comes due. It is often financially easier for a firm to set aside small amounts of money each year than to pay off an outstanding debt out of the revenue of a single year. In addition, the money set aside can earn interest. The annual payment into the sinking fund is calculated so that the sum of the payments plus the accumulated interest will just equal the future sum desired. In the case of bonds, the current interest on the bonds outstanding is paid out of current revenue, not from the sinking fund.

Sinking funds are not restricted solely to the repayment of bonds. They may be employed in order to accumulate sufficient funds to replace a piece of equipment or for some other purpose.

The basic problem with a sinking fund is to determine the periodic payment necessary to accumulate the required sum of money at some specific time in the future. In other words, one needs to know the amount deposited annually which, together with the interest on the deposits, will produce a fund of the proper size when a specific payment must be met. You may recognize this problem as that of an ordinary annuity, and there is a very simple relationship between an ordinary annuity table and a sinking fund table.

$$\text{Sinking Fund Factor} = \frac{1}{\text{Ordinary Annuity Factor}}$$

To facilitate the calculation of the amount to set aside each year, a table such as Table 26.1 is helpful. It tells how much must be set aside at the end of each year in order to have a total of $1.00000 at the end of *n* years at given rates of interest.

Example. Talbott Industries plans to build a new factory in ten years at a cost of $200,000. What annual amount must the company set aside at 5% in a sinking fund to accumulate this amount?

From the ten-year row and 5% column, we find the figure .0795. If we multiply this factor by the amount required, the result is the annual increment needed.

TABLE 26.1

Sinking Fund Factor								
NUMBER OF PERIODS (N)	**INTEREST RATE PER PERIOD**							
	3%	**4%**	**5%**	**6%**	**7%**	**8%**	**10%**	**12%**
1	1.0000	1.0000	1.0000	1.0000	1.0000	1.0000	1.0000	1.0000
2	0.4926	0.4902	0.4878	0.4854	0.4830	0.4807	0.4761	0.4717
3	0.3235	0.3203	0.3172	0.3141	0.3110	0.3080	0.3021	0.2963
4	0.2390	0.2354	0.2320	0.2285	0.2252	0.2219	0.2154	0.2092
5	0.1883	0.1846	0.1809	0.1774	0.1738	0.1704	0.1638	0.1754
6	0.1546	0.1507	0.1470	0.1433	0.1398	0.1363	0.1296	0.1232
7	0.1305	0.1266	0.1228	0.1191	0.1155	0.1120	0.1054	0.0991
8	0.1124	0.1085	0.1047	0.1010	0.0974	0.0940	0.0874	0.0813
9	0.0984	0.0944	0.0906	0.0870	0.0834	0.0800	0.0736	0.0676
10	0.0872	0.0832	0.0795	0.0758	0.0723	0.0690	0.0627	0.0569
11	0.0780	0.0741	0.0703	0.0667	0.0633	0.0600	0.0539	0.0484
12	0.0704	0.0665	0.0628	0.0592	0.0559	0.0527	0.0467	0.0414
13	0.0640	0.0601	0.0564	0.0529	0.0496	0.0465	0.0407	0.0356
14	0.0585	0.0546	0.0510	0.0475	0.0443	0.0413	0.0357	0.0308
15	0.0537	0.0499	0.0463	0.0429	0.0397	0.0368	0.0314	0.0268
16	0.0496	0.0458	0.0422	0.0389	0.0358	0.0329	0.0278	0.0233
17	0.0459	0.0422	0.0387	0.0354	0.0324	0.0296	0.0246	0.0204
18	0.0427	0.0389	0.0355	0.0323	0.0294	0.0267	0.0219	0.0179
19	0.0398	0.0361	0.0327	0.0296	0.0267	0.0241	0.0195	0.0157
20	0.0372	0.0335	0.0302	0.0271	0.0243	0.0218	0.0174	0.0138
21	0.0348	0.0312	0.0280	0.0250	0.0222	0.0198	0.0156	0.0122
22	0.0327	0.0292	0.0259	0.0230	0.0204	0.0180	0.0140	0.0108
23	0.0308	0.0273	0.0241	0.0212	0.0187	0.0164	0.0125	0.0095
24	0.0290	0.0255	0.0224	0.0196	0.0171	0.0149	0.0113	0.0084
25	0.0274	0.0240	0.0209	0.0182	0.0158	0.0136	0.0101	0.0075
30	0.0210	0.0178	0.0150	0.0126	0.0105	0.0088	0.0060	0.0041
35	0.0165	0.0135	0.0110	0.0089	0.0072	0.0058	0.0036	0.0023
40	0.0132	0.0105	0.0082	0.0064	0.0050	0.0038	0.0022	0.0013
45	0.0107	0.0082	0.0062	0.0047	0.0035	0.0025	0.0013	0.0007
50	0.0088	0.0065	0.0047	0.0034	0.0024	0.0017	0.0008	0.0004

Increment = Amount Needed × Sinking Fund Factor (from table)

= $200,000 × .0795

= $15,906

ASSIGNMENT 39 SINKING FUNDS

A. Given the necessary information, find the amount of the annual increment needed to bring about the desired accumulation in each of the problems below.

a. $400,000 needed in 5 years, interest rate is 3%

b. $100,000 needed in 7 years, interest rate is 4%

1. $500 needed in 1 year, interest rate is 6%

2. $2000 needed in 4 years, interest rate is 5%

3. $10,000 needed in 10 years, interest rate is 3%

4. $15,600 needed in 8 years, interest rate is 4%

5. $26,000 needed in 12 years, interest rate is 6%

6. $49,000 needed in 13 years, interest rate is 4%

7. $110,000 needed in 10 years, interest rate is $3\frac{1}{2}$%

8. $750,000 needed in 5 years, interest rate is 5%

9. $990,000 needed in 20 years, interest rate is 6%

10. $1,500,000 needed in 15 years, interest rate is 5%

B. Solve each of the following problems.

1. Clark Sporting Goods Company has issued $100,000 of 8% 10-year bonds. What uniform amount of money must the Company set aside each year at 6% interest to retire the bonds when they mature in ten years?

2. Hardy Boy Manufacturing Company has purchased $150,000 of new machinery. The Company wishes to invest enough money each year so that it will have accumulated a fund of $200,000 at the end of nine years when the machinery will need to be replaced. How much should it invest each year at 5% interest to obtain the desired fund?

3. The Deep Hole Strip Mine must spend $40,000 to fill and landscape their coal mine when it becomes exhausted in ten years. If they expect to invest their funds at 4%, how much must they set aside each year to accumulate $40,000 at the end of 10 years?

4. Ralph Morris wants to buy a house costing about $50,000. If he has a 20% cash down payment for the house, he can obtain a mortgage for the balance. At 7% interest how much must he set aside each year to obtain the down payment in five years?

5. The Grayson Company needs $350,000 to retire a bond issue at the end of five years. How much should they set aside each year at 6% interest?

6. Bronson & Son Company has set aside $22,000 each year at 7% into a sinking fund for the past four years. The management now finds that a new machine must be purchased immediately at $93,000. Will the total amount currently in the sinking fund be enough to cover the cost of the new machine? If so, how much will remain in it for future use?

7. Marin Industries, after placing $15,000 into a sinking fund annually for six years, calculates the total amount in the fund to be $104,675.50. What interest rate was effective for the six-year period?

A. Matching.

_____ 1.	annuity	**(a)**	payments made to insurance companies
_____ 2.	par value	**(b)**	a policy that covers up to 100% of any loss up to the face value of the policy
_____ 3.	payee	**(c)**	an annuity that runs for an uncertain length of time
_____ 4.	interest	**(d)**	periodic deposit of a constant amount of money to insure future payment of a debt
_____ 5.	dividend	**(e)**	promissory notes with some security of payment
_____ 6.	present value	**(f)**	policy that must be paid every year until the death of the insured
_____ 7.	promissory note	**(g)**	printed value placed on a share of stock
_____ 8.	ordinary annuity	**(h)**	amount of money an individual can borrow against his policy
_____ 9.	stockbrokers	**(i)**	that part of the company's profits distributed to its stockholders
_____ 10.	premiums	**(j)**	agents who handle transactions involving stock
_____ 11.	compound interest	**(k)**	charge or fee for the use of money
_____ 12.	discounting	**(l)**	$\text{compound amount} = \dfrac{1}{\text{present value}}$
_____ 13.	reciprocal relationship	**(m)**	a fixed sum of money paid at regular fixed intervals
_____ 14.	bond	**(n)**	written and signed promise to pay a stated sum of money at some specific future date
_____ 15.	pure insurance	**(o)**	the process of adding interest to the principal that in turn earns interest
_____ 16.	contingent annuities	**(p)**	recipient of the note or the borrower
_____ 17.	ordinary fire insurance	**(q)**	an annuity having payments made at the end of each interval
_____ 18.	sinking fund	**(r)**	the process of deducting interest in advance
_____ 19.	loan value	**(s)**	the concept that expected money is worth less than if the money were received now
_____ 20.	straight policy	**(t)**	an annuity having payments made at the end of each interval

B. Given the following information, fill in the blanks.

	PRINCIPAL	RATE	TIME	INTEREST
1.	$700	4% exact	3 yr	
2.	$1400	2% exact	86 da	
3.	$850	6% ordinary	30 da	
4.	$3600	3% exact	60 da	
5.	$7500	5% exact	93 da	

	LOAN ISSUED DATE	LOAN DUE DATE	NUMBER OF DAYS BETWEEN
6.	June 7		60
7.	Jan. 23	Mar. 17	
8.	Oct. 13	Dec. 20	
9.	May 30		83
10.		June 2	30

	PRINCIPAL	RATE	TIME	INTEREST
11.	$800	8% compounded semiannually	4 yr	
12.	$1100	12% compounded quarterly	3 yr	
13.	$1700	6% compounded annually	5 yr	
14.	$8750	12% compounded quarterly	2 yr	
15.	$17000	3% compounded semiannually	2 yr	

C. Compute the principal payments for the first five monthly periods if the principal is $1400, the interest rate is 12%, and the constant total payment is $60.

1.   2.

3.   4.

5.

D. Find the final value of the following annuities.

	TYPE OF ANNUITY	AMOUNT	COMPOUND INTEREST RATE	TIME	FINAL VALUE
1.	Annual annuity due	$4000	5%	3 yr	
2.	Annual ordinary annuity	$1000	3%	1 yr	
3.	Semiannual annuity due	$700	4%	5 yr	
4.	Semiannual ordinary annuity	$2500	2%	4 yr	
5.	Annual annuity due	$13000	6%	2 yr	

E. Solve each of the following problems.

1. Dr. Samuels purchased a 90 day-6% interest-bearing note on August 12. If the face value of the note is $4000, if the maturity date is October 2, and if the discount rate is 4%, what is the maturity value and the proceeds?

2. Savestment Corporation pays an annual ordinary annuity of $45,000 at 4% for three years. How much more or less would they have to pay if the annuity were an annual annuity due?

3. Mr. Daniels purchased an 80% coinsurance policy with a face value of $40,000. The value of his property is $55,000. If he should experience a fire loss of $30,000, how much would he receive from the insurance company?

4. What is the annual uniform investment needed if the Jackson Manufacturing Company hopes to accumulate $70,000 in ten years? The current interest rate is 5%.

PART FOUR

Statistics

CHAPTER 27
Basic statistics

Statistics are an important factor in business decisions in the evaluation of past performance, developing new managerial techniques, and planning for future expansion. One important use of statistics is to summarize data. A particularly useful summary statistic is the average. A detailed discussion of statistics involves considerable mathematics, but a basic explanation of measures of central tendency can be presented with the tools we have already developed.

An *average* of any set of statistical data is a single number which represents all the numbers in the set or list. More formally, an average is a measure of central tendency. Whenever a set of data is not divided into specific classes and each number in the set is considered individually, the data are called *ungrouped data*.

Example. Height in inches of 12 high school students:

70	66
72	70
64	68
71	74
77	67
73	71

If, however, the numbers are placed in specific classes and only classes are considered in the computations, the data are called *grouped data*.

Example. Height in inches of 12 high school students:

	NUMBER OF STUDENTS
From 64 to 66	2
67 to 69	2
70 to 72	5
73 to 75	2
76 to 78	1

Mean

Whenever someone tells us to find the average of a list of figures, we usually think of adding all the figures and dividing the total by the number of items in the list. This, however, is only one type of statistical average, called the *mean*. The mean is the sum total of all the items in a set or list, divided by the number of items in the list.

Example. Find the arithmetic mean (average) of the following list of figures:

4, 12, 6, 5, 5

The mean may be found by using the following formula:

$$\text{Mean} = \frac{\text{Sum of Items}}{\text{Number of Items}}$$

$$\text{Mean} = \frac{4 + 12 + 6 + 5 + 5}{5} = \frac{32}{5} = 6\frac{2}{5}$$

$$X = \frac{32}{5}$$

$$X = 6\frac{2}{5}$$

Array and Median

An *array* is a list of figures in either increasing or decreasing numerical order.

Example. Place the following numbers in an array of increasing order: 4, 3, 6, 14, 7, 9, 2, 10.

2
3
4
6
7
9
10
14

Once the data have been arrayed, the median can be found. The *median* is the number that divides the list exactly in half. In other words, half of the items are below the median and half are above. The position of the median is found by adding 1 to the number of items in the array and dividing by 2. Note that this result is the *position* of the median in the array and not the value of the median. If the position is a whole number, count down the figures in the array until you find the figure in the position you computed. The value of this figure is the value of the median. If, however, the position computed is not a whole number, find the values of the figures in the array that correspond to the next whole position above and below the position calculated. The arithmetic mean of these two values gives the value of the median.

Example. Find the median of the following arrays:

(1) 20
     16      $$\text{Position} = \frac{n + 1}{2}$$
     12
      8              $$= \frac{5 + 1}{2} = 3$$
      4

The median is equal to the 3rd figure, which is 12.

(2) 10
    9
    8
    7
    6
    5
    4
    3

$$\text{Position} = \frac{8+1}{2} = 4.5$$

4th position $= 7$
5th position $= 6$

$$\text{Median} = \frac{7+6}{2} = \frac{13}{2} = 6.5$$

Mode

The *mode* is the number that appears most often in any set of data. It is possible to have more than one mode if several figures appear the same number of times. Similarly, there may be no mode if all the figures appear only once.

Example. What is the mode in each of the following lists?

(a)   4, 5, 1, 3, 4, 7, 2   The mode is 4.

(b)   3, 6, 4, 3, 8, 3, 8, 6, 4, 6   The modes are 3 and 6, and the distribution is said to be *bimodal*.

(c)   9, 7, 5, 3, 1   There is no mode.

RANGE

A city in Arizona had an average annual temperature of 70° Fahrenheit. Sound good? You may change your mind when you learn the average annual temperature is made up of an average summer temperature of 98° and an average winter temperature of 42°. In order to evaluate collections of data, it is useful not only to employ measures of central tendency but also a measure of the degree of dispersion of the data. A simple measure of dispersion is the *range*.

The *range* is defined as the difference between the largest and smallest magnitudes of a frequency distribution. For the distribution of heights given on page 263, the tallest height is 77 inches and the smallest height is 64 inches, so that range equals 13 inches (77 − 64), While the range is easy to calculate, it is based on two extremes of a typical behavior and therefore may not always give a good picture of the dispersion of the data as a whole.

A. Find the mean, median, and mode for the following lists of data.

a.	5	Mean _____		1.	10	Mean _____
	6	Median _____			12	Median _____
	8	Mode _____			8	Mode _____
	12				10	
	1				14	
					10	
					12	

2.	20	Mean _____		3.	36	Mean _____
	15	Median _____			40	Median _____
	16	Mode _____			20	Mode _____
	25				28	
	12				53	
	17					
	16					
	15					
	17					

4.	25	Mean _____		5.	29	Mean _____
	17	Median _____			36	Median _____
	28	Mode _____			41	Mode _____
	32				33	
	24				44	
	18				37	
					48	
					36	

B. Solve the following problems.

1. The White family members have ages of 65, 42, 40, 16, 13 and 8. What is the average age of the six members?

2. Mrs. Hunt's math class received the following scores on a quiz: 98, 92, 74, 79, 52, 68, 85, 70, 80, 73, 95. What is the median of these scores?

3. The ages of students in a certain anthropology class are 18, 19, 22, 25, 20, 20, 21, 18, 19, 23, 19, and 20. What is the mode of the students' ages?

CHAPTER 28
Charts and graphs

Frequently, statistics can be more easily understood and interpreted if they are expressed in graphic form. In many cases, the relationship between sets of data is more evident using these visual aids. More importantly, graphs and charts make it possible for people not trained in statistics to comprehend what is being presented. For the purposes of this discussion, a *chart* is any visual presentation of statistical data. A *graph* is a type of chart that employs two or more scales. The most important types of charts are the simple bar chart, the component bar chart, the pictogram, the pie or circle chart, and the line graph.

SIMPLE BAR CHARTS

The simple bar chart is used to present comparisons of the magnitude of an item. The length of the bar represents the magnitude in each class of the item being presented. The bars may be either horizontal or vertical. Too many scale or grid lines should be avoided.

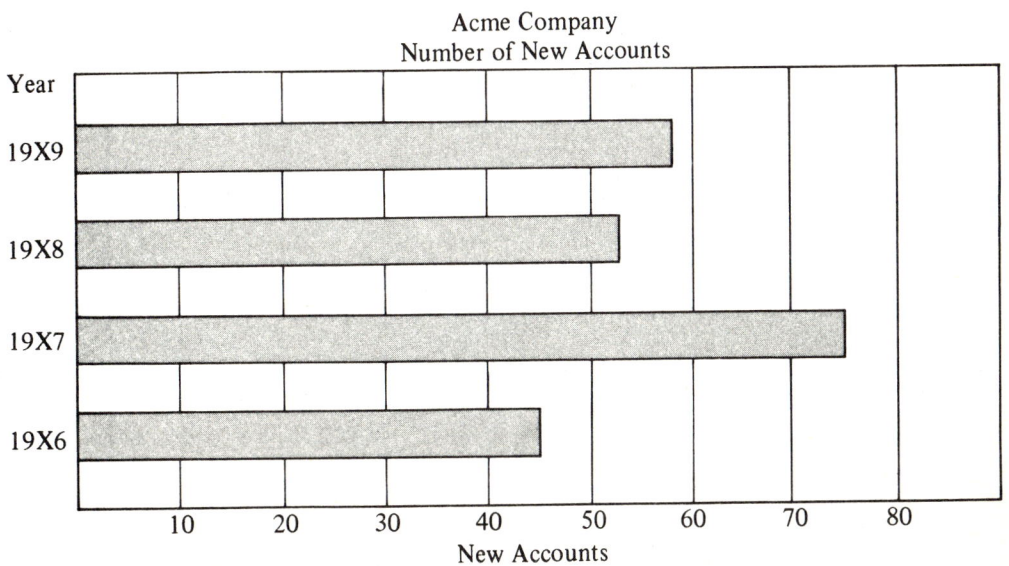

THE COMPONENT BAR CHART

The component bar chart has a characteristic not found in the simple bar chart. Each bar is divided into component parts, so that a relationship within a category can be expressed. When preparing such a chart, remember that the largest value is usually placed at the base and a key is often necessary to aid the interpretation and differentiation of the bar segments. An example of a component bar chart is shown below.

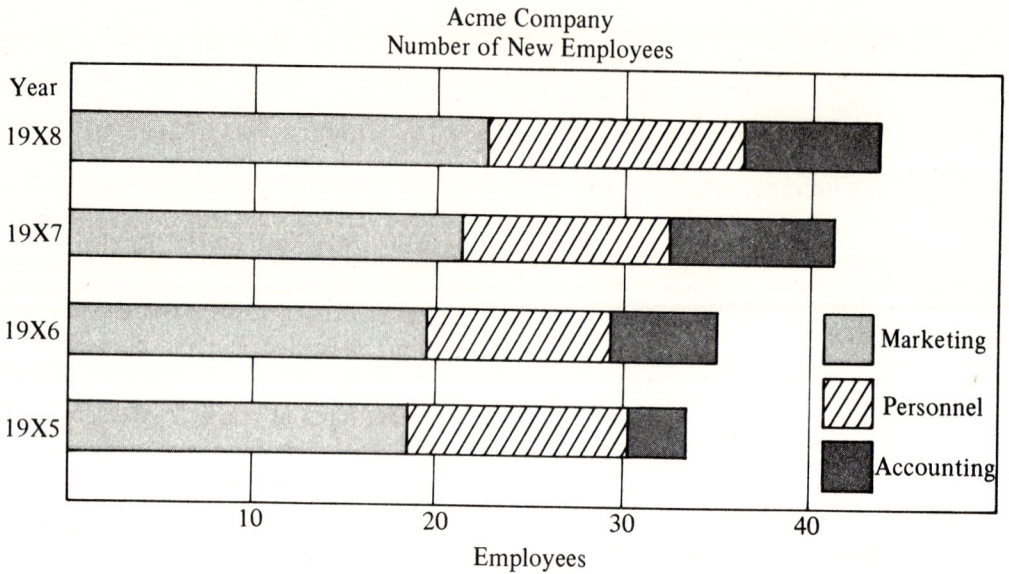

PICTOGRAMS

For dramatic effect, pictograms are often used to express data. Grid lines are not used, and the value of each grouping is dependent on the value of a single symbol.

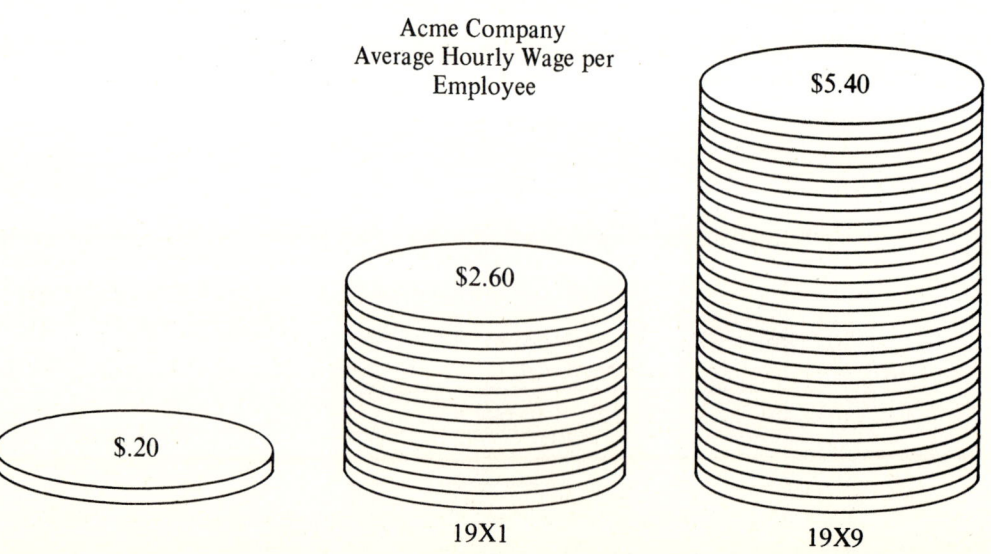

CIRCLE CHARTS

Circle or pie charts are used to express the relationship between fractional parts and the whole. To prepare a circle, express each of the parts as a percent and multiply each by 360°. The result is the number of degrees of the center angle of each of the respective parts. The sum of all the resulting angles must equal 360°. It should also be noted that if any of the angles are very small, the circle should be enlarged enough to make this segment visible.

Example. Waco Company spent $3000 last month. This total can be expressed as follows:

		PERCENTAGE OF TOTAL	EXPRESSED IN DEGREES
Wages	$ 900	30	$.30 \times 360° = 108°$
Purchases	1100	37	$.37 \times 360° = 133°$
Utilities	250	8	$.08 \times 360° = 29°$
Maintenance	750	25	$.25 \times 360° = 90°$
	$3000	100	360°

Weekly Expenditures Expressed as Percents of the Total

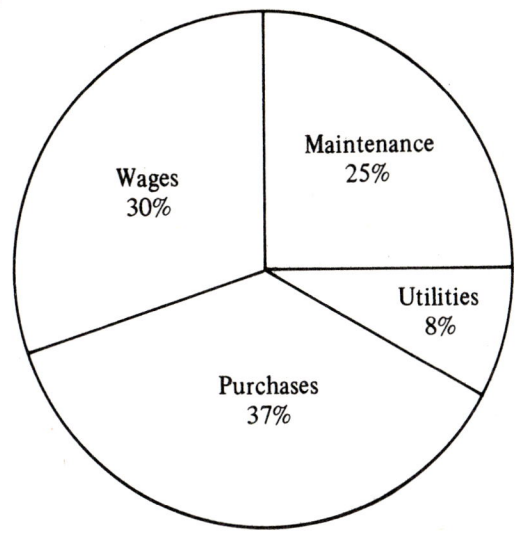

LINE GRAPHS

The line graph is an outstanding device for presenting a limited amount of statistical data. A line graph is constructed first by plotting points with reference to a pair of intersecting lines called *axes*, as shown below, and then connecting the points together with a line. The horizontal line is known as the *x axis* and the vertical line is known as the *y axis*. The point of intersection of the two axes is known as the *origin*. The independent variable is usually measured on the *x* axis. Independent variables are often measures of time. The dependent variable is usually measured on the *y* axis. The dependent variable can be any variable that can be measured over a period of time.

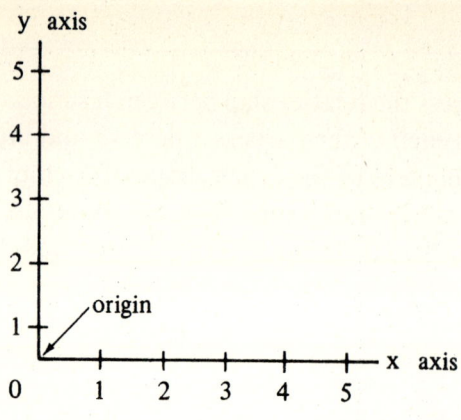

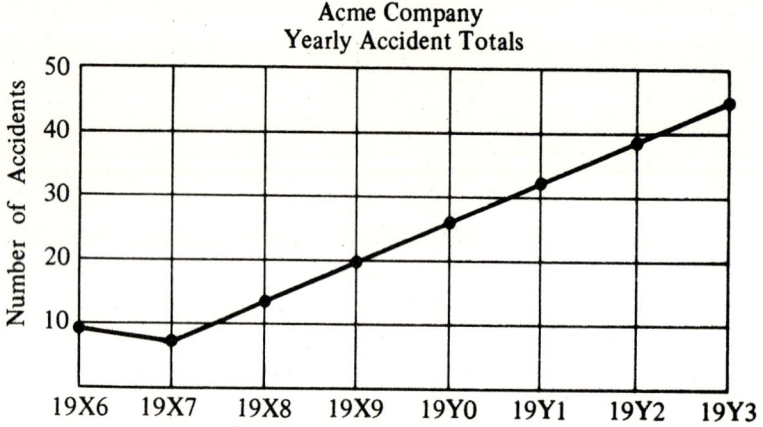

Acme Company
Yearly Accident Totals

Since one advantage of using a chart or graph is its simplicity, usually no more than three lines are plotted on any one graph.

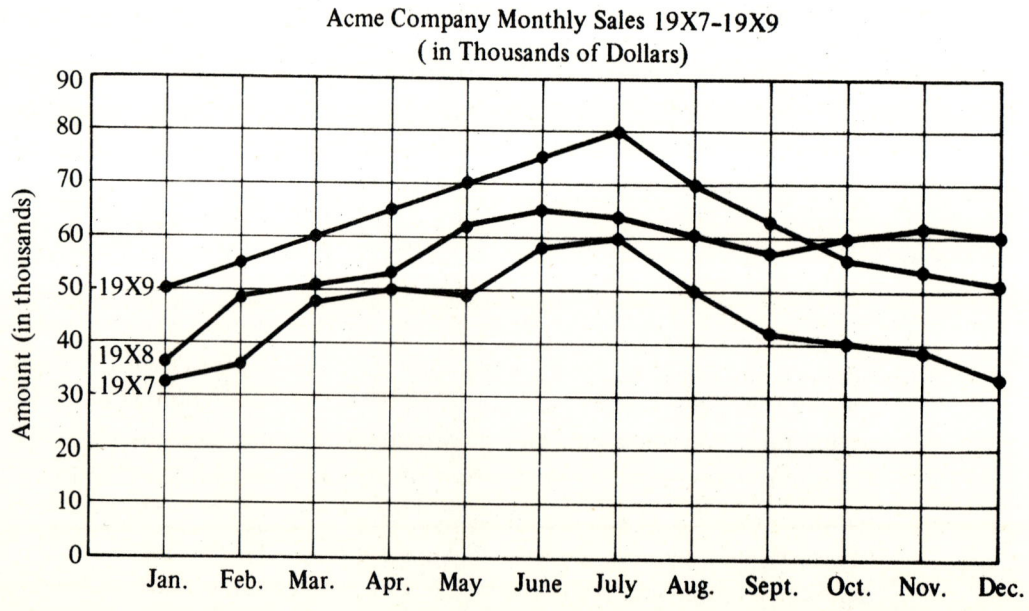

Acme Company Monthly Sales 19X7–19X9
(in Thousands of Dollars)

A. Given below are yearly sales commissions for Beklay Motors. Prepare a simple bar chart and a line graph to express these data. Make a comment on which of the two charts expresses this information better.

19X7: $15,000
19X8: $16,200
19X9: $14,500
19Y0: $15,500
19Y1: $16,000

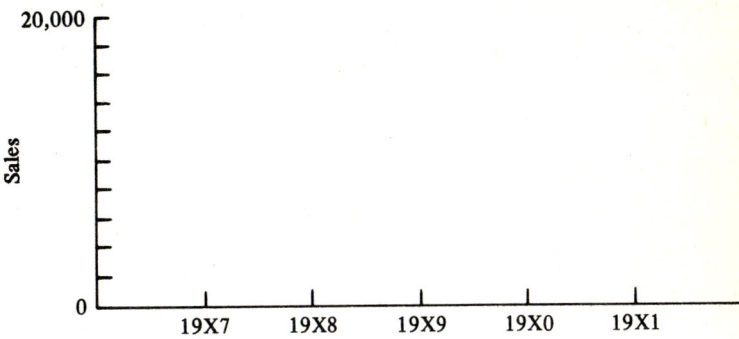

B. Given below are the numbers of people injured at Malcolm Manufacturing in each of the four quarters of 19X9. The totals are divided into male and female groups. Prepare a component bar chart expressing these data.

QUARTER	MALE	FEMALE	TOTAL
I	52	23	75
II	41	30	71
III	22	18	40
IV	20	16	36

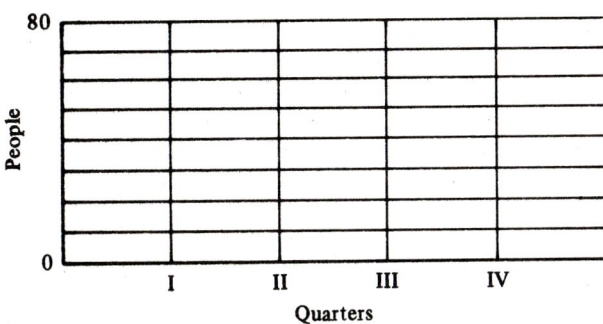

C. Mr. Davis makes $220 a week after deductions. Each week he spends $50 for food, $80 for rent and utilities, $30 for insurance, $30 for recreation, and $30 for savings. Make a circle chart to express the distribution of Mr. Davis' budget expenditures.

D. Jackson's Department Store decided to reevaluate its inventory policy. In order to facilitate this evaluation, a line chart must be prepared from yearly sales totals. Given these totals, prepare such a line chart.

	19X6	19X7	19X8	19X9
Men's furnishings	$17,850	$18,500	$19,000	$18,750
Ladies' furnishings	22,400	23,000	25,500	26,000
Furniture	34,000	35,000	42,000	50,000

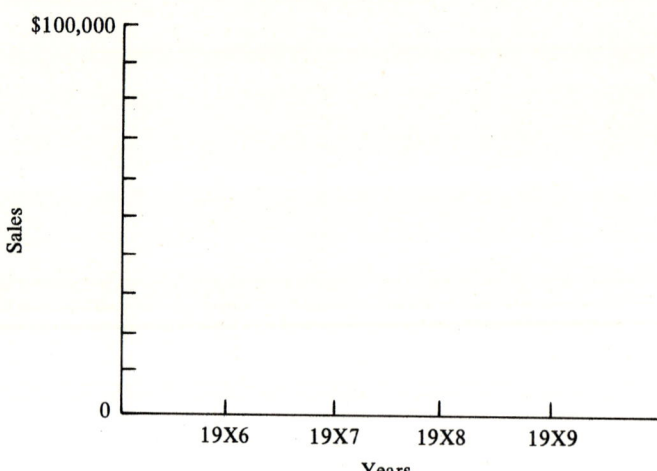

PART FIVE

Financial Statements and Analysis

CHAPTER 29
The balance sheet

Most businesses keep detailed accounts of all transactions. These accounts can be compiled in order to show the financial position of the business at any time. The formal statement showing what the company owns, what the company owes, and the value of the owners' interests, is called a *balance sheet*. What the company owns is listed on the *asset* side, or left side, of the balance sheet. What the company owes is listed on the right side of the statement under *liabilities*. The valuation of the owners' interests is placed under the heading of *stockholders' equity*, also on the right side of the statement. An example of a balance sheet is shown below.

Balance Sheet
Benson–Woodward, Inc.
December 31, 19X9
(In thousands)

Assets			Liabilities		
Current Assets:			**Current Liabilities:**		
Cash	$ 1,500		Accounts Payable	$ 500	
Accounts Receivable	750		Notes Payable	700	
Notes Receivable	500		Federal Taxes Payable	75	
Merchandise Inventory	1,000		Total Current		$ 1,275
Total Current Assets		$ 3,750	Liabilities		
Investments:			**Long Term Debt:**		
Long Term Govt. Securities	$ 60		Mortgage due 1980	$1,500	
Investment in Foreign Subsidiaries	2,000		Promissory Note 1983	500	
Total Investment		$ 2,060			$ 2,000
			Total Liabilities		$ 3,275
Fixed Assets:			**Stockholders' Equity:**		
Property, Plant & Equipment	$11,400				
Less: Accumulated Depreciation	– 2,600		Preferred Stock	$2,000	
			Common Stock	6,000	
Total Fixed Assets		$ 8,800	Paid in Surplus	900	
			Retained Earnings	2,505	
Other Assets:		$ 70	Total Stockholders'		$11,405
			Equity		
Total Assets		$14,680	Total Liabilities and Stockholders' Equity		$14,680

The asset side is broken down into four major divisions: current assets, investments, fixed assets, and other assets. *Current assets* include cash and all assets that could be converted to cash without much difficulty in a short period of time, or those assets that will be consumed during some accounting period. Therefore, such things as inventory (assets that will be sold or consumed in production), notes receivable (debts expected to be paid shortly), and accounts receivable (credit given on open account to be paid shortly), are included under current assets. *Investments* are those assets of a longer-term nature. Included in this classification would be any stocks, bonds, securities or foreign investments not convertible into cash within a certain time period, usually a year. *Fixed assets* include the value of permanent properties such as land, plant, and equipment, less accumulated depreciation. *Other assets* are those entries that do not fit into any other classification.

Liabilities are of two major types: current liabilities and long-term debt. *Current liabilities* include all debts that are to be paid within a certain time, usually a year. *Long-term debt* includes liabilities of a longer-term nature or those debts that will be owed for more than a year.

The stockholders' equity section includes the amount of money received for the stock issued, representing the par value of the stock. In other words, the value of this entry is found by multiplying the par value of the stock times the number of shares issued. When a company issues stock, the money paid by the buyer may exceed the par value of the stock. The amount of money paid over the par value is listed as a separate entry known as Paid-in Surplus or Excess Capital. The final entry is Retained Earnings or the amount of money the company has reinvested into the business since it was established.

The balance sheet gets its name because the left-hand side and the right-hand side of the statement must balance; that is, the total assets must equal the total liabilities plus the owners' equity.

Total Assets = Total Liabilities + Owners' Equity

From the stockholders' viewpoint, their equity is equal to the total assets minus the total liabilities.

Owners' Equity = Total Assets − Total Liabilities

ASSIGNMENT 42 THE BALANCE SHEET

A. Place the following entries in their proper place in the balance sheet below. (*Hint:* The word *payable* indicates a current liability.)

Accounts Payable	$ 50	Notes Payable	$ 100
Capital Stock	1100	Paid-in Surplus	50
Cash	200	Notes Receivable	500
Long-term Municipal Bonds	1000	Property, Plant, Equipment	1430
Accumulated Depreciation	750	Inventory	325
Federal Tax	100	Accounts Receivable	500
Retained Earnings	905	Long-term Debt	700
		Mortgage Payment Payable	200

Robson Rotors
Balance Sheet
December 31, 19X9

Assets

Current Assets:

Liabilities

Current Liabilities:

_____ $1,525

_____ $ 450

Total Assets $3,205

Total Liabilities and
Stockholders' Equity

B. Place each of the following entries in their proper place on the balance sheet and carry out the additions. Note that retained earnings is not given a value; this should be the balancing entry.

Retained Earnings	$	Accounts Receivable	500
Other Assets	200	Federal Tax Payable	50
Plant	300	Preferred Stock	750
Land	700	Cash	700
Long-term Bonds	500	Short-term Securities	200
Common Stock	500	Accounts Payable	300
Mortgage due 1985	1000	Accumulated Depreciation	500
Inventory	800	Equipment	450
Notes Payable	250	Paid-in Surplus	150
Promissory Note due 1983	50	Stock Held in Treasury for Building Fund	200

Joy Manufacturing Company
Balance Sheet
June 30, 19X9

Assets

Current Assets:

Liabilities

Current Liabilities:

Total Assets _____

Total Liabilities and
Stockholders' Equity _____

CHAPTER 30
Income statement analysis

Another important financial statement is the *income statement*. Whereas the balance sheet gives the financial position of a business as of a given *moment*, the income statement reveals what has happened over a given *period of time*. The income statement is concerned with the financial flow of the company's revenues and expenses over a period of time, usually a year. Because this notion of flow is inherent in the income statement, it is concerned with such things as sales, costs, profit, and loss.

The income statement may be prepared in two ways: the single-step form or the multiple-step form. An example of each is given below.

The multiple-step income statement has the advantage of revealing the *gross margin on sales* and *net operating income* in the process of computing net income for the year. These two figures are not shown by the single-step form.

As you can see, the entries on both forms can be placed in one of two categories: revenues or expenses. The income statement shows the revenues minus the expenses. *Revenue* is derived from two sources. The first source, *sales*, represents the products, services, or merchandise the company sold during the period. The entry on the income

---

Single-Step Income Statement

Roger's Hardware Store
Income Statement for
the Year Ending December 31, 19X9

Revenues:		
Net Sales	$60,000	
Other Revenue	5,000	
	$65,000	Total Revenues
Expenses:		
Cost of Goods Sold	25,000	
Operating Expenses	20,000	
Other Expenses	10,000	
	$55,000	Total Expenses
Income Prior to Taxes	$10,000	
Federal Income Tax (22%)	2,200	
Net Income for the Year	$ 7,800	

```
                    Multiple-Step Income Statement
                       Roger's Hardware Store
                         Income Statement for
                     the Year Ending December 31, 19X9

    Net Sales                                          $60,000
    Less:    CGS                                        25,000

             Gross Margin on Sales                      35,000
    Less:    Operating Expenses                         20,000

             Net Operating Income                       15,000
    Less:    Other Expenses minus
                 Other Revenue                           5,000
    Net Income prior to Taxes                          $10,000
    Federal Income Taxes (22%)                           2,200
    Net Income for Year                                $ 7,800
```

statement is *net sales*. This is computed by subtracting sales returns, allowances, and discounts from gross sales.

Net Sales = Gross Sales − Sales Returns, Allowances, and Discounts

The second source is the total of all other income derived from operations unrelated to the main sources. This total is entered on the income statement as *other revenue*. This entry includes such things as dividends and interest earned by the business, rental incomes, and profits gained by the sale of fixed assets such as machinery or land.

Expenses can be grouped into five classifications. The first classification, *cost of goods sold* (CGS), is the summary of the costs of the products sold by the company. Cost of goods sold is computed by first adding purchases to the inventory at the beginning of the period and then subtracting from this the value of the inventory at the end of the period.

Cost of Goods Sold = (Opening Inventory + Purchases) − Closing Inventory

Selling expenses include all expenses incurred in marketing and distributing the products. *Administrative expenses* include the general, day-to-day expenses incurred, such as office salaries, supplies, and utility and maintenance costs. These can be listed separately or grouped under the heading of *operating expenses*. *Other expenses* is the sum total of all expenses not logically placed in any of the other categories, such as interest paid, losses on the sale of assets, or loss from unforeseen accidents such as fire or flood. The final expense is the *Federal income taxes* paid on the income for the period.

ASSIGNMENT 43 THE INCOME STATEMENT

A. On a separate sheet, compile both a single-step and multiple-step income statement from the following list.

Opening Inventory	$ 70,000
Sales Returns, Discounts, Allowances	10,000
Gross Sales	100,000
Selling Expenses	10,000
Other Expenses	15,000
Closing Inventory	50,000
Other Revenue	10,000
Administrative Expenses	5,000
Purchases	30,000
Federal Income Taxes	(22% of net income plus surtax of 26% of net income over $25,000)

B. On a separate sheet, compile both a single-step and multiple-step income statement from the following list.

Closing Inventory	$ 245,000
Purchases	160,000
Other Revenue	17,000
Federal Income Taxes	(22% of net income plus surtax of 26% of net income over $25,000)
Opening Inventory	570,000
Other Expenses	15,000
Sales Returns, Discounts, Allowances	200,000
Administrative Expenses	125,000
Gross Sales	1,200,000
Selling Expenses	115,000

CHAPTER 31
T-account analysis

Since both the balance sheet and the income statement are prepared at the end of an accounting period, some method of recording what goes on during this period is needed. All financial transactions of a firm are recorded in both the journal and the ledger accounts. The *journal* is a running or sequential account of the entries of both the balance sheet and the income statement. This will be seen more clearly after we understand how the accounts work and what they look like.

DEBITS AND CREDITS

The basic operations involved in both journals and ledgers are debit and credit. In accounting, debit refers to the left-hand side and credit refers to the right-hand side of an account. Simple ledger accounts are in the shape of the letter "T" with the left-hand side being the debit side and the right-hand side being the credit side. Each entry on the balance sheet and all expenses and revenues have separate ledger accounts.

Every financial transaction of the firm must involve at least one credit entry and one debit entry. This is known as *double entry bookkeeping*. The procedure for deciding what ledger is to be debited (entering a transaction on the left-hand side) or credited (entering a transaction on the right-hand side) is determined by the following rules.

Rule 1. **For ledger accounts whose titles are entries on the asset side of the balance sheet, any increase is debited and any decrease is credited.**

Account Title							
Date	Item	PR	Debit	Date	Item	PR	Credit

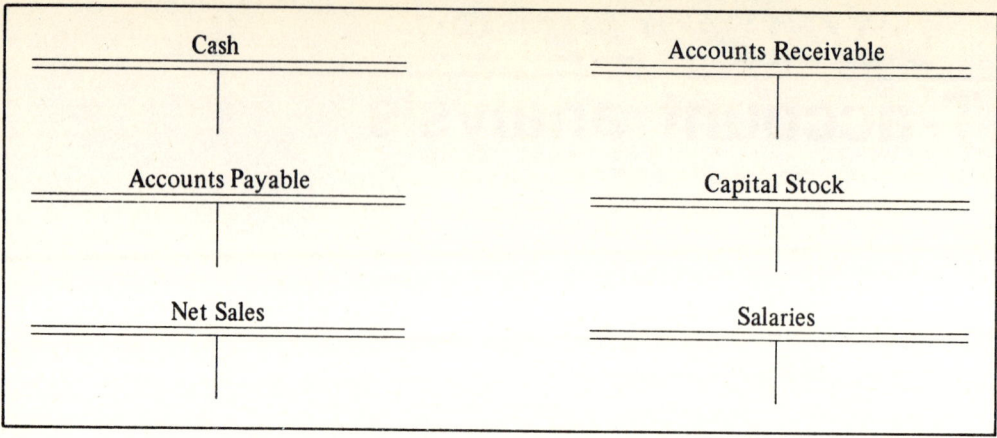

Rule 2. For ledger accounts whose titles are entries on the liability side of the balance sheet, any increase is credited and any decrease is debited.

Rule 3. Expenses are debited and revenues are credited.

An easy way to remember Rules 1 and 2 is to think of the changes graphically.

Balance Sheet			
Assets		Liabilities	
Increase (+)	Decrease (−)	Decrease (−)	Increase (+)
Debit	Credit	Debit	Credit

Example. Show the resulting ledger entries when a company sells some of its goods for $600 cash on February 3.

The fact that the company sold some its goods means that $600 must be credited on the net sales ledger. Net sales are a source of revenue and, according to Rule 3, must be credited. The resulting cash from the sale means that the cash account has increased by $600. According to Rule 1, since cash is an asset and has increased, the result is a $600 debit to cash.

Cash			Sales	
Feb. 3	$600		Feb. 3	$600

Example. Show the resulting ledger entries from the following transactions, using the same ledger accounts as above.

In the example above, the common stock ledger account is credited with $50,000 for two reasons. First, common stock is under stockholder's equity on the right-hand

Feb. 6 Paid employees' salaries, $2,500

	Salary Expense	
Feb. 6	$ 2,500	

	Cash	
Feb. 3	$600	Feb. 6	$ 2,500

Feb. 7 Bought store supplies on credit, $7,000

	Supplies Expense	
Feb. 7	$ 7,000	

	Accounts Payable	
		Feb. 7	$ 7,000

Feb. 10 Issued and sold common stock, $50,000

	Cash	
Feb. 3	$ 600	Feb. 6	$2,500
10	$50,000		

	Common Stock	
		Feb. 10	$50,000

side of the balance sheet. According to Rule 2, any increase in these entries must be credited. Second, the increase in common stock means the creation of revenue. According to Rule 3, any increase in revenue must be credited.

THE JOURNAL

The journal accounts record transactions in a similar manner. The only difference is in the form. Instead of recording the transaction in two separate "T" accounts, both halves of the transaction are recorded together in chronological order. A journal page is shown below with the previous ledger examples recorded.

Date		Entry	PR	Debit	Credit
Feb.	3	Cash		$ 600	
		Sales			$ 600
		Sales of Merchandise			
Feb.	6	Salary Expense		$ 2,500	
		Cash			$ 2,500
		Employee Salaries for Jan.			
Feb.	7	Supplies Expense		$ 7,000	
		Accounts Payable			$ 7,000
		Purchase of Store Supplies			
Feb.	10	Cash		$50,000	
		Common Stock			$50,000
		Sale of Stock to Public			

Between the entry and debit columns is a small column headed "Posting Reference (PR)." The ledger accounts are headed and numbered. The actual practice in an office is, first, a transaction is recorded in the journal, then the same transaction is recorded in the ledger and the numbers of the ledger accounts involved are entered in this PR column. This process is known as *posting to the general ledger*.

THE TRIAL BALANCE

The final area in T-account analysis is the trial balance. Since the ledger accounts are the entries used in the balance sheet and income statement, they also must balance

Debit	Cash	Credit
$5,000		$ 750
1,000		2,000
250		
500		
$6,750		$2,750

Cash account carries a $4,000 debit balance.

$6,750
-2,750
$4,000   Debit Balance

Trial Balance
Ajax Manufacturing Co.
June 30, 19X9

Account	Debit	Credit
Cash	$ 4,000	
Accounts Receivable	14,000	
Inventory	21,000	
Property, Plant & Equipment	75,000	
Accounts Payable		$ 12,500
Salaries Payable		6,000
Notes Payable		20,000
Common Stock		60,000
Sales		40,000
Interest Income		250
Salary Expense	10,000	
Rental Expense	8,750	
Depreciation Expense	6,000	
	$138,750	$138,750

at any given time or some error has been made. This balance is verified by first determining the debit or credit value of each account.

The second step is to list all the ledger accounts and their respective debit or credit balances. These balances are placed in either a left-hand or right-hand column depending on whether they are debit or credit balances. A sample trial balance is shown on page 286.

A. Given the following transactions, record the resulting ledger changes.

   a. Paid utilities on June 6: $400
   1. Made partial payment to Ajax Co. on account payable: $250
   2. Sold merchandise on account: $6000
   3. Sold common stock to the public: $75,000
   4. Purchased new turret lathes: $2500
   5. Paid advertising bill: $575

Cash	Utilities	Accounts Payable	Advertising

Plant and Equipment	Sales	Accounts Receivable	Common Stock

B. Given the following transactions, record the resulting journal entries.

   a. March 8—Wages were paid: $900
   1. March 12—Purchased merchandise to add to inventory: $12,000
   2. March 15—Paid administrative expenses: $560
   3. March 15—Paid part of a note due 1983: $5000
   4. March 23—Received a check to pay a bill on account: $700
   5. March 31—Sold merchandise for cash: $1140

Date		Entry	PR	Debit	Credit

C. Given the information below, record the necessary journal entries and post to the general ledger. Then prepare a trial balance.

1. Feb. 6—Sold merchandise for cash: $1200
2. Feb. 8—Purchased supplies: $900
3. Feb. 15—Paid office salaries: $900
4. Feb. 17—Sold merchandise on account: $5500
5. Feb. 25—Purchased equipment and issued noninterest bearing note to cover the cost: $15,000

JOURNAL

Date		Entry	PR	Debit	Credit

LEDGER

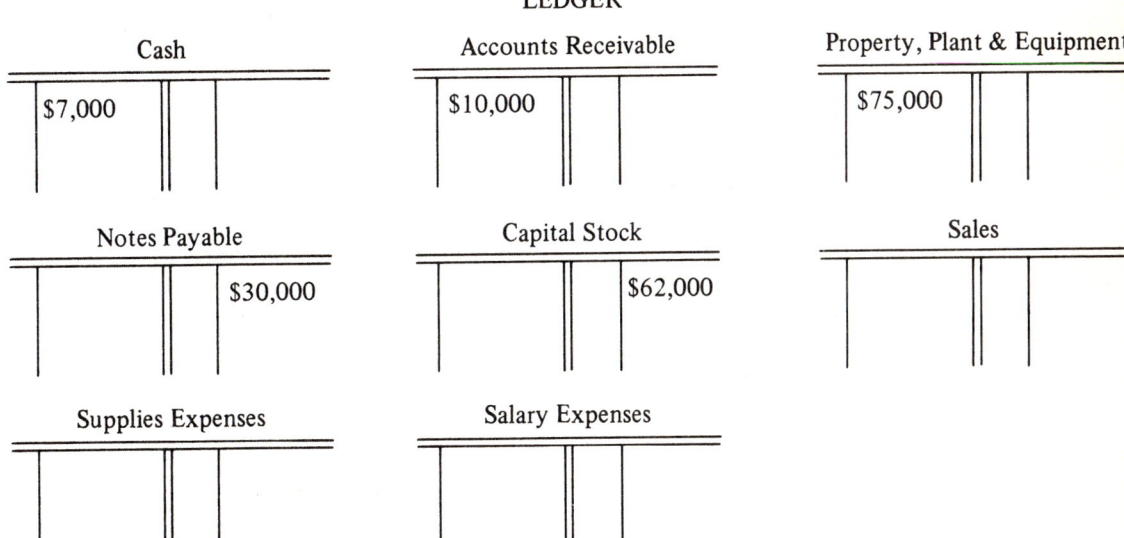

TRIAL BALANCE

Account	Debit	Credit

CHAPTER 32
Financial ratios

In the previous chapters, discussion was concerned primarily with the actual structure of the various accounts used by businesses. Attention should also be given to how these statements can be used to help the firm make future decisions. The successful business-man analyzes certain ratios carefully and compares these business ratios to past years and to other firms in the industry. A *ratio* is defined as the proportional relationship of one number to another. The term ratio implies division in much the same way that a fraction implies division. The Balance Sheet and Income Statement below will be used to explain the most common business ratios.

R.C. McCormick, Inc.
Balance Sheet
December 31, 19X9

Assets			Liabilities	
Current Assets:			**Current Liabilities:**	
Cash	$ 5,000		Accounts Payable	$ 7,000
Accounts Receivable	5,000		Dividends Payable	4,000
Inventory, at cost	20,000		Federal Income Tax Payable	1,500
Notes Receivable	1,000		Notes Payable	2,000
	$31,000			$14,500
Investments:			**Long Term Debt:**	
Long Term Govt. Securities	$ 7,000		4% Promissory Note due 1982	$20,000
			Mortgage due 1985	21,500
			Total Liabilities	$56,000
Land & Buildings $70,000				
Less Depreciation 25,000	$45,000		**Stockholders' Equity:**	
			Common Stock	$15,000
Other Assets:	$ 2,000		Surplus Capital	1,500
			Retained Earnings	12,500
				$29,000
			Total Liabilities and	
Total Assets	$85,000		Stockholders' Equity	$85,000

```
                        R.C. McCormick, Inc.
                         Income Statement
                          Dec. 31, 19X9

        Net Sales*                              $90,000
          Cost of Goods Sold                  -  60,000
        Gross Margin on Sales                   $30,000
          Operating Expenses                  -  20,000
        Net Operating Income                    $10,000
          Other Expenses, Other Revenues      -   2,000
        Net Income Prior to Federal Tax        $ 8,000
          Federal Income Taxes                 $ 1,760
              Net Income for 19X9              $ 6,240

        *Note:  Credit sales accounted for $30,000.
```

BUSINESS RATIOS

Current Ratio. This ratio is obtained by dividing current assets by current liabilities.

Example. Current Ratio $= \dfrac{\text{Current Assets}}{\text{Current Liabilities}}$

$$= \dfrac{\$31,000}{\$14,500}$$

$$= 2.13$$

The resulting ratio is a test for solvency or, in other words, the extent to which a company is able to pay off all current debts should they come due concurrently. In our example below, for each $1.00 of debt the company owes, it has $2.13 of current assets with which to pay. Should Current Liabilities be greater than Current Assets (the ratio being less than 1), the company is in financial trouble and has incurred too many debts. Likewise, should the ratio be very large, the company is holding a larger amount of current assets than is necessary. In the first case, the company may be in danger of bankruptcy, while in the second case, the company is not utilizing its assets most efficiently. Generally, the current ratio should fall between 2.00 and 3.00, but this may fluctuate according to the industry.

Net Income to Net Sales. This ratio is obtained by dividing net income for the period by net sales for the period.

Example. Net Income to Net Sales $= \dfrac{\text{Net Income}}{\text{Net Sales}}$

$$= \dfrac{\$6240}{\$90,000} = 6.93\%$$

This ratio is an important test for profitability and real improvement. It would be useless for a businessman simply to compare two companies on the basis of volume of business because costs for the two companies may not be proportionately equal. Similarly, the fact that a company increases its volume does not necessarily mean the company improved its profits. This ratio, then, allows the cost factor to be accounted for and makes the comparisons between firms or between years meaningful.

Capital Turnover. This ratio is obtained by dividing net sales for the period by stockholders' equity.

Example. $\text{Capital Turnover} = \dfrac{\text{Net Sales}}{\text{Stockholders' Equity}}$

$$= \dfrac{\$90,000}{\$29,000}$$

$$= 3.10 \text{ times}$$

This ratio gives a measure of the number of times invested capital turns over or, in other words, the amount of money invested in relation to sales. In this case, $1.00 invested accounted for $3.10 of net sales.

Net Income to Net Worth (Equity). This ratio is obtained by dividing net income for the period by stockholders' equity.

Example. $\text{Net Income to Net Worth} = \dfrac{\text{Net Income}}{\text{Stockholders' Equity}}$

$$= \dfrac{6240}{29,000}$$

$$= 21.5\%$$

This ratio is a criterion for profitability. It represents a rate of return on invested capital.

Collection Period. This period is obtained by dividing net sales on credit by accounts receivable. The resulting figure is then divided into 365 days (if days is the desired measure) or 12 months (if months is the desired measure).

Example. $\text{Number of Collection Periods} = \dfrac{\text{Net Credit Sales}}{\text{Accounts Receivable}}$

$$= \dfrac{30,000}{5000}$$

$$= 6$$

Example. $\text{Collection Period} = \dfrac{365}{6}$

$$= 60.8 \text{ days}$$

This result tells you that, on the average, any credit extended today will be paid back in 60.8 days. This is helpful in both estimating the collectibility of accounts and planning for the future.

Some other important business ratios are presented in Table 32.1.

TABLE 32.1

FINANCIAL RATIO	SIGNIFICANCE
Working Capital (= Current Assets − Current Liabilities)	A measure of the available funds to carry on day-to-day operations.
Net Income ÷ Working Capital	Provides an indication of management's ability to turn working capital into profit.
Net Sales ÷ Working Capital	Provides a measure of management's efficiency in utilizing working capital. Too high a ratio, however, may indicate a shortage of working capital. Normal ratio indicates amount of working capital needed for a given level of sales.
Net Sales ÷ Inventory	Provides an indication of merchandising efficiency and quality of the inventory (see Chapter 8).
Fixed Assets ÷ Net Worth	A measure of creditors' protection. The higher this ratio, the less is the owner's contribution to current assets.
Current Liabilities ÷ Net Worth	Provides a measure of a firm's protection to its short-term creditors.
Total Liabilities ÷ Net Worth	Provides an indication of the relative positions between owners and creditors and is a measure of financial strength.
Inventory ÷ Working Capital	An additional measure of liquidity and inventory balance, normally varies between .75 and 1.00 in most industries.
Current Debt ÷ Inventory	Shows how much the firm relies on selling its inventories in order to meet its obligations.
Funded Debt ÷ Working Capital	A measure of how much creditors contribute to working capital of firm. Should not exceed 1.0 for most industries.

COMPARISONS

Financial ratios are useful in the evaluation of a firm's improvement, profitability, and rate of return over a period of years, but alone they do not give insight into how well the firm compares with other firms or industries. These comparisons, however, can be achieved by obtaining the ratios for other firms. For example, Dun & Bradstreet, Inc.,

TABLE 32.2

Selected Business Ratios

Line of business (and number of concerns reporting)	Current assets to current debt (Times)	Net income on net sales (Percent)	Net income on tangible net worth (Percent)	Net income on net working capital (Percent)	Net sales to tangible net worth (Times)	Net sales to net working capital (Times)	Collection period (Days)	Net sales to inventory (Times)	Fixed assets to tangible net worth (Percent)	Current debt to tangible net worth (Percent)	Total debt to tangible net worth (Percent)	Inventory to net working capital (Percent)	Current debt to inventory (Percent)	Funded debts to net working capital (Percent)
RETAILING														
5611† Clothing & Furnishings, Men's & Boys' (215)	4.48 **2.71‡** 1.91	4.62 **2.47** 1.11	13.64 **7.52** 2.87	16.08 **8.96** 3.37	4.43 **3.30** 2.26	5.25 **3.71** 2.63	* * *	4.9 **3.6** 2.8	4.4 **10.9** 21.4	24.2 **52.7** 87.7	56.1 **106.2** 160.6	71.6 **108.9** 146.7	34.4 **56.5** 84.7	10.2 **23.5** 54.3
Discount Stores (169)	2.29 **1.86** 1.46	3.00 **1.87** 1.04	20.80 **14.16** 7.69	28.56 **18.70** 9.78	10.30 **6.95** 4.84	14.54 **8.85** 5.81	* * *	7.3 **5.6** 4.2	11.5 **27.5** 50.4	61.8 **97.4** 154.8	91.3 **142.7** 206.4	108.2 **161.2** 228.8	58.7 **76.8** 98.9	16.7 **41.9** 74.8
5651 Family Clothing Stores (80)	4.93 **2.78** 1.99	3.46 **1.79** 0.70	11.09 **6.33** 2.03	14.62 **7.38** 2.20	4.42 **3.09** 2.02	5.44 **3.57** 2.18	* * *	5.3 **3.9** 3.1	5.1 **13.2** 37.6	23.0 **51.7** 82.4	70.5 **95.9** 189.0	67.6 **94.6** 119.7	34.9 **57.8** 108.7	15.6 **39.6** 57.0
5712 Furniture Stores (187)	5.74 **3.07** 1.79	4.86 **2.16** 0.69	11.20 **6.01** 2.01	11.94 **6.33** 2.05	4.72 **2.49** 1.60	5.03 **2.71** 1.65	57 **111** 209	6.6 **4.8** 3.7	3.8 **9.2** 22.0	20.4 **46.3** 105.6	47.2 **98.2** 165.2	32.2 **60.2** 106.5	55.5 **90.2** 143.7	9.1 **20.0** 41.5
5541 Gasoline Service Stations (63)	3.48 **2.31** 1.44	6.55 **2.73** 1.14	16.40 **8.57** 4.24	40.80 **18.65** 8.85	4.56 **3.38** 2.12	10.53 **7.43** 4.40	* * *	20.9 **10.7** 6.1	18.9 **46.3** 71.1	19.1 **34.8** 69.2	50.0 **79.6** 138.3	34.3 **64.3** 131.4	61.6 **114.9** 256.8	20.1 **58.2** 119.4
5511 Motor Vehicle Dealers (98)	2.56 **1.96** 1.59	1.82 **0.94** 0.47	13.37 **7.51** 3.74	20.15 **9.97** 5.19	11.40 **8.07** 4.83	15.95 **11.20** 6.79	* * *	11.1 **8.1** 5.9	8.3 **18.4** 41.1	42.1 **77.4** 119.5	87.4 **117.5** 183.4	84.2 **130.2** 183.9	66.5 **79.9** 95.8	9.0 **33.0** 74.2
WHOLESALING														
5095 Beer, Wine & Alcoholic Beverages (84)	3.23 **2.04** 1.53	2.01 **1.18** 0.43	14.54 **7.40** 3.73	22.87 **12.17** 5.38	10.39 **7.14** 5.39	13.67 **9.59** 6.63	11 **22** 39	17.9 **9.3** 6.0	4.9 **15.2** 44.6	29.4 **65.0** 139.7	78.5 **141.2** 212.0	67.2 **100.8** 160.0	57.6 **94.5** 140.6	10.5 **34.4** 55.8
MANUFACTURING AND CONSTRUCTION														
2731-32 Books; Publ., Publ. & Printing (43)	3.52 **2.63** 2.01	8.14 **5.20** 2.65	17.52 **10.44** 5.63	25.20 **16.13** 8.19	3.18 **2.32** 1.69	5.02 **2.86** 1.95	41 **58** 78	10.6 **4.1** 2.5	9.4 **28.8** 55.9	30.2 **45.7** 73.3	51.8 **77.2** 113.8	52.0 **71.4** 88.2	49.7 **85.4** 164.2	6.1 **28.1** 86.5
3671-72-73-74-79 Electronic Components & Accessories (95)	3.42 **2.75** 1.94	7.59 **4.23** 1.86	21.75 **14.83** 6.40	30.49 **18.57** 6.57	4.40 **3.27** 2.34	5.62 **4.09** 3.27	38 **51** 70	7.8 **5.3** 4.0	24.9 **39.0** 63.2	29.0 **48.1** 71.6	53.0 **100.2** 166.5	54.9 **81.3** 99.2	63.8 **84.2** 110.6	28.1 **53.2** 84.2
1511 General Building Contractors (187)	2.09 **1.52** 1.29	2.71 **1.35** 0.59	16.75 **9.89** 4.43	29.88 **16.33** 7.03	11.98 **7.82** 4.85	19.05 **12.34** 7.83	** ** **	** ** **	10.1 **22.9** 45.5	56.8 **111.5** 198.3	84.3 **162.9** 271.4	** ** **	** ** **	17.6 **29.8** 72.8
3321-22-23 Iron & Steel Foundries (59)	3.73 **2.62** 1.76	5.73 **4.17** 2.54	13.98 **9.23** 6.55	37.18 **23.66** 12.03	3.47 **2.66** 1.98	9.57 **5.94** 4.21	30 **37** 51	21.6 **9.5** 6.6	43.6 **60.9** 75.3	18.0 **24.9** 44.8	47.2 **58.4** 92.4	33.9 **60.0** 83.3	67.6 **102.0** 218.4	30.6 **46.5** 80.2

* Not available.   ** Not applicable.

† The four-digit number refers to the Standard Industrial Classification for each line of business.   ‡ The figure in boldface is the median ratio.

a private management service organization, prepares such ratios on an industry-wide basis. These reports are readily available to the public. The reports first classify firms into four broad groups: retailing, wholesaling, manufacturing, and construction. They then combine firms along business lines and list fourteen ratios for each line of business.

To compile these figures, questionnaires are sent to representative companies. All like ratios from the firms in the sample are listed in decreasing order. The ratio figure falling exactly in the middle of this list is the *median* ratio for that business group; i.e., half the number of firms sampled had ratios higher and half lower than this figure. The ratios shown above and below the median in Table 32.2 are the upper and lower *quartiles*. One quarter of the firms had ratios higher than the upper quartile, and one quarter had ratios lower than the lower quartile. These quartiles provide some estimate of the acceptable variation in the various ratios reported. With the help of these ratios, an individual firm can better analyze how well its operations are doing in relation to those in the rest of its industry.

A. From the following list of entries, derive a balance sheet and income statement.

Fixed Assets	$100,000	Cash	$ 10,000
Accounts Payable	11,800	Promissory Note	50,000
Retained Earnings	13,200	Other Revenue	5500
Other Expenses	7500	Depreciation	59,000
Federal Inc. Tax Expense	3200	Accounts Receivable	7000
Inventory	35,000	Common Stock	10,000
Dividends Payable	8000	Net Sales	130,000
Capital Surplus	5000	Operating Expenses	22,000
Cost of Goods Sold	90,000	Notes Receivable	4500
Federal Taxes Payable	1000	Current Assets	56,500
Other Assets	1500	Net Income After Taxes	12,800

B. Using the balance sheet and income statement in Problem A, compute each of the following business ratios.

1. Current Ratio

2. Net Income to Net Worth

3. Net Profit on Net Sales

4. Collection Period

5. Capital Turnover (Net Sales to Stockholders' Equity)

6. Net Sales to Inventory

7. Current Debt to Inventory

8. Working Capital

C. Assume that this firm is a retail family clothing store. Using Table 32.2, what can you say about its operations in relation to other firms in the same line?

D. Solve the following problems.

1. The Blucher Company sold $45,900 on credit during 197X. The accounts receivable for that year totaled $5100. What was the average collection period for credit offered during 197X?

2. The A & J Company possesses total liabilities of $94,890 and net worth of $141,350. The Bryce Company has total liabilities of $66,480 and net worth of $109,000. Which company would you say is financially stronger, judging from these respective ratios?

3. The Woodward Company's net income for 197X was $50,960 and net sales amounted to $1,295,000 that year. The following year, 197Y, net income for Woodward's totaled $27,380 and net sales

were $675,000. Using the net income to net sales ratio, determine which year was actually more profitable for the Woodward Company.

4. The Jeffreys' retail men's clothing store has net sales of $42,700 and working capital of $5260. Summer's Men's Clothing Store has net sales of $35,410 and working capital of $2060. Compare the net sales to working capital ratios for both companies with those given in Table 32.2. Which company would you say was using its working capital in a more efficient manner? Is there any need for a change in the amounts of working capital for either firm?

5. The Grady Furniture Store has a current debt of $68,730 and an inventory of $40,440. What is the current debt to inventory ratio here? Referring to Table 32.2, do you think that Grady's depends on selling its inventories to finance its current debt more than might be advisable?

A. Matching.

_____ 1. mean

_____ 2. fixed assets

_____ 3. capital turnover

_____ 4. graph

_____ 5. income statement

_____ 6. assets

_____ 7. array

_____ 8. working capital

_____ 9. balance sheet

_____ 10. journal

_____ 11. number of collections periods

_____ 12. administrative expenses

_____ 13. liabilities

_____ 14. current ratio

_____ 15. average

_____ 16. cost of goods sold

_____ 17. chart

_____ 18. selling expenses

_____ 19. double entry bookkeeping

_____ 20. current assets

(a) summary of the costs of the products sold by a firm

(b) formal statement showing the company's financial worth at a given moment

(c) a company's total possessions

(d) total claims against a company

(e) cash and all assets that can be easily converted to cash

(f) permanent properties such as buildings, land, and equipment

(g) statement showing the financial flows of a company

(h) part of operating expenses

(i) cost of marketing and distributing a company's products

(j) running account of the entries of both the balance sheet and the income statement

(k) at least one debit and one credit

(l) $\dfrac{\text{current assets}}{\text{current liabilities}}$

(m) $\dfrac{\text{net sales}}{\text{stockholders' equity}}$

(n) $\dfrac{\text{net credit sales}}{\text{accounts receivable}}$

(o) current assets − current liabilities

(p) a single number that represents all the numbers in a list or set

(q) $X = \dfrac{\text{sum of items}}{\text{number of items}}$

(r) a list of numbers in either increasing or decreasing order

(s) any visual presentation of statistical data

(t) type of chart that employs two or more scales

B. On a separate sheet, compile both a balance sheet and an income statement, given the following information.

Federal Tax Expense	$ 400,000	Inventory	$ 705,000
Paid-in Surplus	120,000	Other Assets	825,000
Net Sales	1,685,000	Current Assets	2,055,000
Common Stock	1,200,000	Promissory Note (due in 2 years)	1,500,000
Net Income	400,000	Accounts Payable	650,000
Depreciation	250,000	Retained Earnings	610,100
Cash	300,000	Dividends Payable	300,000
Other Expenses	35,000	Notes Receivable	150,000
Other Revenue	10,000	Operating Expenses	110,000
Fixed Assets	1,750,000	Federal Taxes Payable	200,000
Cost of Goods Sold	750,000	Accounts Receivable	900,000

C. Using the balance sheet and the income statement prepared for Problem B, compute the following business ratios.

1. Capital turnover

2. Current ratio

3. Net income to net sales

4. Net income to net worth

5. Working capital

6. Net sales to working capital

7. Net sales to inventory

8. Inventory to working capital

9. Current liabilities to net worth

10. Current debt to inventory

D. Set up a ledger and show the ledger entries resulting from the following financial transactions.

1. Purchased turret lathes on open account: $17,500

2. Paid administrative salaries: $43,000

3. Issued a note to cover the costs of the turret lathes in 1

4. Received a check in payment for merchandise sold: $1270

5. Sent a check to cover part of the note issued in 3: $8000

E. From the data below, answer the following questions.

1. What is the mean?

2. What is the median?

3. What is the mode?

4. What is the range?

HEIGHT IN INCHES OF 30 HIGH SCHOOL STUDENTS									
65	66	72	64	73	69	61	70	61	67
67	74	68	60	62	71	67	68	72	65
66	65	61	74	65	63	73	65	69	66

Final examination

A. Matching.

_____ **1.** check   **(a)** sum total of items in a list divided by the number of items in the list

_____ **2.** current assets   **(b)** general administrative and selling expenses incurred in normal business operations

_____ **3.** mean   **(c)** allocating the cost of an asset with more than one year of useful life over its entire lifetime

_____ **4.** liter   **(d)** an order or draft to pay someone

_____ **5.** overhead   **(e)** process of balancing a bank statement

_____ **6.** depreciation   **(f)** .1¢ or $.001

_____ **7.** premiums   **(g)** cash and all other holdings that could be easily converted into cash

_____ **8.** reconciliation   **(h)** $\dfrac{1}{c}$

_____ **9.** reciprocal   **(i)** unit of volume

_____ **10.** mills   **(j)** policy payments made to insurance companies

B. Perform the indicated operations.

1. $\dfrac{1}{2} + \dfrac{7}{6} + 3\dfrac{5}{8}$

2. $6.3 + 27.12 + .061 + 14.03$

3. 1400 articles @ $4.60

4. 2 gal, 2 pt plus 3 qt, 1 pt

5. 531 centimeters converted to meters

C. Find each of the following.

1. Single equivalent discount rate of 30%, 20%, and 5%

2. 18% of $2300

3. Simple interest on $1600 at 4% for 5 years

4. Annual ordinary annuity of $1000 at 4% compound interest for 3 years

5. The mean of 75, 212, 83, and 46

D. In each of the problems below, fill in the missing answers.

1. Inventories   3/26/197X $ 54,000
                  9/25/197X   61,000
     Goods sold   716,000
     Turnover rate   _____

2. $R =$ _____, $B = 165$, $P = 210$

3. List price, $480
Discounts, 15%, 10%, 5%
Net price _____

4. $c =$ Cost Price = $460
   $m = 20\%$ Markup (based on Cost Price) =
     $s =$ Selling Price =

5. Cost of building, $12,000
Estimated life, 10 years
Salvage value, $2000
Depreciation for first year computed by SOYD, $_____

6. Needed revenue, $1,650,000
Assessed value, $72,500,000
Property tax rate in mills, _____

7. $P = \$4000$ $R = 3\%$ $T = 60$ days
Ordinary interest = $_____

8. Amount of loan, $4000
Time of loan, 3 months
Discount rate, 6%
Bank discount _____
Proceeds _____

9. Amount of money needed, $100,000
Time allowed to accumulate, 6 years
Current interest rate, 4%
Annual increment to sinking fund _____

10. 36   Mean _____
    18   Median _____
    26   Mode _____
    30
    21
    24
    30

E. Solve each of the following problems.

1. Mr. Donaldson plans to paint his game room. If the areas of the four walls are 100, 100, 80, and 80 sq ft, how many gallons of paint will he need to cover the room if one gallon covers 85 sq ft?

2. Mr. Jarvis' installment payments are similar to an annual annuity due. He must pay $600 at the beginning of each year for ten years and also interest at the rate of 6% per year. What is the total amount of his annual payments (annuity due)?

3. In 19X9 the Malcolm Manufacturing Company's balance sheet revealed current assets of $85,000 and current liabilities of $100,000. Compute the firm's current ratio and analyze the result.

4. Textile Plus Inc. decided to distribute $150,000 of its net profit to its stockholders. If they had 15,000 preferred shares of 4% stock with a par value of $50, how much would be distributed to both preferred and common stockholders as dividends?

5. If Mrs. Richards is able to borrow $10,000 at 6% for six years and can invest it at the same rate compounded quarterly at 7%, how much profit can she make?

6. Mrs. Steele works 46 hours at $3.80 per hour. She is paid on the basis of a 40-hour work week, with time-and-a-half overtime allowance. What are her gross total wages for that pay period?

7. Mr. Cox is a salaried executive who earned $23,500 in 1978. Using the Social Security tax rate of 6.05%, determine:

   a. the total amount of tax paid by Mr. Cox in 1978
   b. the tax paid per week
   c. how many weeks he paid this tax

8. Joe Blake expects to receive $3800 in seven years. If the annually compounded interest rate is 6%, what is the present value of this amount?

APPENDIX

Federal professional and administrative careers examination (PACE)

The Federal Professional and Administrative Careers (PACE) Examination is an important avenue of entry into employment with the Federal government. The material covered in this book is sufficient to permit one who has mastered it to pass the quantitative part of the Examination. The Examination consists of problems covering such subjects as fractions, decimals, percent, interest, taxation, measurement and interpretation of graphs. All these areas have been covered in this volume, making it useful as a study guide for the quantitative section of the Examination.

Three sample tests are presented below similar to those found in the Examination. The number enclosed in parentheses after each question refers to the particular chapter in this book where the methods necessary to answer this type of question are discussed. Read the questions carefully. If any question appears too difficult, a review of the appropriate chapter should enable you to arrive at the correct solution. An answer key is given at the end of the Examination.

Sample Part (Quantitative Section) of the Federal Professional and Administrative Careers (PACE) Examination

Directions.
To answer the following questions, perform the operations indicated or determine what operations are needed to solve the written problems and then perform them. Use the blank space on the pages to do any figuring. Then select your answer from the alternatives and mark the appropriate space on your answer sheet. *All answers are neither truncated nor rounded; they are exact answers unless otherwise specified in the question.*

Time.
35 minutes for each sample test. If you finish before before 35 minutes has elapsed, check your work.

1. $59.896 + .63 + 19.6122 =$ (3)
   - (A) 80.2282
   - (B) 81.1482
   - (C) 80.1382
   - (D) 81.2372
   - (E) None of these

2. $254,322 \overline{)635,805}$ (3)
   - (A) 2.512
   - (B) 2.53
   - (C) 25
   - (D) 2.5
   - (E) None of these

3. $372.39 - 144.6378 =$ (3)
   - (A) 226.7422
   - (B) 226.7522
   - (C) 227.7522
   - (D) 228.7532
   - (E) None of these

4. $67\frac{2}{9} + \frac{4}{5} + 4\frac{7}{9} =$ (2)
   - (A) $72\frac{4}{5}$
   - (B) 72.42
   - (C) 72.31
   - (D) $72\frac{5}{9}$
   - (E) None of these

5. $780,968 \overline{)488,105}$ (3)
   - (A) .6252
   - (B) .625
   - (C) .0625
   - (D) 6.253
   - (E) None of these

6. The combined area of two lots of equal width is 285 sq. rods. One lot is 22 rods long, and the other is 35 rods in length. What is their width? (1)
   - (A) 4 rods
   - (B) 5 rods
   - (C) 6 rods
   - (D) 12 rods
   - (E) None of these

7. Mr. Powell is older than his wife. In fact, by adding his son's age to his wife's age, Mr. Powell's age is given. Six years from now Mr. Powell will be 3 times as old as his son, and at the same time his age will be twice the difference between his wife's and his son's ages. How old is Mr. Powell? (1)
   - (A) 28 yr.
   - (B) 30 yr.
   - (C) 36 yr.
   - (D) 42 yr.
   - (E) None of these

8. A manufacturer makes an article at a cost of $4.80. He sells it at a profit of $17\frac{1}{2}\%$ on sales to a wholesaler. The wholesaler sells it at a profit of 20% on sales to a retailer. The retailer sells it at a profit of $33\frac{1}{3}\%$ on sales to a customer. What does the customer pay for the article? (9, 10)
   - (A) $8.00
   - (B) $8.99
   - (C) $10.91
   - (D) $10.99
   - (E) None of these

9. The large size of a dishwashing liquid sells for 35¢ for 12 oz. The economy size of the same brand sells for 69¢ for 22 oz. How much is saved in buying 132 oz. of the better buy?   (3)
   (A) 25¢
   (B) 29¢
   (C) 32¢
   (D) $1.03
   (E) None of these

10. A traveling salesman fills his car with gasoline one morning. During that day he drives a total of 221 mi. When he fills the car with gasoline the next morning, he finds that it takes 15.3 gal. of gasoline. On the average, how far did he drive on 1 gal. of gasoline?   (3)
   (A) 24.2 mi.
   (B) 24.3 mi.
   (C) 24.4 mi.
   (D) 24.5 mi.
   (E) None of these

11. $47\frac{13}{29} + 156\frac{17}{31} =$ (2)
   (A) $189\frac{23}{60}$
   (B) $201\frac{96}{899}$
   (C) $203\frac{896}{899}$
   (D) $207\frac{896}{901}$
   (E) None of these

12. $936) 471,757 =$ (3)
   (A) $54\frac{11}{936}$
   (B) $504\frac{1}{72}$
   (C) $504\frac{11}{936}$
   (D) $507\frac{5}{72}$
   (E) None of these

13. $57.609 + 995.3482 + 4.986 + 29.4578 + 970.43 =$ (3)
   (A) 205.7831
   (B) 2157.831
   (C) 2367.831
   (D) 3057.941
   (E) None of these

14. $\dfrac{(217 + 53 - 8)191}{26 + (49 + 8)7 - 163} =$ (1, 2)
   (A) -12473
   (B) 123
   (C) 191
   (D) 217
   (E) None of these

15. $37,654 \times 498 =$ (1)
   (A) 18,751,692
   (B) 18,751,693
   (C) 187,516,932
   (D) 187,516,392
   (E) None of these

16. If a train goes 150 yd. in 10 sec., how many feet can it go in one-fifth of a second?   (2)
   (A) 3
   (B) 5
   (C) 9
   (D) 13.7
   (E) None of these

17. A glass packer is paid 8¢ for each article packed but is fined 25¢ for each one he breaks. His net earnings for a day in which he successfully packed 10 more than 30 times as many articles as he broke were $18. How many articles did he successfully pack that day?   (3)
   (A) 200
   (B) 225
   (C) 240
   (D) 250
   (E) None of these

18. A home owner paid a tax of $28.00 on a house assessed at $25,000. What was the assessed valuation of the house on which the tax was $22.40? (3, 14)

(A) $15,000   (B) $15,680
(C) $16,000   (D) $18,000
(E) $20,000

19. A woman owning 725 shares of stock sold 20% at one time and later sold 10% of the balance. How many shares had she left? (9, 25)

(A) 495   (B) 512
(C) 522   (D) 622
(E) None of these

20. In a certain city a sociologist finds the ratio of the number of residents 30 years of age or older to the number under 30 to be 3:2. He plans to interview a sample of 250 residents. How many persons of the older age group must he select if his sample is to have the same age distribution as the city's population? (2, 32)

(A) 100   (B) 150
(C) 160   (D) 90
(E) None of these

21. $364,095 \div 465 =$ (1)

(A) 692   (B) 779.3
(C) 782.9   (D) 783
(E) None of these

22. $\dfrac{29(462 + 19 - 6)}{210 + 5(67 - 14)} =$ (1, 2)

(A) $2\frac{7}{11}$ (B) 2.9
(C) 29   (D) 43
(E) None of these

23. $103\dfrac{7}{13} - 97\dfrac{31}{39} =$ (2)

(A) $4\frac{2}{3}$ (B) 5
(C) $5\frac{23}{39}$ (D) $6\frac{29}{39}$
(E) None of these

24. $37\dfrac{5}{7} \times 25\dfrac{23}{66} =$ (2)

(A) 832.7   (B) 956
(C) 963.11   (D) 2178
(E) None of these

25. $7006.02 - 938.467 =$ (3)

(A) 6.6735   (B) 606.735
(C) 6067.53   (D) 6067.533
(E) None of these

26. Eight men can finish a job in 6 days. How many men will be needed to finish it in half a day?   (2)
    (A) 48   (B) 56
    (C) 96   (D) 104
    (E) None of these

27. One vegetable oil contains 6% saturated fats and a second contains 26% saturated fats. In making a salad dressing how many ounces of the second must be added to 10 oz. of the first if the percent of saturated fats is to be 16%?   (9)
    (A) 10   (B) 12.3
    (C) 14   (D) 16.7
    (E) None of these

28. Each of twenty-four 4-room apartments is rented for $240 per month, and twelve 3-room ones for $180. If yearly expenses are $4500, the average monthly profit per room is most nearly   (6)
    (A) $35   (B) $55
    (C) $60   (D) $65
    (E) $150

29. In his wallet Mr. Sewell has $1, $5, and $10 bills totaling $117. He has the same number of $5 bills as $1 and $10 bills put together. If he has 30 bills in all, how many $10 bills does he have?   (1)
    (A) 3   (B) 5
    (C) 7   (D) 9
    (E) None of these

30. If a train travels 444 mi. in 8 hr. 40 min., the time in which it can run 1250 mi. at the same rate is most nearly   (6)
    (A) 24 hr.   (B) 24 hr. 23 min.
    (C) 24 hr. 24 min. (D) 25 hr.
    (E) 25 hr. 30 min.

STOP

1. $54.917 + .81 + 21.7133 =$ (3)
   - (A) 77.4403
   - (B) 77.4303
   - (C) 77.44
   - (D) 77.4313
   - (E) None of these

2. $275{,}601 \overline{)\, 385{,}841.4}$ (3)
   - (A) 1.414
   - (B) 1.44
   - (C) 1.444
   - (D) 1.4
   - (E) None of these

3. $472.38 - 156.5762 =$ (3)
   - (A) 314.8038
   - (B) 314.7038
   - (C) 315.7038
   - (D) 315.8038
   - (E) None of these

4. $73\frac{2}{7} + \frac{2}{5} + 8\frac{5}{7} =$ (2)
   - (A) $82\frac{2}{5}$
   - (B) 82.54
   - (C) $82\frac{3}{5}$
   - (D) 82.61
   - (E) None of these

5. $612{,}328 \overline{)\, 76{,}541}$
   - (A) 1.255
   - (B) .1255
   - (C) .01252
   - (D) .125
   - (E) None of these

6. The price per pound of pears is 40¢. The price per pound of apples is 25¢. If a shopper buys 12 pounds of apples how many pounds of pears can he or she buy with the same amount of money?   (3)
   - (A) 6
   - (B) 9
   - (C) 7
   - (D) 6.5
   - (E) 7.5

7. Two rectangular fields of equal lengths are 15 meters and 20 meters wide. If the total area of the two fields is 350 square meters, what is the length of each field?   (1)
   - (A) 5 meters
   - (B) 10 meters
   - (C) 15 meters
   - (D) 20 meters
   - (E) None of these

8. A pile of phonograph records is 5.5 feet high. Each record is .125 inches thick. The number of records in the pile is (3, 6)
   - (A) 528
   - (B) 626
   - (C) 438
   - (D) 275
   - (E) None of these

9. On a map, 288 square feet is represented by $\frac{1}{4}$ inches. What is 192 square feet represented by on the map?   (2, 4)
   - (A) $\frac{1}{4}$ inches
   - (B) $\frac{1}{6}$ inches
   - (C) $\frac{1}{2}$ inches
   - (D) $\frac{1}{3}$ inches
   - (E) None of these

10. How many boxes 8 inches × 6 inches × 9 inches can be put into a space 10 feet × 6 feet × 4 feet?   (1, 6)
    - (A) 1406
    - (B) 108
    - (C) 240
    - (D) 2160
    - (E) None of these

11. $\dfrac{27 \times 13}{(17 + 33)2} =$ (1, 3)

(A) 3.515
(B) 3.51
(C) 3.41
(D) 3.5152
(E) None of these

12. 435,822 (1)
$\times$ 1,374

(A) 598 719 428
(B) 598 820 428
(C) 598 819 428
(D) 598 819 328
(E) None of these

13. $2.1456 \div 2235 =$ (3)
(A) .0000962
(B) .00096
(C) .00965
(D) .000965
(E) None of these

14. $455\dfrac{8}{16} - 65\dfrac{3}{31} =$ (2)

(A) 390.4
(B) 390.38
(C) $390\frac{25}{62}$
(D) $390\frac{13}{31}$
(E) None of these

15. 31.461 (3)
.7131

(A) 22.4348391
(B) 22.5348391
(C) 22.4358391
(D) 22.5348291
(E) None of these

16. A clock gains 12 minutes in 2 days. If the clock is set at 9 A.M. on Monday, what time will it read at 1 P.M. (real time) the next day? (6)
(A) 1:02 P.M.
(B) 1:07 P.M.
(C) 1:10 P.M.
(D) 1:11 P.M.
(E) None of these

17. In order to obtain admission into a special school program, all applicants must take a special exam, which is passed by three out of every five applicants. Of those who pass the exam, one-fourth are finally accepted. What is the percentage of all applicants who *fail* to gain admission into the program? (2, 9)
(A) 55
(B) 60
(C) 75
(D) 85
(E) None of these

18. A stenographer does typing work at the following rate: 5¢ per sheet of typing paper used and $3.00 per hour of typing. He can type 60 words a minute, and types on paper which holds 30 lines per page, and 10 words per line. How much will he charge to type an 1800-word paper, with two carbon copies? (3, 6)
(A) $2.40
(B) $4.10
(C) $6.50
(D) $9.15
(E) None of these

19. The mileage on a car was 3740 when the gas tank was one-half full. When the tank was empty the mileage was 3890. If the car averages 15 miles to the gallon, how much can the gas tank hold? (2)
(A) 20 gallons
(B) 15 gallons
(C) $22\frac{1}{2}$ gallons
(D) 10 gallons
(E) None of these

20. John eats $\frac{1}{8}$ of a pie. The next day his sister Jean and her friends eat $\frac{4}{5}$ of the remaining pie. What percent of the original pie is left? (2, 9)
(A) $7\frac{1}{2}\%$
(B) $17\frac{1}{2}\%$
(C) 30%
(D) 70%
(E) None of these

21. $\dfrac{3876 \times 4}{(499 + 39)18 + 6} =$ (1, 3)

(A) 1.732
(B) 1.65
(C) 1.675
(D) 1.6
(E) None of these

22. $32\dfrac{1}{8} \div 1\dfrac{1}{4} =$ (2, 4)

(A) 25.7
(B) 25.75
(C) 2.57
(D) 2.575
(E) None of these

23. $65.2245\overline{)88.70532}$ (3)

(A) 1.3645
(B) 1.36
(C) 1.355
(D) 1.3
(E) None of these

24. $713\dfrac{1}{20} \times 31\dfrac{1}{10} =$ (2, 4)

(A) 22175.855
(B) 21175.855
(C) 22175.755
(D) 22175.85
(E) None of these

25. $\dfrac{(49 \times 12) + 12}{497 + 34 - 8 + 2} =$ (1, 2)

(A) $1\frac{2}{7}$
(B) 1.141
(C) 1.14
(D) $1\frac{1}{7}$
(E) None of these

26. A shirt costs $3.75. If Jay buys 3 shirts, how much change does he get from a $20 bill? (3)

(A) $8.75
(B) $9.00
(C) $9.25
(D) $9.50
(E) None of these

27. Phil has a sheet of paper 8 inches long and 3 inches wide. How many strips of paper 6 inches long and 1 inch wide can be cut from this sheet? (1)

(A) 3
(B) 4
(C) 6
(D) 24
(E) It cannot be determined from the given information.

28. A Mid-Western railway company charges $3.75 per pound for each item 10 lbs or less, shipped one mile, and $3.25 per pound for each item over 10 lbs, shipped one mile. The fee the company will charge per one mile shipment of 20 forty pound items sent in 5 equal one-mile shipments is (3)

(A) $520
(B) $640
(C) $580
(D) $720
(E) None of these

29. It takes Bill 4 hours to do a job. It takes Joe 2 hours to do the same job. How many such jobs could they do together in 4 hours? (1)

(A) 1
(B) 3
(C) 5
(D) 7
(E) None of these

30. The Skoie River flows eastward for 42 miles. Then it flows southward for 24 miles. Then it flows eastward again for 30 miles. It flows eastward at 6 miles per hour. It flows 4 miles per hour southward. Assuming no outside interference, how long would it take a raft to flow down this stretch of the Skoie River? (1)

(A) 16 hours
(B) 18 hours
(C) 24 hours
(D) 36 hours
(E) None of these

STOP

1. Find the product: 987.234   (3)
   × 5467.08

   (A)   53,972,872.5672   (B)   539,728.25652
   (C)   5,397,287.25672   (D)   7,397,287.25672
   (E)   None of these

2. $503\frac{9}{17} - 29\frac{29}{34} =$ (2)

   (A) $473\frac{23}{34}$ (B) $475\frac{21}{34}$
   (C) $483\frac{23}{34}$ (D) $574\frac{12}{17}$
   (E)   None of these

3. $34.9\overline{)1075.84} =$ (3)
   (A) $29.8\frac{17}{349}$ (B) $38.2\frac{16}{349}$
   (C) $3.08\frac{92}{349}$ (D) $30.8\frac{92}{349}$
   (E)   None of these

4. $3001.92 - 983.8932 =$ (3)
   (A)   3018.0268   (B)   2008.676
   (C)   2018.1278   (D)   2118.0268
   (E)   None of these

5. $\frac{45(77 - 21)}{1100 - 417} =$ (1, 2)

   (A) $3\frac{9}{11}$ (B) $3\frac{7}{13}$
   (C) $3\frac{7}{11}$ (D) $2\frac{9}{11}$
   (E)   None of these

6. A mechanic repairs 16 cars per 8 hour day. Another mechanic in the same shop repairs $1\frac{1}{2}$ times this number in $\frac{3}{4}$ the time. Theoretically, how long will it take to repair 16 cars in the shop?   (2)
   (A) $2\frac{2}{3}$ hours   (B) $2\frac{9}{10}$ hours
   (C)   3 hours   (D) $2\frac{1}{2}$ hours
   (E)   None of these

7. A man, wishing to fence around a piece of ground with some posts, found that if he set them a foot apart there would be 150 too few, but if he placed them a yard apart, there would be 70 posts to spare. How many posts did he have?   (1)
   (A)   180   (B)   190
   (C)   200   (D)   215
   (E)   None of these

8. If the sum of two numbers is 60 and their ratio is 3:2, then the larger number is   (1, 32)
   (A)   20   (B)   25
   (C)   30   (D)   35
   (E)   None of these

9. A boy has 12 apples. He gives half of these to his mother and half of the rest to a friend. (2) How many apples does he have left for himself?
   (A) 8   (B) 2
   (C) 4   (D) 3
   (E) None of these

10. The number of days in 30% of 3 weeks 4 days 8 hours is (6, 9)
   (A) 7   (B) 7.5
   (C) 7.6   (D) 8.1
   (E) None of these

11. $499\frac{3}{7} + 501\frac{2}{17} =$ (2)

   (A) $901\frac{35}{119}$ (B) $1000\frac{5}{17}$
   (C) $1001\frac{5}{17}$ (D) $1002\frac{2}{7}$
   (E) None of these

12. $\dfrac{(418 + 56 - 8)313}{77 + (50 + 9)7 - 24} =$ (1, 2)

   (A) -12378 (B) 310
   (C) 313   (D) 1246.649
   (E) None of these

13. $509\overline{)\,45,304} =$ (3)
   (A) $79\frac{3}{17}$ (B) $87\frac{3}{509}$
   (C) $89\frac{5}{509}$ (D) $91\frac{5}{19}$
   (E) None of these

14. $221\frac{1}{19} \times 10\frac{11}{35} =$ (2)

   (A) 80.3   (B) 2510.0
   (C) 2510.1   (D) 2280
   (E) None of these

15. $150.03 - 39.958 =$ (3)
   (A) 110.072   (B) 111.072
   (C) 111.75   (D) 112.05
   (E) None of these

16. A package of 12 paper plates costs 39¢. Another package of 10 paper plates costs 31¢. The difference in cost per plate is (3)
   (A) 0.1¢   (B) 0.12¢
   (C) 0.15¢   (D) 1.4¢
   (E) None of these

17. In 1936, New Mexico had 18 Indian pueblos with a population of 10,565, an increase of 22% in 20 years. The Indian population in 1916 was most nearly (9)
   (A) 2324   (B) 7635
   (C) 8241   (D) 8659
   (E) 8661

18. A watch lost 1 min. 18 sec. in 39 days. How many seconds did it lose per day?   (6)

(A) 2   (B) $2\frac{1}{2}$
(C) 5   (D) $7\frac{1}{2}$
(E) None of these

19. In a test a woman scored 115 on a scale of 0–160. Her score converted to a scale of 0–100 is approximately   (4)

(A) 69   (B) 70
(C) 71   (D) 72
(E) 73

20. A metal foundry has some gun metal which is 15% tin, the rest being copper. The number of pounds of pure tin needed to mix with 600 lb. of the 15% gun metal to produce a grade of gun metal containing 20% tin is   (9)

(A) 30   (B) 35
(C) 37.5   (D) 40.2
(E) None of these

21. $1\frac{7}{15} + \frac{5}{12} + \frac{11}{36} + \frac{4}{9} =$ (2)

(A) $1\frac{47}{90}$ (B) $2\frac{43}{90}$
(C) $2\frac{93}{180}$ (D) $2\frac{47}{90}$
(E) None of these

22. $252\overline{)13{,}860} =$ (3)

(A) 49.72   (B) 51.3
(C) 54.93   (D) 61.7
(E) None of these

23. $\dfrac{5039 - (7 \times 54 - 337)}{56(127 - 118) + 133} =$ (1, 2)

(A) $3\frac{5}{637}$ (B) $7\frac{11}{13}$
(C) $9\frac{17}{31}$ (D) $9\frac{7}{57}$
(E) None of these

24. Find the sum: 3.597   (3)
Find the sum: 42.65
                   784.3809
                     6.748
                11,948.37
                   29.486
                   ───────

(A) 12,815.2319   (B) 13,815.2319
(C) 12,815.2329   (D) 12,816.2319
(E) None of these

25. $14\frac{4}{25} \div 52\frac{4}{9} =$ (2, 4)

(A) 0.27   (B) 1.37
(C) 2.43   (D) 3.06
(E) None of these

26. A man agrees to build a garage to be owned jointly by himself and his neighbor, each to share equally in the cost. The man does all the labor himself, working 200 hours, and the neighbor contributes $500 worth of material. If the man's labor is worth $1.50 an hour, how should settlement be made? (3)
    (A) Man reimburses neighbor $150 for materials.
    (B) Neighbor pays $150 additional for labor.
    (C) Neighbor pays $50 additional for labor.
    (D) The cost has been equally divided by labor and materials provided.
    (E) None of these

27. How many sheets 0.375 in. thick are in a stack $4\frac{1}{2}$-ft. high?   (4)
    (A) 694   (B) 144
    (C) 12   (D) 102
    (E) None of these

28. A new union contract gave employees who had been working a 38 hour per week a wage increase of 40¢ per hour and a reduction in work-hours. As a result, each employee worked 3 hours less, but earned $8 more, each week. What was the hourly wage under the new contract?   (3)
    (A) $2.00   (B) $2.40
    (C) $3.75   (D) $4.62
    (E) None of these

29. If the lengths of a pair of opposite sides of a square are each increased by 7 ft. and the lengths of the other pair of sides are each decreased by 2 ft., the resulting rectangle has a perimeter of 70 ft. The length of a side of the square is   (1)
    (A) 10 ft.   (B) 12 ft.
    (C) 15 ft.   (D) 18 ft.
    (E) None of these

30. A house is insured for 60% of its assessed value of $17,500. If the insurance rate is $\frac{1}{4}$% per year, what is the insurance premium for 3 years?   (4, 9, 24)
    (A) $70.00   (B) $72.50
    (C) $78.75   (D) $83.25
    (E) None of these

STOP

ANSWER KEY

Sample Test I

1.	C	7.	B	13.	E	19.	C	25.	D
2.	D	8.	C	14.	C	20.	B	26.	C
3.	C	9.	B	15.	A	21.	D	27.	A
4.	A	10.	E	16.	C	22.	C	28.	B
5.	B	11.	C	17.	D	23.	E	29.	A
6.	B	12.	B	18.	E	24.	B	30.	C

Sample Test II

1.	A	7.	B	13.	B	19.	A	25.	D
2.	D	8.	A	14.	C	20.	B	26.	A
3.	D	9.	B	15.	A	21.	D	27.	A
4.	A	10.	D	16.	B	22.	A	28.	A
5.	D	11.	B	17.	D	23.	B	29.	B
6.	E	12.	C	18.	A	24.	A	30.	B

Sample Test III

1.	C	7.	A	13.	E	19.	D	25.	A
2.	A	8.	E	14.	D	20.	C	26.	E
3.	D	9.	D	15.	A	21.	E	27.	B
4.	E	10.	C	16.	C	22.	E	28.	B
5.	C	11.	E	17.	D	23.	B	29.	C
6.	A	12.	C	18.	A	24.	A	30.	C

ANSWER KEY FOR *a* AND *b* PROBLEMS

Assignment 1

    A.   **a.**   XXVIII or XXIIX   **b.**   CMXLVI

    B.   **a.**   102   **b.**   1,228

    E.   **a.**   Rule 2   **b.**   Rules 15 and 16

    F.   **a.**   6   **b.**   24

Assignment 2

    A.   **a.**   152   **b.**   13,995

    C.   **a.**   59   **b.**   373,777

    E.   **a.**   3,196   **b.**   16,191,882

    G.   **a.** $3\frac{1}{2}$ **b.** $171\frac{545}{561}$

Assignment 3

    A.   **a.** $71.20   **b.** $1,037.38

    B.   **a.** $86.30   **b.** $653.38

    E.   **a.** $4.93

    F.   **a.**   980 sq yd

Assignment 4

    A.   **a.** $1\frac{1}{2}$ **b.** $3\frac{1}{3}$

    B.   **a.** $\frac{43}{6}$ **b.** $\frac{719}{10}$

    C.   **a.** $\frac{3}{7}$ **b.** $\frac{16}{21}$

    D.   **a.** $\frac{6}{8}, \frac{5}{8}$

Assignment 5

    A.   **a.** $\frac{18}{30} + \frac{15}{30} + \frac{20}{30} = \frac{53}{30} = 1\frac{23}{30}$ **b.** $\frac{1129}{18} + \frac{15}{18} + \frac{22}{18} = \frac{1165}{18} = 64\frac{13}{18}$

    B.   **a.** $\frac{3}{4}$ **b.** $7\frac{2}{5} - 3\frac{1}{3} = (7 - 3) + (\frac{2}{5} - \frac{1}{3}) = 4\frac{1}{15}$

    C.   **a.** $\frac{28}{99}$ **b.** $\overset{3}{\underset{1}{\frac{21}{5}}} \times \overset{5}{\underset{1}{\frac{25}{7}}} \times \frac{17}{2} = \frac{225}{2} = 112\frac{1}{2}$

    D.   **a.** $\frac{1}{2} \times \frac{3}{1} = \frac{3}{2} = 1\frac{1}{2}$ **b.** $\overset{69}{\underset{4}{\frac{345}{8}}} \times \overset{3}{\underset{23}{\frac{6}{115}}} = \frac{207}{92} = 2\frac{1}{4}$

Assignment 6

    A.   **a.**   .7   **b.**   1002.0102

    B.   **a.**   seventy-four and one tenth

          b.   one thousand six hundred twenty-four, and one thousand six ten-thousandths

    C.   **a.**   .70

    D.   **a.**   .001

    E.   **a.** $\frac{85}{100}$

    F.   **a.**   7.2

               9.64

                .8

            12.

           ——————

          29.64

    G.   **a.**   2.396

           −.947

          ——————

          1.449

Assignment 7

    A. **a.** .2592   **b.** 96.92298
    B. **a.** .02030252   **b.** 60.15409
    C. **a.** .02
    D. **a.** 8.66
    E. **a.** 589

Assignment 8

    A. **a.** .714   **b.** .992
    B. **a.** $\frac{17}{100}$ **b.** $\frac{8}{1,000}$
    C. **a.** $\frac{65}{72}$, or $(.833 \times .333) + .625 = .902 = .90$

Assignment 9

    A. **a.** $\frac{13}{32}$, or $.969 - 563 = .406$
    B. **a.** $\frac{7}{1,024}$, or .684

Assignment 10

    A. **a.** $21   **b.** $1,026.13

Assignment 11

    A. **a.** $7   **b.** $170
    B. **a.** $9   **b.** $110
    C. **a.** $3   **b.** $70
    D. **a.** $50   **b.** $29
    E. **a.** $30   **b.** $84

Assignment 12

    A. **a.** 4 sq yds   **b.** 34 in.
    B. **a.** 2 meters   **b.** 5.31 meters
    C. **a.** 2 hr, 10 min, 11 sec

Assignment 17

    A. **a.** 10%   **b.** $\frac{1}{5}$
    B. **a.** 15%   **b.** .33
    C. **a.** $\frac{3}{10} = .3$ **b.** $\frac{125}{100} = 1.25$
    D. **a.** 3,600   **b.** $2\frac{1}{30} = 2.033 = 2.03 = 203\%$
    E. **a.** 73.5¢
              b. $\frac{\$5200}{.04} = \$130,000$
                   $\$130,000 + \$5200 = \$135,200$

Assignment 18

    A. **a.** $c = 100\%$ Cost Price = $263.00
               $m = 20\%$ Markup = $52.60
               $s = 120\%$ Selling Price = $315.60
    B. **a.** $c' = 75\%$ Cost Price = $460.00
               $m' = 25\%$ Markup = $153.33
               $s' = 100\%$ Selling Price = $613.33
    C. **a.** $s' = \$285$
    D. **a.** $d = \$4.15$
               $s' = \$23.49$

Assignment 19

A. a. $750 \times .25 = \$187.50$ discount, $750 - \$187.50 = \$562.50$ net price
B. a. $435 \times .85 = \$369.75$ net price, $435 - \$369.75 = \$65.25$ discount
C. a. $295 \times .25 = \$73.75$ discount, $295 - \$73.75 = \$221.25$
$221.25 \times .10 = \$22.12$ additional discount
$221.25 - \$22.12 = \$199.13$ net price
alternatively the chain discount Table 11.1 could have been used
$295 \times .675 = \$199.125 = \$199.12$ net price, the difference in the two answers is due to rounding.
D. a. $365 \times .8075 = \$294.74$ net price, employing Table 11.1.

Assignment 20

A. a. .4988
b. .7909, using 10–5% row and $7\frac{1}{2}$ column, remembering that the order of taking the discounts does not affect the result.
B. a. A 2 percent cash discount is granted if paid within 15 days, and the balance must be paid within 60 days.
b. A 5 percent cash discount is granted if paid within 10 days, and the balance must be paid within 60 days.
C. a. cash discount = $13.00; net amount paid = \$637.00

Assignment 21

A. a. $1,065.67

Assignment 23

A. a. $(\$32,000 - 4,000) \times \dfrac{6}{21} = \underset{3}{\overset{4,000}{\cancel{28,000}}} \times \dfrac{\overset{2}{\cancel{6}}}{\underset{1}{\cancel{21}}} = \$8,000$

First year SOYD depreciation = $8,000
C. a. 20% applicable—yes
Initial allowance = $20\% \times \$10,000 = \$2,000$

First and second year straight-line depreciation $= \dfrac{\$120,000 - \$20,000 - \$2,000}{10 \text{ yr}}$

$= \dfrac{\$98,000}{10}$

$= \$9,800$ annual depreciation

b. 20% applicable—yes
Initial allowance = $20\% \times \$10,000 = \$2,000$

First year SOYD depreciation $= (\$120,000 - \$20,000 - \$2,000) \times \dfrac{10}{55}$

$= 98,000 \times \dfrac{\overset{2}{\cancel{10}}}{\underset{11}{\cancel{55}}} = \dfrac{196,000}{11} = \$1,781.82$

Second year SOYD depreciation $= 98,000 \times \frac{9}{55} = 19,600 \times \frac{9}{11}$

$= \$1,603.64$

Assignment 24

A. a. Taxpayer should itemize deductions:
$3000 - \$2200 = \$900$
$12000 - \$900 = \$11100$ taxable income
Tax liability from table = $1293; $1740 - \$1293 = \$447$ refund

Assignment 25

A. a. @ 3% sales tax = $0.83   b. @ 3% sales tax = $192.38
       @ 4% sales tax = $1.10   @ 4% sales tax = $256.50
       @ 5% sales tax = $1.38   @ 5% sales tax = $320.63

B. a. $105   b. $47.20
C. a. 50.5 mills   b. 42.0 mills
D. a. $631.25   b. $525.00

Assignment 27

A. a. $45
B. a. $9
C. a. $700 \times .04 \times \frac{73}{365} = \$5.60$
D. a. $\$40 \times \frac{.04}{.06} \times \frac{80}{60} = \$35.56$

Assignment 28

A. a. 30 days   b. 133 days
B. a. August 8   b. May 16
C. a. 71 days
D. a. April 7
E. a. June 6, $3,015

Assignment 29

A. a. $0.33
B. a. $20.25
C. a. 23 days, $4.14

Assignment 30

A. a. $\$3,000 \times .06 \times \frac{120}{360} = \$60$
Discount: $60
Proceeds: $3,000 − 60 = $2,940

C. a. $\dfrac{24 \times [(36 \times 300) - 8000]}{800 \times (36 + 1)} \times \dfrac{24 \times 2,800}{8,000 \times (36 + 1)} = 22.7\%$

Assignment 31

A. a. $1,050.62 amount, $50.62 interest
B. a. $597
C. a. $1806 − $1762.34 = $43.66
D. a. $129,274.07

Assignment 33

A. a. $862.60

Assignment 34

A. a. $p_1 = 8$ yr, $p_2 = 7$ yr
p_2 is preferred investment

B. a. $P_1 = \dfrac{\$300}{(1 + .06)} + \dfrac{\$300}{(1 + .06)^2} + \dfrac{\$300}{(1 + .06)^3} + \dfrac{\$300}{(1 + .06)^4} + \dfrac{\$300}{(1 + .06)^5} = \$1,263.72,$

$\dfrac{1263.72}{760} = 1.81$

Solve using the Present Value table on p. 211

$$P_2 = \frac{250}{(1 + .06)} + \frac{250}{(1 + .06)^2} + \cdots + \frac{250}{(1 + .06)^6}$$

$$P_2 = \$1,229.35, \frac{1229.35}{250} = 4.92$$

P_2 is preferred investment.

Assignment 35

A. a. Ordinary annuity = \$1753.06
B. a. \$7,142
C. a. \$2,987.50 − \$2,818.50 = \$169.00

Assignment 36

A. a. \$100.80
B. a. Semiannual = \$21.73
Quarterly   = \$11.08
Monthly   = \$ 3.71

Assignment 37

A. a. \$64.80
B. a. \$29.12
C. a. \$17,307.69 = \$17,308

Assignment 38

A. a.

200 × \$24	= \$4,800.00
20 × 24⅛	= 482.50
Round lot commission (2 × 31) =	62.00
Odd lot commission	= 9.83
Transaction charge	= 15.00
Total cost	= \$5,369.33

B. a. $\dfrac{70 + 10}{950} = 8.42\%$

Assignment 39

A. a. \$75,320 per year   **b.** \$12,660 per year

Assignment 40

A. a. Mean   = $6\frac{2}{5}$
Median = 6
Mode   = none

Assignment 44

A. a.

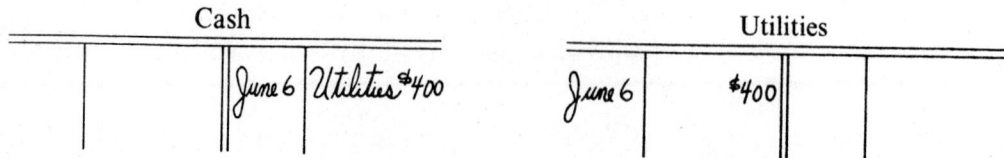

B. a.

Date		Entry	PR	Debit	Credit
March	8	Wages		$900	
		Cash			$900

INDEX